O9-BSA-690

SHADOW AND EVIL
IN
FAIRY TALES

By

Marie-Louise von Franz

1974

Spring Publications
c/o Postfach 190
8024 Zürich
Switzerland

ACKNOWLEDGEMENTS

The text of this book is comprised from two lecture series given by Marie-Louise von Franz at the C. G. Jung Institute, Zürich; the first, "The Problem of the Shadow in Fairy Tales," during the Winter Semester, 1957; and the second, "Dealing With Evil in Fairy Tales," Winter Semester, 1964. We are grateful to Miss Una Thomas for her transcription of the lectures.

Editing for Part I, Charles Kruger; Part II, Robin Van Löben Sels; Index by Austin Delany and Dendron Boden; Production by Valerie Donleavy and Angela Wierwille; Cover by Jeffrey Isaac.

Copyright © 1974, Marie-Louise von Franz

Spring Publications, The Analytical Psychology Club of New York, Inc.

ISBN 0-88214-109-0

Composed, Photo-offset and Manufactured in Switzerland
by Buchdruckerei Schrumpf, 8123 Ebmatingen Zürich
for Spring Publications, Postfach 190, 8024 Zürich

CONTENTS

PART ONE: SHADOW

PART TWO: EVIL

PART ONE

THE PROBLEM OF THE SHADOW
IN FAIRY TALES

CHAPTER I

SHADOW AND FAIRY TALE

The psychological definition of the shadow, which we must bear in mind before going into our material, can vary greatly and is not as simple as we generally assume. In Jungian psychology, we generally define the shadow as the personification of certain aspects of the unconscious personality, which could be added to the ego complex but which, for various reasons, are not. We might therefore say that the shadow is the dark, unlived, and repressed side of the ego complex, but this is only partly true. Dr. Jung, who hates it when his pupils are too literal minded and cling to his concepts and make a system out of them and quote him without knowing exactly what they are saying, once in a discussion threw all this over and said, "This is all nonsense! The shadow is simply the whole unconscious." He said that we had forgotten how these things had been discovered and how they were experienced by the individual, and that it was necessary always to think of the condition of the patient at the moment.

If someone who knows nothing about psychology comes to an analytical hour and you try to explain that there are certain processes at the back of the mind of which people are not aware, that is the shadow to them. So in the first stage of approach to the unconscious the shadow is simply a "mythological" name for all that within me of which I cannot directly know. Only when we start to dig into the shadow sphere of the personality and to investigate the different aspects, does there, after a time, appear in the dreams a personification of the unconscious, of the same sex as the dreamer. But then this person will discover that there is in this unknown area still another kind of reaction called the anima (or the animus), which represents feelings, moods and ideas, etc.; and we also speak of the concept of the Self. For practical purposes, Jung has not found it necessary to go beyond these three steps.

Most people get stuck when it is a question of practice and not just theory. To integrate the anima or animus is a masterpiece and nobody can claim to have succeeded. When we speak of the shadow we have therefore to bear in mind the personal situation and even the specific stage of consciousness and inner awareness of the person in question. Thus at the beginning stage we can say that the shadow is all that is within you which you do not know about. In general, when investigating it, we discover that it consists partly of personal and partly of collective elements. Practically, when we first meet it the shadow is simply a conglomeration of aspects in which we cannot make out what is personal and what collective.

As a practical example, let us say that someone is born of parents quite different in character and inherits from both parents certain characteristics which, so to speak, do not mix well chemically. For instance, I once had an analysand who had inherited a fiery and brutal temperament from her father and an oversensitive touchiness from her mother. How could she be both people at the same time? If someone annoyed her she was filled with two opposing reactions. In a child there are opposite possibilities which do not harmonize with each other. In the course of development generally a choice is made between them so that one side becomes more or less established. Then comes education, which adds to this, and then habit, for by always choosing one quality and giving that attitude preference, it becomes "second nature" and the other quality is swept under the table, though it still exists. From these repressed qualities, which are not admitted or accepted because they are incompatible with those chosen, the shadow is built up. With a certain amount of insight, and with the help of dreams, and so on, it is relatively easy for people to recognize these elements, and that is what we call making the shadow conscious — and with that analysis usually comes to a stop. But this is no achievement, for then comes the much more difficult problem where most people have great trouble: they know what their shadow is, but they cannot express it much or integrate it into their lives. Naturally, those in the immediate surroundings do not like a person to change, for that means that they also have to re-adapt. A family will be simply furious when a hitherto mild and lamb-like member suddenly becomes aggressive and says *No* to their demands. It leads to much criticism and, as the ego of the person concerned does not enjoy this either, the integration of the shadow may go wrong, and the whole problem gets stuck.

To have the courage to accept a quality which one does not like in oneself, and which one has chosen to repress for many years, is an act of great courage. But if one does not accept the quality, then it functions behind one's back. To see and admit the shadow is part of the problem, to say something has happened to me, something has leaked out; but the great ethical problem begins when one makes up one's mind to express the shadow consciously. That requires great care and reflection if it is not to have a disturbing reaction. I want here to give you an example.

Feeling types are apt to be cruel and narrow-minded in their judgments of their friends. On one side they feel their way very well through to people, but behind their own and other people's backs they have the most negative thoughts and jùdgments about them. The other day I was in a hotel with a feeling type. I am myself a thinking type, and it happened that when we first met I was in a tremendous hurry and just rushed past her with a brief greeting, whereupon she made up her mind that I hated her, was furious with her, and that I did not want to spend the day with her — that I was a cold and unrelated person, etc. The feeling type had suddenly switched into a negative thinking and had produced a number of negative thoughts with a whole explanation of why I had rushed by.

In the beginning stage the shadow is the whole unconscious — a rush of emotions, judgments, and so on. You might say that my friend was engaged in negative animus thinking — but actually, it was an outburst of negative thoughts (here the inferior function), brutal emotion (the shadow), and certain destructive judgments (animus in this case). If you study such negative outbursts you can distinguish between the figure which we call the shadow and the judgment faculty which, in a woman, we call animus. After a time people discover these negative qualities in themselves and succeed not only in seeing but in expressing them, which means giving up certain ideals and standards, aṇd entails a lot of consideration and thought if nothing is to be destroyed in the surroundings. Then, since we can also discover in dreams things which seem not to be personal, we say that the shadow consists partly of personal and partly of impersonal and collective material.

All civilizations, but especially the Christian, have their own shadow. This is a banal statement, but if you study other civilizations you can see where they are better than we are. In India, for example, they are far ahead of us in their spiritual and philosophical attitude in general, but their social behavior, to our minds, is shocking. If you walk through the streets of Bengal you will see numbers of people obviously starving to death; they are in extremis, yet no one takes any notice for that is their

7

"karma," and people must attend to themselves, to their own salvation; to look after others would only mean being involved in worldly considerations. To us Europeans, this social attitude spoils the whole country, for it is revolting to see people starving and ignored. We would call this plight the shadow of Indian civilization. Their extraversion is below the mark and their introversion above. It could be that the light side is not aware of the dark side, which is so obvious to another civilization.

If one lived quite alone it would be practically impossible to see one's shadow because there would be no one to say how you looked from the outside. There needs to be an onlooker. If we take into consideration the onlooker's reaction we could speak of the shadows of the different civilizations. For instance, most Eastern people think that our group attitude is absolutely unaware of certain metaphysical facts and that we are naively caught in illusions. That is how we appear to them, but we do not see it. We must have a shadow which we have not yet realized, of which we are unconscious; and the collective shadow is particularly bad because people support each other in their blindness — it is only in wars, or in hate for other nations, that an aspect of the collective shadow reveals itself.

Therefore you can say that the European has certain bad or incompatible qualities which have been repressed by the individual and that he also has the bad or inferior qualities of the group of which he forms a part — qualities of which he is generally unaware. The collective shadow also appears in another form: certain qualities within us are diminished when in a small group, or when we are alone, and increased suddenly if we are in a bigger group. You see this compensatory phenomenon typically with retiring introverts who have a great longing to be brilliant and the big bug in a crowd. The extravert is the contrary. When alone, the introvert says that he is not ambitious and does not care, he will not make ambitious intrigues, he will really be himself and content in his introversion. But put him in a crowd where there are ambitious extraverts, and right away he catches the infection. It is comparable to the woman who rushes to a shop to buy something cheap and all the other women run after her and when they get home say, "Why on earth did I buy this? "

If a person is caught by ambition only when in a group, you could say that it was a collective shadow. Sometimes you feel quite all right within but you can come into a group where the devil is loose and get quite disturbed, as happened to some Germans when they went to Nazi meetings. Thinking things over at home, they would be anti- Nazi, but when they went to a meeting something switched and they became, as one man said, "as though possessed by the devil." They were temporarily caught by the collective rather than the personal shadow.

The collective devil is still personified in the religious system by belief in the devil or evil demons. A medieval person who had returned from such a meeting would say that the devil had caught him and that now he was free again. The devil himself exemplifies such a personification of a collective shadow. On the other hand, we could say that as long as such collective demons get us, we must have a little bit of them in us; otherwise they would not get us, for then our psychic door would not be open to infection. When parts of the personal shadow are not sufficiently integrated, the collective shadow can sneak through this door. Consequently, we have to be aware that these two aspects exist, because this is an ethical, practical problem that otherwise we may inflict too much on people.

Suppose an analysand behaves outrageously in a group. If we try to make him see that that was all his fault, he is too crushed and, objectively, that would not be right, for a part was the group shadow. Otherwise there might be too great a feeling of guilt, and there is a kind of secret inner norm of how much of the shadow a human being can stand. It is unhealthy not to see it, but just as unhealthy to take too much of it. One cannot function psychologically if one takes on too much. As long as one has a bad conscience, one should take more; but the worst thing is that one often does not see where one's conscience is, it is blurred by looking at the shadow too closely — and then there is a very subtle problem.

I say all this to make clear that when we speak of the shadow there is a personal individual aspect and also a collective aspect, the group shadow. The latter naturally would in some way be the sum of the shadows, and also within the group be something which does not disturb the group and which is apparent only to outer groups. Practically put, if you put together three or four typical intellectuals of the same intellectual interests, they will say that they have spent a wonderful evening in intellectual discussions and not notice that the contact was otherwise bad; but a peasant boy placed with them would say it was a dreadful evening. If all have the same problem it feels wonderful! Probably all Europeans have many qualities

9

which we do not notice for to us they are normal. That is the normal awareness in individuals and also in groups.

I would like to correct one point. Earlier I said that only when a group
comes up against another group does it realize its shadow; but I was not
fully accurate, since in many civilizations religious rituals tend to make a
group aware of its group shadow. In our Christian civilization these would
correspond to the Black Mass where one would curse the name of Christ,
kiss an animal on the anus in the name of the devil, and so on, and the
point of it all would be to do exactly the reverse of what one thought was
holy. These counter-religious festivals have died out and tend to be forgotten, but they were an attempt to show the crowd its shadow. In many primitive civilizations there is a group of jesters who have to do everything contrary to the group rules. They laugh when one should be serious, cry when
others laugh, etc. For instance, in certain North American tribes someone
is elected to perform in a ritualistic way shocking things contrary to the
group standards. There is here probably the vague idea that another side
should also be brought into the open. It is a shadow catharsis festival. If
you want to see genuine remnants of such things in Switzerland, go to the
Basel Fastnacht, (although now too many foreigners go and disturb the
atmosphere); there you can see the way in which a group brings out its
group shadow in a genuine and beautiful way. In the Swiss Army one
speaks of the Company Calf, who is unconsciously selected by a company
to play the scapegoat, the man selected usually being someone with a weak
ego complex who acts out the collective shadow under compulsion. It can
be quite a tragic constellation. You see the same pattern in the family black
sheep who is forced to carry the shadow of the others.

Now we can look at a related problem: What do fairy tales represent and
what do they not, and how far can we take them as psychological material?
To understand this we have to ask ourselves about the probable origin of
fairy tales and about their function within our civilization. Since the Jung
Institute is a school, one is unfortunately obliged to repeat certain funda-
mental teachings. It is like putting the gramaphone on — so you must for-
give me if this time I give you only a short sketch.

In former times, until about the seventeenth century, fairy tales were not reserved for children, but were told among grown-ups in the lower layers of the population — woodcutters and peasants, and women while spinning amused themselves with fairy tales. There were also (and they still exist in a few villages in Switzerland) professional fairy-tale tellers who were repeatedly asked to relate a few stories. These people are sometimes half-wits and a bit unbalanced, neurotic individuals, and others, on the contrary, are particularly healthy and normal individuals — it is a mixed lot. If you ask them why they do this, some reply they have inherited the function, and others say they learnt it from a cook, or that it is a tradition handed down from one individual to another. We know now that there are fairy tales which are of a collective kind and handed on, like the old traditions, from one generation to another — it is a kind of common knowledge. Theories as to the origin of fairy tales are very different: some say that they are degenerated remnants of religious myths and doctrines, others that they were once a part of literature which degenerated into fairy tales. It has also been asserted that they are a kind of dream, later told as a story. To my mind, the origin can be seen by the following typical example.

In a Swiss family, there was, in the time of Napoleon, a family chronicle in which a miller went out to shoot a fox that then began to talk, saying that the miller should not kill him for he had helped him with the mill. When the miller returned home he found the mill turning by itself. Shortly afterwards he died. Recently, a student of folklore went to this village and asked the old people there if they knew anything about the mill, and picked up various versions of the old story. One gave the same story but said that the fox had run crossways through the miller's legs which produced a fatal infection and inflammation of the skin. Now in that part of the country, a fox is supposed to cause such illnesses. To the original story something new had been added. Another variant said the miller went on to a dinner party where his wineglass broke and then he knew that the fox was the witch soul of a dead aunt. (Witches' souls are said to go about in the souls of foxes.) The story had thus amplified itself with other fitting archetypal material exactly as rumors do.

So you can see how a story originates: there is always a nucleus form of a parapsychological experience or a dream. If it contains a motif that exists in the neighborhood, then there is a tendency to amplify. Now we have the story of a miller who was chased by a former witch that he nearly

11

shot, and then the witch killed him. It is not yet a fairy tale, but just the beginning of one. The name of the miller always stayed unchanged. But supposing the kitchen maid goes to another village and tells the story there, then the miller might be given a different name, or might only be called the Miller. All the elements which are not interesting to that village will be dropped and what is archetypal in the story will remain in the memory. I am always struck by the fact that I can remember archetypal material better than other things — it makes an eternal impression so that one remembers it. A young teacher tried out an experiment on this point. He told two stories, only one of which contained mythological elements, and made his pupils write both out three days later. It was obvious that of course the mythological tale was better remembered.

As long as such layers of the population had no radios and newspapers, the stories formed their great interest, and one sees how a myth originated. I believe this is how fairy tales came about. I do not reject, however, the theory that they are sometimes remnants of degenerated literature. You can find the watered-down story of the Hercules myth in modern Greece, for instance. It has been reduced to its basic structure and the archetypal material remains, and it is these elements of religious forms of the past which reappear in fairy tale material. Different elements come together and the stories are told because they are still interesting and exciting, even if not understood. The fact that we have now relegated them to children shows a typical attitude — I could even call it a definition of our civilization — namely, that archetypal material is looked upon as infantile. If this theory of origin is true, then fairy tales would mirror the most basic psychological structures of man to a greater extent than myths and literary products. As Jung once said, when you study fairy tales you can study the anatomy of man. The myth in general is more embedded in civilization. You cannot think of the *Gilgamesh Epic* apart from the Babylonian-Sumerian civilization and you cannot think of the *Odyssey* apart from the Grecian, but the fairy tale can migrate better for it is so elementary and so reduced to its basic structural elements that it appeals to everybody. A missionary was once sent to one of the Polynesian islands and the first contact he was able to make was by means of a fairy tale, it was the common link. This is true, however, only *cum grano salis*.

Having studied fairy tales for quite some time, I have come to believe that there are typical European and African brands of fairy tales, and though I may be tricked by the changed names, their close relationship is still obvious. Fairy tales are also somewhat influenced by the civilization in which they first appeared, but much less so than myths because of their more basic structure. Investigators of animal behavior have seen that certain rituals in animal life contain basic structural elements. All kinds of drakes perform a certain dance before mating consisting of certain movements of the head and wings and several other little movements: it is the ritual way of wooing the female duck. Behaviorists wondered if it might have to do with the genes and they succeeded in crossing different kinds of ducks, and making a new species and watching how they behaved. They discovered that sometimes the old original duck dance ritual was accepted which had not belonged to either of the varieties crossed, or that the duck dance of one of the partners was repeated in a reduced form, or that there was a combination of two forms. Certain structural elements in the dance of the male duck were always present and certain other elements varied.

If we apply this to man, we could say that there are certain basic structures of the psychological behavior which belong to the human species in general and others which are more developed in one group or race and less prominent in another. Fairy tales are very generally human in their structure. In each type they play a great role because you can study the most basic structures of behavior; but for me there is another practical reason: by the study of fairy tales and mythological myths you come to know of certain structural complexes, and are more apt to recognize what is individual and what is not and to see possible solutions. For example, if you study the myth of the mother complex, i. e., the affection and the instinctive behavior of the male child with his mother and all the psychological results of this relationship as mirrored in myths, you can distinguish typical features. The male child tends to develop the features of the hero, of rather a feminine young man of the type of Attis or Adonis or Baldur, who dies young and has a tendency to refuse life, especially with its dark side. According to these myths the young hero who loved his mother was killed by a dark brutal chthonic male being, which means that there is the crucial moment for a young man in that situation when he is either psychologically killed by the wild boar, or, if he refused to accept his shadow, when he will probably — in modern times — become a pilot and crash, or go to the mountains and fall.

13

If you have a case in which the myth does not appear, in which the dreams are personal, you will probably recognize mythological features in which the young man will dream of a friend who is like Mars, or of a wild boar. He will have a personal name, but you can see the basic pattern and the possible solution and development — if you know the myth. You must not preach it, that would be imposing a mythological idea, but you will have a better understanding. One naturally is still influenced by mythological thinking when dealing with this dark male shadow figure of the analysand. One may perhaps tell the myth, and say this reminds me of the Attis-Adonis myth and bring to life the whole solution. Such a person then feels that his problem is not unique and insoluble, but that it has been solved dozens of times in certain ways; it also reduces conceit, because one feels that one is in a general situation and not a unique neurosis. The myth also has a magical impact on layers which cannot be reached by intellectual talk; it imparts the feeling of *déjà entendu* and yet is always new and awakening.

The consideration of the shadow in fairy tales, then, must focus not on the personal but on the collective and group shadow. We can therefore establish only a general view of the way in which the shadow behaves, yet that, to my mind, is very valuable. People are apt to think of *my* ego and do not realize that the ego is also a general structure and an archetype, to our way of thinking. It is an archetype in that it is based on a general inborn disposition to develop an ego and produce certain types of reactions and representations. You could say that in most civilizations everywhere, in different degrees, there is this tendency to develop an ego complex: what is known as "I" is a general inborn human structure. In the early phases of childhood a lot of energy goes into building up the ego complex, and if there are disturbances in the milieu the process is disturbed and the urge may, among other things, cause extreme egotism. This inborn tendency would be the non-personal aspect of the complex, but there is also another inborn tendency, though much less strong, to split off from the ego; and this split creates an archetypal aspect of the shadow figure. Only these general structures mirror themselves in fairy tales, and they can be influenced by the civilizations in which the tales originate.

The fairy tale I want to take first is a German one related by the Grimm Brothers, who were the first to collect fairy tales and arouse interest in other countries to do the same. The story runs as follows:

14

THE TWO WANDERERS

Mountain and valley do not meet, but human beings sometimes do — both good and bad. So it happened that a tailor and a shoemaker met in their wanderings. The tailor was a small, good-looking, amusing and merry sort of fellow. He saw the shoemaker on the other side of the road and greeted him with a joke. But the shoemaker did not like jokes and made a sour face and looked like fighting the tailor, but the little fellow began to laugh and handed him his bottle, saying, "No harm meant — have a drink and swallow your rage." The shoemaker took a big draught and suggested that they should walk on together. "All right," said the tailor, "if you want to go to a big town where there is plenty of work."

The tailor, always merry and fresh and red cheeked, had no trouble in getting work, as well as a kiss behind the door from the master's daughter, and when he met the shoemaker always had more money than he. Although the surly shoemaker was not so fortunate, the tailor laughed and shared what he had with his companion. When they had been some time on the road they came to a big forest through which a way led to the king's city. But there were two paths, one took seven days and the other only two, and they didn't know which was which and debated as to the quantity of bread they should take. The shoemaker wanted to take enough for seven days, but the tailor was ready to take a risk and trust in God. It was a long way. By the third day the tailor had finished his bread, but the shoemaker had no pity on him. By the fifth day the tailor was so hungry that he asked the shoemaker for some bread for he was quite white and exhausted. The shoemaker agreed but said that in exchange the tailor must let him put out one of his eyes. The unhappy tailor, who didn't want to die, could only agree, and the heartless shoemaker cut out his right eye. The next day the tailor was again hungry and on the seventh day too exhausted to stand. The shoemaker then said that he would have pity on him and give him more bread but that in return he must have the tailor's other eye.

Then the tailor begged God's forgiveness for the light-hearted way in which he had lived, and told the shoemaker that he had not deserved such treatment at his hands for he had always shared everything with him and without his eyes

15

he would not be able to sew and could only beg, and he asked that he might not be left there to die alone in his blindness. But the shoemaker, who had shut God out of his heart, took his knife and cut out the left eye. Then he gave the tailor a piece of bread, cut him a stick, and led him away. When the sun went down they came out of the wood by some gallows. There the shoemaker led the blind tailor and left him. Worn out with pain and hunger the tailor fell asleep and slept through the whole night. When he woke in the morning he did not know where he was. On the gallows hung two poor sinners and on the head of each sat a crow. The two crows began to talk and one told the other that the dew which during the night had fallen on them from the gallows would give back sight to anyone who washed with it. When the tailor heard that he took his handkerchief and soaked it in the dew on the grass, washed his eye sockets with it, and had two healthy eyes.

Soon the sun rose and in the plain before him was the king's city, with its beautiful gates and hundreds of towers. He distinguished every leaf on the trees, saw the birds fly by and the midges dance in the air. He got out a needle, and when he saw that he could thread it as well as ever, his heart jumped for joy, and he knelt and thanked God. Then he picked up his bundle and went on, singing and whistling. Soon he met a brown colt running about in the field. He seized it by the mane meaning to jump on it and ride into town. But the colt begged for its freedom saying it was too young, that even a light tailor would break its back, and to let him be until he was strong enough and perhaps some day he would be able to repay him. So the tailor let the colt go.

But the tailor had not eaten since the previous day. He then saw a stork and seized it by one of its legs meaning to cut its head off so that he could have something to eat. But the stork said that he was a holy bird which never harmed anybody and was of great use to the human race and begged to be allowed to live. He told the tailor that he would make it up to him another time. So the tailor let him fly away. Then the tailor saw on a pond two little ducks. He caught one and wanted to wring its neck to have something to eat. But the old duck swam out of the bushes and implored him to have pity on her dear children. "Think," she said, "what your mother would say if someone wanted to make an end of you!" So the good-tempered tailor said she should keep her children and put the duck back in the water. When he turned round he saw an old, hollow tree where the bees flew in and out. "That will reward me for my good deeds," he said, but the queen bee came out and said, "If you touch my people and destroy my nest, we will sting you with ten thousand glowing needles. Leave us in peace and go your way and in return we will one day do you a service." So the tailor went away and came hungry into the town. As it was midday he entered an inn and ate and then he looked for work and found a good job. Since he was a very good tailor he soon became famous and everybody wanted a coat made by him — and at last he came to be appointed court tailor.

But, as happens in life, on the same day his old comrade was made the court shoemaker, and when the latter saw the tailor with two healthy eyes, his conscience began to trouble him and he planned to destroy the tailor before he could tell his story. So, in the evening when he had finished his work, he went to the king and told him that the tailor was an insolent fellow who had boasted that he would find the golden crown which had been lost in olden days. So the next morning the king had the tailor brought to him and ordered him to produce the crown or leave the town forever. The unhappy tailor packed his bundle and prepared to leave the city, though he was sorry to leave the place where everything had gone so well. When he came to the pond where he had met the ducks, there was the old duck cleaning its beak at the bank. The tailor told it what had happened to him. "Is that all? " said the duck. "The crown fell in the water and is lying at the bottom of the pond. Just lay your handkerchief out on the bank!" Then she dived down with her twelve children and after five minutes came up again with the crown lying on her wings and the twelve little ducks round her holding it up with their beaks. So the tailor wrapped it up in his handkerchief and took it to the king, who gave him a golden chain as a reward.

When the shoemaker saw that his plot had failed, he went again to the king and said that the tailor had boasted that he could produce a model of the royal castle in wax, with everything that was in it. The king ordered the tailor to do this and said that if there was even a nail missing the tailor should be imprisoned under the earth for the rest of his life. The tailor thought that things got worse and worse and nobody

17

could stand that and again he went away. But when he came to the hollow tree the queen bee flew out and asked if he had a stiff neck since he was hanging his head so low. Then the tailor told the story. All the bees began to hum and the queen bee said he must go home and come again tomorrow at the same time with a big cloth. When he arrived the next day the bees had made a perfect model. The king was delighted and gave the tailor a fine stone house.

But the shoemaker went a third time to the king and said that the tailor had boasted that he could make a spring of water well up in the king's courtyard as high as a man, and as clear as crystal. This the tailor was ordered to do under pain of having his head cut off. Once more the tailor prepared to leave with the tears running down his cheeks. But the colt came running to him and said he knew what was the matter, the tailor must just sit on his back, and he galloped to the courtyard and round it three times like lightning and the third time threw himself down, at which time there was a tremendous crash and a great ball of earth flew up into the air and over the castle, and immediately after water jetted up as high as man and horse and as clear as crystal. When the king saw it he embraced the tailor before everybody.

But the good luck again did not last. The king had many daughters, one more beautiful than the other, but no son, and the wicked shoemaker went once more to the king and said that the tailor had boasted that he could bring the king a son through the air. The king called the tailor and told him that if within nine days he could bring him a son, he should marry his eldest daughter. So the tailor went home and wondered what on earth he should do. Again thinking nothing was to be done, he made up his bundle and went, saying, "I will leave this place for here I cannot live in peace." But when he came to the meadow his old friend the stork greeted him. When he had told his story the stork said he should not grow any gray hairs over that since for long he had brought babies to the town and for once he could also fetch a little prince out of the well. The tailor should go home and be quiet, and in nine days time he should go to the court, where the stork would come. The tailor went home, and to the castle at the right time, and soon the stork came knocking at the window. The tailor opened the window and in came long-legs walking carefully over the marble floor,

18

carrying in his beak a child like an angel. It stretched its little hands out to the queen. The stork laid it on her lap, she was overjoyed, and the tailor married the eldest daughter.

And the shoemaker had to make the shoes in which the tailor danced at the wedding feast, whereafter he was ordered to leave the city forever. His road through the forest led to the gallows. Worn out with anger and the heat of the day, he threw himself down, and when he shut his eyes and wanted to sleep the two crows flew down with loud cries and picked out his eyes. He ran round like a crazy man in the wood and must have perished there for nobody ever heard or saw him again.

CHAPTER II

DESTRUCTION OR RENEWAL OF THE KING

At first glance you might say that in "The Two Wanderers" the optimistic nice tailor represents the conscious side and the shoemaker the shadow, compensatory side, and actually this is an interpretation given even by people who work on fairy tales and Jungian psychology. They take it as a typical story representing the ego and the shadow. I think this is in a way true, but, in my experience, if you start with such a hypothesis you get stuck; consequently, I would like to warn you against taking Jungian concepts and pinning them on to mythological figures, saying this is the ego, this the shadow, and this the anima, because you will see that this works only for a time and that then there come contradictions — and finally distortions as people try to force the figures in the story into a definite form. It is much better, instead of jumping to conclusions, to look at the two figures and their functional aspects in the story and the way in which they are constellated in regard to the other characters, and to follow the rule not to interpret any archetypal figures before we have also looked at the context. Then we will come to slightly different conclusions than if we just took them arbitrarily as ego and shadow.

The tailor is a well-known figure in fairy tales. In the famous story of "The Valiant Little Tailor," there are certain similarities, for the tailor in this other story is also gay and light-hearted, of a small, slight build and not physically very strong, and he defeats a giant and later tricks a furious unicorn. In this story a unicorn is annoyed and attacks the tailor, who jumps behind a tree, and the unicorn runs his horn into the tree and then cannot free himself. From this amplification we can conclude that the tailor has something to do with the archetype of the trickster who overcomes his enemies by his intelligence and quick wit.

According to medieval ideas most crafts were connected with certain planets, and every planet protected certain crafts. The planet Mercurius protected cooks and tailors. So here we have the connection: the tailor belongs to Hermes, i. e. , Mercurius, the trickster God, with all his qualities of versatile intelligence, quick wit, and ability to change. In those days the

trade of a tailor was a wise choice for small rather effeminate men who
compensate their weaknesses by their wit and skill. Moreover, the tailor
makes clothes for other people. Generally, we interpret clothes as having
to do with the persona, and to a certain extent this is correct, for we cover
up the naked truth of our personality and show to the surrounding world
a more decent facade, nicer than we really are. The idea of clothes as the
persona is well illustrated by the Hans Anderson fairy tale of "The Emperor's New Clothes." The emperor offers a large reward to the man who
can make the best clothes for him, and a witty little tailor goes to him and
says he can make very special, delicate and beautiful clothes which have
the magic quality that only honest and decent people can see them. The
emperor orders the clothes. He cannot see them but does not give this
fact away, and the rumor spreads in the town that he will appear in his
new magic clothes. Everybody admires him until a small child cries out,
"But he has nothing on!" And then everybody begins to laugh. Again
the tailor is the trickster who shows up the stupidity of the emperor's
persona.

On the other hand, if we think of the mystery cults of late antiquity
and of the initiations and rituals of many civilizations, we see that people
also put on clothes not to represent the persona, but to express an attitude.
For instance, in the baptismal ceremonies of the early Christian Church,
people were totally immersed and then given white garments to manifest
their newly acquired innocent attitude, or their candid (*candidus*: white) *candidate*
attitude. Also in the Mithraic initiations and the Isis mysteries the male
initiates wore certain clothes to represent the sun God and make inner
archetypal transformation manifest to other people. In an alchemical
parable, the spirit Mercurius is described as a tailor of men. Since he has
scissors and cuts men into their right shape, he therefore shapes the people themselves, not only their clothes, and is thus a kind of transformer
of men, a would-be psychotherapist who changes people into their true
and right shape.

We can say, then, that the tailor has to do with an archetypal power
capable of transforming man and giving him a new attitude, a power
which has to do with intelligence and the ability to outwit others. Giants,
known for their size and outstanding stupidity, represent, in general, stupid
emotions. As soon as you are gripped by an affect you become stupid.

21

Mythologically, giants are connected with earthquakes. The unicorn, with his aggressive horn, represents the aggressive attitude, and the tailor knows how to contend with this. He also represents the typically human psychological qualities of wit and intelligence by which one can overcome primitive emotion and attain higher consciousness.

The tailor in "The Two Wanderers" is moreover a very pious man, for every time he is in any difficulty he prays to God, in whom he has great faith and confidence, for he optimistically believes that the Godhead will help him out of his difficulties. So we may conclude that the human way of overcoming affect by wit and intelligence is here combined with the Christian religious attitude, the Christian *Weltanschauung*.

The shoemaker also has to do with clothing, but only for the feet, and therefore the difference between clothes in general and shoes has to be specified. If the clothes represent attitudes, then their interpretation must vary in accordance with the part of the body which they cover. You might say that trousers have to do with the sexual attitude and the brassiere with the maternal attitude — a woman often dreams of a brassiere to represent a criticism of this attitude. A German proverb says that a man's shirt is closer to him than his coat, it is closer to the skin and therefore represents an intimate attitude. Aigremont wrote a book on the symbolism of the shoe from the Freudian standpoint, but I do not agree with his conclusions. Sartori has also written an article on the same subject. Aigremont comes to the conclusion that the foot is a phallic symbol, for which there is some support, the shoe representing the female organ surrounding the foot.

The sexual aspect is implicitly contained in the symbolism of the shoe, but it is not an outstanding aspect: we can assume that people of the layer of society depicted in this fairy tale would speak more directly and would say sex if that was what they meant, so there is a slightly different meaning. If we start from the hypothesis that the shoe is simply the article of clothing for covering the foot and that with it we stand on the earth, then the shoe is the *standpoint*, or *attitude towards reality*. There is much evidence for this. The Germans say when someone becomes adult that he "takes off his childish shoes," and we say that the son "steps into his father's shoes" or "follows in his father's footsteps" — he takes on the same attitude. There is also a connection with the power complex for one "puts one's foot down" if one wishes to assert power, as the victorious

22

soldier, illustrating that he now has power, puts his foot on the neck of his conquered foe. In German there is an expression "the slipper hero," referring to the man who is under his wife's domination — she puts her foot down and he is subordinate to her in the house. Therefore you might say that our standpoint towards concrete reality always has to do with the assertion of power because we cannot take the standpoint of reality without, to a certain extent, asserting ourselves; when it comes to reality you have to make a choice, to make one side decisive. So the shoemaker would represent an archetypal figure similar to that of the tailor, but one specially concerned with the standpoint towards reality.

The shoemaker's trade is regarded as one of the simple professions, even more simple than the tailor's, though neither are socially on a high level according to the bourgeois level of these fairy tales. There are many legends and stories which have to do with the simple level of the shoemaker. There is a legend that St. Anthony, who saw an angel of God, got the idea that he had achieved something and become a great saint, but one day an angel told him that there was a still more saintly man in Alexandria. St. Anthony, feeling jealous, wanted to see the man, and the angel led him to a very poor quarter of Alexandria and to a miserable hovel where an old shoemaker, who had a miserable wife, sat making shoes. St. Anthony was amazed, but began to talk to him and, wanting to find out in what way he was more saintly, asked him about his religious views and attitude towards religion; but the shoemaker just looked up at him and said that he was just making shoes to earn money for his wife and children. St. Anthony thereupon was enlightened. The story shows how the shoemaker has to do with the standpoint towards reality in contrast to St. Anthony, who strove only to become more and more holy. The shoemaker had a completely human and humble contact with reality, which is what most saints lack and was what the angel of God told St. Anthony. There is a proverb which says, "Shoemaker, stick to your tools" for, if he leaves them, things go very wrong, which has to do with the relation to reality for we have to be completely realistic and remain within our own limits. The shoemaker does this, and according to the proverb is right.

Now that we have established the two aspects of our two figures, I would like to speak of the method of interpreting fairy tales which I think important, for the method of approach should be understood, and guessing which figure is which should be replaced by a more scientific approach.

After wandering about, at the decisive point shoemaker and tailor become servants of the king, and the shoemaker starts his intrigues and the tailor in the end marries the princess, which is unusual. In other fairy tales where the simple man marries the princess it is implied that through marriage he becomes the new king, but here the stork brings the king a son who will probably be his heir (not the tailor) unless the child dies, which is not likely according to fairy tale atmosphere. Perhaps we should ask ourselves what it means in general if a simple man like a peasant or a half-wit, or a tailor or a shoemaker, or the only child of a widow, marries the princess and thereby becomes the future king, so we must go into the symbolism of the king.

It would be jumping to conclusions to say that the tailor represents the conscious part and the shoemaker the shadow; you could just as well say both were the shadow of the king. Everybody is everybody's shadow in fairy tales, the whole cluster of figures is compared one with another, and all the figures have a compensatory function. One must, therefore, use the word "shadow" *cum grano salis*.

For the symbolism of the king I refer you to Jung's *Mysterium Coniunctionis* where there is a whole chapter on this subject. The king represents on a primitive level a personification, or is a carrier of the mystical life-power of the nation or tribe, which is why in many primitive civilizations, as you can read in Frazer's *The Dying God*, the health and physical and spiritual power of the king guarantees the power of the tribe and he has to be killed if he becomes impotent or ill. He is deposed after a certain number of years because the carrier of this power has always to be young. He is an incarnated Godhead, the living strength of the tribe. Among the Shilluks in the Upper White Nile this is clearly expressed by the fact that the old king when he is to be killed is shut up in a hut with an untouched virgin and starved to death with the girl; the so-called throne (a primitive little chair) is put in front of the hut, and his successor sits there: at the moment of death the life spirit of the old king enters the body of the new king. From then on he is the king and carrier of this principle.

Again jumping to conclusions, you might say that the king has all the aspects of a symbol of the Self, but this is too general and inaccurate in fact, though the king is the life principle and image of God and the center

24

of physical and spiritual organization and in that way carries the projection of the Self, the regulating dominating center of the aspect of totality. But that is not right in so far as the archetype of the Self is, according to our experience, not so much bound to time as that. Also we have the image of the dying king, or the sick or old king who has to be deposed, which does not fit with the idea of the Self as regulating center of the psyche and which does not have to be deposed. Therefore in what way is he and is he not the Self? The answer is given in the ritual of the Shilluks which I described to you. The king is not the Self, but a manifested symbol of that archetype. That is, the king of our civilization is Christ, he is a symbol of the Self, he is the specific formulated aspect of the Self which dominates our civilization, the King of Kings, the dominating content. I would say that Buddha is the formulated aspect of the symbol of the Self in the Buddhist civilizations. Thus the king is not the archetype of the Self but a symbol of the Self, which has become a central dominating representation in a civilization.

It seems an archetypal law of general validity that every symbolism which has taken shape and form in collective human consciousness wears out after a certain time and resists renewal due to a certain inertia of consciousness. Most inner experiences after ten or twenty years lose some of their strength and, especially in collectivity, most religious symbols tend to wear out in form. Think of all the children who should relate to the symbol of Christ and be Christian and who by the time they are six years old are already bored and shut their inner ear because to them it has already become a kind of slogan and makes no more sense, it has lost its numinous qualities and its value. I have also been told by parsons and priests that it is practically impossible always to write a sermon into which they can put themselves for there will inevitably be days when the man is tired, or has quarrelled with his wife, when this "wearing out" effect will be visible. If Christ were completely numinous to him that would not happen. It seems a tragic fact that human consciousness tends to be unilateral and single track, not always adapted to inner processes, so that certain truths are formulated and adhered to for too long.

The same thing applies to the inner evolution of an individual — someone has an inner experience and lives it for a while, but then life changes, and the attitude should change, but this is not noticed until dreams show

25

that a readaptation must be made. In middle life, consciousness tends to persist in certain attitudes and does not notice quickly enough that, now the inner thing has changed, consciousness should also change for approaching death. Religious contents also, as soon as they become conscious and spoken of, lose their immediate freshness and their numinosity, for which reason the great religious systems undergo movements of renewal, or there is a complete change and renewal or re-interpretation so that the system regains its immediacy and original meaning. The ageing king who has to be replaced by a new king expresses this general psychological law. Whatever has reached general recognition is, in a way, already doomed; it would only be wisdom to know that and always be ready for a change of attitude. But, just as the individual generally perseveres in his old attitude, so does the collective, and to a much greater extent. Then you have to face the inertia which can be dangerous to the content. The mystery of the renewal of the king refers to this.

The king has another aspect: he is not only the profound hope of a civilization, but at the same time the religious representative. An effort was made to evade the unavoidable tragedy of the king having to die from time to time by doubling the power, that is by having a medicine man *and* a king. The medicine man is not so much involved in the earthly activities of organization, for his task is to cope with the immediacy of the religious experience. Therefore, in many primitive tribes, there is discord between king and medicine man, who is the "Grey Eminence" behind the king, or who is kept down by the absolute rule of the chief. This is a squabble which was carried on in our own history when the Catholic Church tried to be the power over the king, or certain kings tried to replace the pope, or to govern him and rule the religious life of the Catholic Church. The idea behind the division of power was to keep the two separate, so that the religious aspect should have the possibility of renewal, and organization should keep to its own duties. In this way it might be possible to keep balanced the opposites, the tendency towards the continuity of consciousness and the necessity for constant inner renewal. The drawback is the danger of a quarrel and split between the two powers, which really belong together in the psyche.

In fairy tales it is often the simple person who becomes the next king, after many inner processes and peripeteias. We must investigate what this

26

means. If the prince becomes king he is the right person by inheritance, and we could call that renewal within the same dominant, like that of the Order of St. Francis of Assisi within the Catholic Church. There was a moment of danger for the Catholic Church when the Order of St. Francis might have formed a movement of its own, but within the Catholic Church it was a rejuvenating movement of spiritual life and of the same dominating stamp; this would be analogous to the prince becoming king. On the other hand, if the fairy tale says that a very anonymous and unexpected person becomes king, then the renewal of the dominant of collective consciousness comes from an angle, both sociological and archetypal, from which it was least expected. The dogma of the assumption of the Virgin Mary provides such an example, for in some circles of theology this new dogma was rather looked down upon. The pope emphasized that it was the general popular wish that it should take place, but he met with great opposition and referred to the visions of Fatima in Spain, for the assumption of the Virgin Mary is based more on a feeling movement among the simple people than on theological thought. The pope himself is said to have had visions (though this is not officially stated), but from an unexpected corner such as the pope's unconscious such a thing came to light: the renewal comes from the unexpected place.

In general, we might conclude that if the fairy tale tells us of a simple man becoming king, it describes a process of renewal of collective consciousness which comes from the unexpected and officially despised part of the psyche, and from the simple people, for in a population, in a confused way, the latter suffer more than the learned people from the undercurrents of archetypal development. For example, in universities and all educated circles it is argued that there is too much technique and not enough relation to nature in the life of modern man. The more dominant classes are aware of this, but a simple peasant boy who leaves his village to work in a factory is not, yet suffers from it much more immediately and may become desperate and perhaps hate his fellow men and not know that he is suffering from the disease of the time. In his psyche a longing for a change of attitude may be constellated and expressed quite symbolically. He may try to overcome his trouble by going to a renewal meeting for he sees things on a very primitive level and he may try to cure his sickness in this way. Such vague suffering may be solved in a symbolically demon-

27

strated form, or, he may feel that his life is meaningless and drink himself
to death. One could say, therefore, that the moods, secret longings, and
needs of the simple people within the population express in a clear form
the needs of our time. When analyzing people of that level I am always
amazed at the archetypal material in their dreams which seem much more
concerned with the problem of our time than those of educated people.
A poor girl who is full of fears and anxieties, and whose horizon is clouded,
does not see that she may be a victim of the time and may dream of our
present problem in a most clear and amazing way. You could call such
dreams visions of the time working within the dreamers' souls. What one
can learn through analyzing a charwoman or a half-wit!

During the interval I have been asked two questions: one is why a simple person should have such particularly clear visions of the problems of
our time. We concluded that they suffer much more helplessly than do
the upper classes who can build a holiday resort somewhere so that they
can escape and compensate the time situation. Also, educated people see
the situation in which they are and try to help themselves and do not take
it in the same way. They are not obliged, for instance, to live miserably in
a noisy street from which they cannot get away. Poor people are more exposed to the problem, and, since they suffer more from it, the instinctive
healing reaction is more intensified.

I have been asked to give illustrations: A woman school teacher had
the following vision. She went to the neighboring town and attended an
anthroposophic meeting in a world-famed cathedral. She went out of the
meeting house where the parson was holding a conference and saw dark
clouds and an earthquake, as if it were the end of the world. At the top
of the tower of the cathedral, on the upper-most point, she saw a bronze
figure of death on a horse, and a voice said, "Death is coming down and is
beginning to ride into the world." The tower began to writhe like a woman
in childbirth and the figure of death shook. The woman rushed back to the
meeting and said, "Come and see, death is getting loose." The amplification was that there would be many deaths by disease and war, but when she
looked back she saw that the tower was restored after death had jumped
down, and now uppermost was a beautiful female figure in stone which

gave her more confidence.

You can understand the dream from the personal angle: she had a very Christian attitude with ideas of self-mortification; she never allowed herself anything and had a secret wish to die. Since she thought that she herself did not matter, she made up her mind to help others, and gave up her own life completely, building it up again on the principle of death, with the result that she ruined herself psychologically and physically with a Christian attitude of self-mortification. That was the personal aspect of the vision, the uppermost principle being the Christian attitude which served death rather than life. She was living the life of the *Imitatio Christi*, which means that you have to die at about thirty or thirty-two, and lived it with bitter consequences to herself. Also she was animus possessed and completely excluded the feminine side of life, which lack also corresponds to the Christian principle.

In such a case the death principle must be replaced by a female Goddess. So the vision had a personal implication. Moreover at that time she thought she had the beginnings of cancer. On the other hand, it shows the problem of our time in all its implications, even with the dogma of the assumption of the Virgin Mary. The woman had a collective fate and the collective unconscious appears completely naked in her unconscious. The same person dreamt that once when sitting out of doors she heard a humming noise and saw a huge round disc flying in the sky — a metal spider full of human beings. Within the spider a hymn or prayer was repeated which said, "Keep us down on earth, guide us up to heaven"; and the thing went on hovering over a parliament building, something like a UFO, and the people inside were so frightened that they quickly signed the treaty of peace, and then the dreamer discovered that she was not dressed. She had a schizoid disposition, but on top of that is the illustration of the time situation. These would be examples of naive dreams or visions.

I also analyzed a charwoman of a rather suicidal type who was absolutely convinced that her visions were religious revelations meant to be told in our time. She made up her mind to write a libretto and send it to Walt Disney, and from the sketches she made it was not at all stupid. The plan is not as negative as it sounds and Walt Disney might be able to write it up, for the visions which she has and wants to use are distinctly meant to cure our present day difficulties. The problem here is that the woman hasn't the education to bring the thing out properly, and therefore it gets stuck and becomes morbid. Such people have to be helped in a concrete way, but the great question is whether there is sufficient vitality. Had the charwoman been a very vital person, which she was not, I would have told her to attend Migros classes and study and then to serve and be loyal to her vision, and that would have kept her occupied and living for a goal. Unfortunately a schizoid type often has not sufficient vitality, so you can only help with your own vitality or find someone else, but often such people are in a physically miserable state and for that reason cannot bring the thing into shape. There are such types in history who succeed, like Jakob Boehme, who was a shoemaker and who wrote religious revelations based on his visions, though you can see that he was not learned enough to put them in quite the proper form. But he had a great effect on his time and his inner experiences became meaningful for others. Such latent "Jakob Boehmes" exist more frequently than we know.

If therefore such constellations in a society are strong enough, things can happen, as, for instance, in the Christian religion when overnight, as it were, and through the lower layers of the population, a completely new religious attitude arose. Christianity did not at first reach the upper layers of Roman society, it began among the slaves. People had visions of Christ at that time and a very personal relation which spread like a fire among the simple people and expressed their need to be saved from slavery and given a new goal: that would be renewal from below. The king was replaced by a workman or a slave, and that became the dominant symbol. It is even literally expressed in the description of Christ as the King of Kings and at the same time the servant of man.

In our story the king is not yet deposed. The tailor does not become a prince but marries into the royal family and both tailor and shoemaker are at one time servants at the court. So, if we look at the whole structure, we have a king, neither good nor bad, but rather on the decline — which may be concluded from the fact that he has to have help in getting a son and that his crown is lost. He is therefore already approaching the state of the decaying king, but is still potent enough to keep his position and his court; in the realm of collective consciousness and its dominant repre-

30

sentations two opposite factors turn up and play the king against each other. First the shoemaker and then the tailor wins the king's confidence. The former plays the devilish or Luciferian role, like Satan in the Book of Job who complains of Job by saying that he is rich and therefore pious, but take away his goods and then see what happens! The shoemaker, on a smaller scale, functions in exactly the same way in this story: he wins the king's confidence and the tailor is put under tremendous pressure from above.

I would assume that the king represents the dominant collective symbol of our era, i. e., of Christianity, though I could not say exactly of what age, whether in the 16th, 17th or 18th century. The period is difficult to guess in fairy tales, even if you have the outer forms. If pistols are mentioned that gives an indication, but no definite proof. The fact that we have a type of fairy tale similar to that of "Amor and Psyche" shows that the basic structure might be 2,000 years old or more, so the date can perhaps be proved from inner if not from outer evidence, by the archetypal situation. We could say that the king would represent the dominant Christian attitude which has not reached the state of having to be completely deposed or renewed, but where it is no longer strong. Two archetypal factors turn up, two Gods, Mercurius and Saturn; they have constellated at court, and it is a question as to which will win out. In fairy tales, where there is no such thing as the shadow, there is the doubling of an archetypal figure, one half being the shadow of the other. The shadow is the same thing in an individual, but not personally constellated. All the complexes and general structures, i. e., collective complexes which we call complexes, have a light and a dark side and a polarized system. A model of an archetype can be said to be composed of two spheres, one light and the other dark. With the archetype of the Great Mother you have the witch, the devilish mother, the beautiful wise old woman, and the Goddess who represents fertility. In the archetype of the spirit there is the wise old man and the destructive or demonic magician represented in many myths. The archetype of the king can indicate the fertility and strength of the tribe or nation, or the old man who suffocates new life and should be deposed. The hero can be the renewal of life, or the great destroyer, or both. Every archetypal figure has its own shadow. Is that shadow a genuine phenomenon or does it come from the way we look at it? We do not know what

31

an archetype looks like in the unconscious, but when it enters the fringe of consciousness, as in a dream which is a half-conscious phenomenon, it manifests the double aspect. Only when light falls on an object does it throw a shadow.

Probably complexes in the unconscious are the neutral thing — a *complexio oppositorum* — and then they tend to double into a Yes and No, a plus and minus, which is due to consciousness falling on the object. The twin motif in mythology shows that there is always a double, one more introverted and the other extraverted, one male and the other female, one more spirit and the other more animal — but one is not morally better than the other; and then you have myths where one is good and the other evil. I think where there is an ethical attitude in consciousness then the attitude of the twins is ethically discerned, but if there is no ethical consciousness this is not so. In our story there is a difference between good and evil. The Judeo-Christian attitude sharpened the ethical conflict in man, and therefore in our civilization there is a tendency to judge in that way and not to leave things blurred. If an archetypal figure doubles, then it doubles also morally; it appears not only as good and evil, but as lighter and less light — that is the sharpening of ethical response through our religious system.

The contrast of extravert and introvert is held between the tailor and shoemaker. The latter gets bread for seven days because they might be hungry, and the tailor has the extraverted rather light attitude which goes from one situation to the other without too much forethought: they are opposed to each other in this specific way. If we refer this to the symbolism of the king as the Christian dominant, two figures are constellated, one tending towards disagreeable introversion and the other to light extraversion. Are we fantasizing or has Christianity presented such a problem? I think it has. Christian symbolism, especially if you look at its American ramifications (which are characterized by a certain amount of extraverted drive), has an optimistic outlook on life, a great confidence in God, the basic Christian optimism; and that is one kind of Christian attitude because Christianity judges God as good, and evil only as the non-existence of good, which creates an attitude of confidence in oneself and God, a tendency to ignore and not over-emphasize the reality of evil in oneself and others, and the helpful attitude. You have the counter development in Calvanism and other pessimistic sections of Christianity with a specific attitude towards

32

Christianity marked by its mercantile spirit, a completely un-Christian, un-charitable severity of ethical attitudes, a dark melancholy temperament to be found in certain ramifications of Christian thinking. That would correspond to the shoemaker type which has one eye on the hardships of reality. If you study such austere movements within the Christian religion you see that there is no joy of life: people must be sad, must repent their sins, must not enjoy good food because that would be displeasing to Jesus Christ...this type is to be found everywhere, and this kind of tradition. Such people are wealthy, they have "put their foot down," they are sceptical, realistic and distrustful, and are more rooted in the darkness of this world than the others because their warnings against evil and the dark side of life make them so. The optimistic people tend not to see difficulties and get shot from behind for either they are shot at by others, or their own destructive shadow pops out.

   We can say therefore that the tailor also represents a simple kind of naive attitude within the Christian world with a hopeful outlook and trust in God, and that the shoemaker is the opposite, the shadow of that attitude. Both are tendencies within the Christian civilization of a certain time.

33

5 Sept 95
after Thompson Bldg.
r Fri 27th A
2nd reading.

CHAPTER III

RENEWED DOMINANT CONSCIOUSNESS

Last time we tried to amplify the symbolism of the shoemaker and the tailor and to understand the opposite principles which they represent. We considered their functions in relation to the king. There is still more to be said. In *Mysterium Coniunctionis* you will find that the king is the dominant of the collective conscious, a symbol of the Self which has become manifest and worshipped within a community.

Every powerful symbol of the Self unites the opposites, but if it loses its strength it can no longer function in this way and the opposites begin to fall apart. If the king were completely powerful, which he is not, he could reconcile the shoemaker and the tailor and would rule so that they could not afford to quarrel but would have to cooperate — that they get into opposition evinces his weakness. Here he gives his confidence to the shoemaker and listens to the evil insinuations which precipitate the tailor into difficulties. The king is not just, and no longer rules as he should but listens to whatever anybody says. In the end it works out well, but not exactly as expected. We could say that represented here is still a powerful dominant of collective consciousness, but that it has lost its power to unite the opposites properly since they begin to separate and play against each other. This weakening would refer to a situation in our civilization where the opposites begin to fight each other. You could illustrate it with the following diagram:

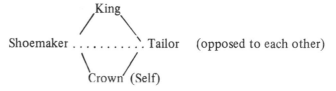

If the king begins to lose power, then the axis of opposition increases, the tension consolidates, and the king waivers between the two, first placing his confidence in one and then in the other: the unifying symbol begins to weaken. I would not refer this to personal psychology, but there is an analogy to individual development, i. e., as long as the attitude of the ego is powerfully engaged in life and is in tune with the instincts, it can hold the opposites together. There are always phases where one is filled with life and the problem of the opposites is not so acute; one knows one has a shadow and that there is always a plus and a minus, but somehow the opposites do not bother one much. Then, for some reason, the ego gets stuck, loses its possibilities and its creative ability, and the opposites fall apart and all sorts of conflicts arise. Then the ego, wavering between the two like the king, strives to identify with one side or the other. It cannot hold a middle place but listens to insinuations and takes sides.

That is typical of an analytical situation, but it is a normal process in life too when the ego is not in union with the deeper layers of the instinctive personality, for then it gets torn between the opposites. If the ego could relate directly to the Self or a unifying symbol, the conflict would fade and the ego would function again in wholeness. That is the normal way in which the opposites function and the main impulse is again the flow of life, the ego serving or moving along the flow of life which comes from the totality. A conflict is never really solved, but the emotion invested in it diminishes, one outgrows it by suffering and it becomes absorbed in a new form of life with the result that one looks back dispassionately on it from a different angle. The king, then, cannot hold the opposites together if he takes sides and no longer really rules.

The tailor and the shoemaker go along together, the tailor happy, and the shoemaker lonely and envious, with the result that when they go through the woods the tragedy begins and the shoemaker wreaks his revenge on the tailor. The shoemaker has saturnine, introverted qualities, like Prometheus. He looks ahead and takes more bread with him than the tailor who, as the Epimethean man, learns only by experience. That is the difference between introvert and extravert: the introvert worries through life, always looking ahead, with the danger of becoming acid, and the extravert jumps first and looks afterwards when he discovers that he has fallen into a hole, whence he struggles out saying that he never saw it. Naturally both attitudes if they become too one-sided are destructive. Here the two get lost in the woods and are hungry and the shoemaker has the bread which he sells to the tailor at the price of his eyes, i. e., he tries to destroy the tailor's beauty, of which he is jealous.

35

You might say that the counter-tendency of the unconscious, the melancholic, suspicious, introverted attitude, blinds the other side and takes away his capacity to see things. As an example, a successful businessman with a strong extraverted drive slowly acquires a suspicious nature brought on through the neglect of his introverted side. If he does not turn to the shadow figure and endeavor to see where his moods originate, he will be blinded and make one mistake after another, for the shadow will force him to change his attitude — if not voluntarily, then involuntarily. He will have failures in his business, or he will fall ill and so be forced to develop the other side. I remember a very extraverted lawyer who had been successful in that extraverted attitude, but he began to have fits of unhappiness and negative moods. When talking to him once I said that it might be a good idea to go for a holiday alone and look at the other side. But he turned the suggestion down, saying that if he was alone he got melancholic and overwhelmed with depression. Then he had a bad accident, he broke his hip and was in the hospital for eight months, so that he had his lonely holidays inescapably forced on him — the other side imposed itself upon him. This would be the mechanism which plays between the opposites as with the shoemaker and the tailor, and which ends in the former leaving the tailor blind under the gallows.

The gallows with the two poor devils hanged on them form an interesting motif which we should follow up. The habit of killing bad criminals by hanging them on trees is a very archaic one. It was originally practiced as a sacrifice: Germans in olden days, for instance, hanged people as sacrifices to the God Wotan. They hanged not only criminals but also enemies captured in battle. The victor would say to his prisoner, "Now I will dedicate you to Wotan." Wotan himself is the God who hangs on the tree, for he hung on the oak Yggdrasil for nine days and nights and then found the runes and acquired secret wisdom. It is an old Germanic idea that suspension on a tree is a sacrifice to that God. In Christianity you meet this archetypal idea in the form of the crucifixion of Christ, and in the area of Asia Minor Attis is suspended on the fir tree. He is killed and his picture is hanged on a fir tree, and in the Spring festivals the image of the suspended Attis is shown. It is pre-Christian and is found in Germanic

36

and Mediterranean mythological circles. Everybody crucified or hanged is
dedicated to such a God.

We have to ask what lies behind the idea of killing an enemy not as
social revenge or in judgment, but by the more archaic form of a sacrifice
to the Gods. I think that there is a much deeper and more meaningful idea
than that of just punishment. If one has to fight against demonic evil in a
human being, what strikes one most is that if people are outstandingly destructive, not just through the small mistakes of laziness and cheating, etc.,
which take place with every human being, but if they are seriously destructive, one's immediate reaction is that it is inhuman, especially in psychosis
or psychotic states where one sometimes meets destructiveness so cold and
inhuman and demonic, and concomitantly so "divine," that one is overwhelmed. It sends a grim cold shiver down one's spine that one cannot
deal with — it is too horrible, too shocking; and this shocking, horrible
thing in people enables them to commit cold-blooded murder.

I have never dealt with anybody who committed an actual murder, but
I have met people who could have, and that makes one shudder, and one
thinks "Hands off," yet, at the same time, one has the feeling that it is
something Godlike, no longer human. We use the word "inhuman" but
one could equally well say "demonic" or "divine." The primitive idea
that somebody who commits a murder or an outstanding crime is really
not himself but performs something which only a God could do, expresses
the situation very well. In the moment when someone commits a murder
he is identical with the Godhead and is not human. People become the
instruments of this darkness. At such a time, they are possessed, or completely identical. The very fact that somebody imagines that he can kill a
fellow being, someone of the same substance as himself, which is not normal among warm-blooded animals, transcends human nature and in that
way the deed has this demonic or divine quality. That is why, for instance,
in the ritual executions in primitive tribes, you see that though they kill the
criminals there is no element of moral judgment about it, the criminal simply bears the consequences of his deeds. The primitive says that if a human
being acts as though divine, then he suffers the fate of a God, is treated as
a God and hanged, killed, or dismembered, and so on. One cannot be in
human society and behave like a divine being who can kill *ad libitum*.

Someone lent me a paper about the execution of a member of a North

37

American Indian tribe. A medicine man made the mistake of asking too high fees of people and made such an abuse of this habit that he became inhuman. From a widow he took everything and left her ruined – he went beyond human limits. These acts aroused suspicion in the tribe, but it did not mature for a long time; instead, the suspicion went beneath the surface. The medicine man continued in this way, and feeling the criticism in his surroundings, became more and more demanding, probably to compensate the uncertainty in himself. He claimed to be the best medicine man, etc., until the whisperings in the tribe that he must be possessed by an evil spirit became louder and louder.

One day the elders of the tribe told him that the tribe believed him to be possessed by evil. As the medicine man did not deny it, they took him into the desert for trial by ordeal to find out if it was true. They made sand paintings and drawings and all the medicine men invoked the spirits saying that the medicine man was possessed by evil demons and did they wish to save him. The accused medicine man prayed with the others. Since no answer came, he was executed – quartered by four horses. He agreed with the sentence himself. To him it was not a question of being morally condemned but simply of having fallen inextricably for the Gods of evil, of losing his humanness. He was absolutely at peace with himself. This is the natural behavior towards the evil forces in man, which seems impressive and close to the psychological truth of these things. This closeness probably reveals why criminals often are executed in a way by which they are identified with a God; one recognizes that they have fallen into the hands of the dark Godhead and therefore have to suffer their bitter fate.

The symbolism of the suspended God, the gallows, and the cross should be examined. Such fates normally overtake that part of the Divinity most interested in man; the philanthropic part of the Godhead falls into the tragedy of suspension, and has to do with the bringing of civilization – as in the Wotan myth where after suspension on the tree Wotan discovers the runes, an implication of a progress in consciousness. We have first to go into the symbolism of the tree. You probably all know the chapter on "The Philosophical Tree" in Jung's *Alchemical Studies*. Jung shows there that the tree symbolizes human life and development and the inner process of becoming conscious in the human being. You could say that it symbolizes

38

in the psyche that something which grows and develops undisturbed within us, irrespective of what the ego does; it is the urge towards individuation which unfolds and continues without reference to consciousness. When a child is born a tree is planted at the same time and will die when the human dies. There is the strange idea that the tree provides an analogy of human life, that the tree carries life, like the lights on the Christmas tree, and that the sun rising at the top of the tree implies growth towards higher consciousness. There are many mythological writings which liken the tree to the human being, or in which the tree appears as a man-tree. The Self is the tree — that which is greater than the ego in man.

Part of our life passes like a drama written by a novelist biographer, but behind that there is a mysterious process of growth which follows its own laws and takes place behind the biographical peripeteias of life and goes from childhood to old age. In a mythological connection, the greater human being, the anthropos, is likened to a tree. The human being is suspended on the tree because the conscious human constantly pulls away, trying to free himself and to act freely and consciously and he is then painfully pulled back to the inner process. The struggle reveals a tragic constellation if it is represented in this painful form. That is why the whole philosophy of the Christian religion has a tragic view of life: to follow Christ we have to accept mortification and repress certain natural growth. The basic idea is that human life is based on conflict and strives towards spiritualization which does not come of itself but is brought forth with pain. The same idea is represented in a more archaic form in the Wotan myth — Wotan hanging on the tree. He is the eternal wanderer who roams all over the earth, the God of impulsiveness, of rage, of poetic inspiration, that element in the human being in constant restlessness, bursting out into affect; and if this God is suspended on the tree for nine days and nine nights, he consequently discovers the runes of writing by which civilization based on the written word is founded.

Whenever the conscious and animal personality is in conflict with the inner process of growth, it suffers crucifixion; it is in the situation of the God suspended on the tree and is involuntarily nailed to an unconscious development from which it would like to break away but cannot. We know the states one falls into when nailed down to something greater than ourselves which does not allow us to move and which outgrows us.

39

The Attis myth, which is older than the myth of the crucified God in Christianity, represents this in specific form. Attis, the beloved son of the Great Mother and himself the type of divine being that does not grow old and decay, represents the pattern of the *puer eternus*, the perennially young God, eternally beautiful, the figure which cannot suffer sadness, human restriction, disease, ugliness and death. Like this God, most young men who have a decided mother complex feel, at some moment in their lives, that the process of life does not allow for such a state to be eternal; it has to die. In the plenitude of life, life lies ahead with its meaningfulness and splendor; but we know that this never lasts — it is always destroyed by the other side of life. Therefore this young God always dies early, nailed to the tree, which is again the mother; the maternal principle which gave birth to him swallows him back in the negative form and he is reached by ugliness and death.

You see this sometimes in the case of a young man who should marry or choose a profession, or who discovers that the fullness of youth is leaving him and that he has to accept the ordinary human fate. Many at that moment prefer to die either by an accident or in war, rather than become old. At the critical time, between thirty and forty, the tree is growing against them, their inner development is no longer in tune with the conscious attitude, but grows against it, and in that moment they have to suffer a kind of death; it should mean a change of attitude, but may mean actual physical death, a kind of disguised suicide, because the ego cannot give up its attitude — that is the crucial moment where they are sacrificed by a process of inner development which has turned against them. When the inner growth is the enemy of consciousness something within the man wants to outgrow him that he cannot follow and therefore has to die; for the self-will of the conscious personality has to die and surrender to the process of inner growth. Christ was crucified because that was the normal and most humiliating punishment for run-away slaves and criminals in the Roman Empire. This symbol has always been behind the Christian motif.

Another aspect of hanging as a means of killing something is that in most mythological systems the air is the place in which ghosts and spirits roam about, like Wotan and his army of ghosts of the dead that fly through the air, especially on stormy nights, and hunt with the dead. They live in the air. Therefore if you hang someone you turn him into a ghost and he must now ride with the other dead, with Wotan in the air. In the cult of

Dionysus gifts were put on swings on the tree with the idea that Dionysus was a spirit and would see them; the gifts could thus be lifted up into the air and given to the spiritual beings who lived there. An expression illustrates this situation from a certain angle: we speak of suspension. When an inner psychological conflict gets too bad, life gets suspended; the two opposites are equal, the Yes and the No are equally strong, and life cannot go on. You wish to move with the right leg and the left refuses, and vice versa, and you have the situation of suspension, which means a complete stoppage in the flow of life and intolerable suffering. Stuck in sterile conflict, nothing happening, is the most painful form of suffering.

When the shoemaker has blinded the tailor where the two criminals are hung, we might say that that symbolizes a suspension of conflict where the process of life has stopped. The opposites have clashed and life has stuck. The two dead people on the gallows mirror the shoemaker and tailor now in a state of sterile suspension. Naturally, as we have referred the whole story to the situation of the collective Christian era, we have to ask who these two are. If it were one suspended man the idea would be close at hand as a hidden form of the symbol of Christ, the basic symbol of the Christian religion, the God hanging on the cross, but there are two sinners and therefore we have to ask who the second could be?

There are several, especially German, fairy tales which represent the evil spirit nailed to a tree or wall. Or the two people might in the same way allude to Christ suspended on the cross and Wotan on the tree, the good God suspended on the cross and the other God on the tree. This is not too far-fetched because the motif of the two divine beings nailed to the tree or the cross occurs in many Christian legends and in the legends of the Arthurian circles and the circle of the Holy Grail where Perceval has really a feeling of Christ and has not only to find the Grail containing his love but also the stag, or stag's head, nailed to an oak tree, from which he has to take it down. In the main legend he does not forget and he finds the Grail before finding the stag's head and brings *it* to a divine female figure; or the stag is represented as an evil doer, a destroyer of the woods and Christ's shadow. The stag with its beautiful antlers, an unnecessary decoration which hampers its movements and whose object is to impress the female deer, suggests the idea of an arrogant creature and therefore represents the shadow of the Christian principle, an incredible arrogance

41

and superciliousness which we have acquired and which seems one of the worst shadow attitudes spread by Christian teaching.

A concrete illustration of what this arrogant shadow means often crops up in analysis: under the cloak of being Christian and kind to our fellow men we do not speak of our resistances, but, instead, produce a lot of negative assertions and judgments with a sweet Christian attitude, until a dream shows what has happened. The analysand has not spoken of resistances because that might lead to difficulties and anyway the analyst has "already been forgiven." That is arrogance! It would be much simpler to say, "I blame you for this and that, what have you to say about it? " That would be being human, modest, and normally related. But instead, animus arguments hide under the cloak of "forgiveness" and a virtuous and superior attitude and the knowledge that "the analyst is a human being and has negative sides." That is the poison of the wrong Christian attitude. I have often met with this and resent the forgiveness and sweetness of people and would prefer that they were more naturally related and would say straight out what they thought so that one could get to a human understanding. This shadow of the Christian attitude is symbolized by the stag hung up in the tree in the medieval legends. If someone just pardons a fellow human being, then nothing happens, the negative assumptions remain for the next ten years! Such people will keep their negative judgments of the analyst for three or four years of analysis and have neither the courage nor decency to discuss the thing, they are sure the other could not take it and that it would be un-Christian to bring it up. The negative assumption then gets stuck and the positive attitude of "politeness and forgiveness" remains. If an analysis gets stuck you may be sure that something like this has happened. You cannot always catch it but it is there and neither the good nor the evil side can evolve. Through discussion relationship could re-establish itself and the whole thing would flow again. That is a place where one generally has to interfere and perhaps suggest that the analysand go to a colleague, and generally then there is a big outburst that gives material on which to proceed. Usually there is a false attitude in the conscious personality and the idea that "this is something with which I can deal myself," and so the person's own inner development is hindered through narrowness and prejudice.

While the tailor sits under the gallows, on the head of each of the men

42

hanging above him is a crow, and the two begin to talk. The first one says
that the dew which this night has fallen over them from the gallows will restore the eyesight of anyone who washes in it. If the blind knew that, many
who do not think it possible could have their sight restored. Here is a general and archetypal representation found in many civilizations and religious
creeds: the remains of an executed criminal are potent medicine. It con-
firms the idea that execution is a deification, that the criminal had the
arrogance to assume the role of the Gods and so is given back to them; and
what was negative in the living human becomes positive in the Beyond,
what was destructive in the human state is again constructive when back in
its proper place. The right power behind the divine and the human is re-
established and through that a potent medicine is produced, so that the
rope on which the human being was hung was used for healing purposes.
"Take a piece of the rope on which a man has been hung, or nail parings,
etc., and you will find a potent medicine." The healing power in the
relics of the saints has the same idea. The fact that executed criminals
are treated like saints shows what the common idea is.

The birds, which in Germanic mythology belong to Wotan, and in the
Mediterranean to Apollo, represent the capacity for divination. Apollo is
the owner of the Delphic oracle and the revealer of truth, and the same
applies to Wotan. The birds, the ravens and crows, are believed capable of
knowing the future and of telling the hidden truth. In part this evolved
since ravens and crows often assemble in places where a battle takes place,
or on a house where someone is dying. When many crows or ravens frequently assemble in a place, people say that someone will die and that the
crows know it. From that hook came the projection that they knew the
truth and the future. Wotan had two ravens, Hugin and Munin, his sources
of secret information. Birds in general represent intuition: creatures which
fly in the air, in the medium of the spiritual world, and have therefore to
do with secret hunches, the involuntary thoughts which are revealed to be
true. These two birds are the spirits of truthfulness. In the end the shoemaker finishes up under the gallows and the crows pick out his eyes. The
birds represent that invisible truth of the unconscious which fulfills itself;
the shoemaker does not come to his end by human power but by the unconscious truth.

If we observe unconscious processes we see that wrong deeds do not

43

have to be avenged by other human beings for they are punished from within. The murderer ultimately kills himself. This is a terrible truth again and again confirmed. Frequently one is shocked by the injustice of human life, when the evil man prospers and the good man does not, but, psychologically, this is not true and it sometimes makes one shudder to realize what people risk. They may succeed in the outer world, but they incur terrible psychological punishment.

Jung once told of a woman who had committed murder. She put poison in the soup of another woman who was in love with her lover, and she was not found out. She came to confession absolutely destroyed. She felt cut off, for people had begun to avoid her without knowing why. She lost all her maids and servants and nobody wanted to live near her. She lived quite alone. She rode everyday, but then the horse would bolt and would not carry her, and when one morning she called her dog and the dog put its tail between its legs and slunk away, she had to confess. She was slowly and cruelly ruined from within. This secret truth, the law of inner truth, is here expressed by the crows who are the spirit of truth and also have to do with healing power. In the tale of Apollo and Coronis, from who's union resulted the birth of Aesclapius, the crow too gave valuable information. It is the crows who call the tailor's attention to the cure for his eyes.

Dew in general carries the projection of manifesting an act of divine grace. In the Bible we have the story of Gideon's fleece on which the dew falls, an act by God which showed his grace. This has also been interpreted as a prefiguration of the Holy Ghost falling on the Virgin Mary. In North American civilization, dew and rain are *the* great blessings on which depend the fertility of the earth. One must perhaps have lived in such a country to know the feeling of the dew or rain that is experienced as divine grace, for by it everything comes to life. Now that these sinners have paid for their sins the grace of God falls on them again; in the Beyond there is a reconciliation of the opposites and therefore the dew has healing power. Psychologically, dew represents the first beginning of objective psychological manifestations in such a state of suspension.

Let us return to the conflict as it reaches its climax. There is the state of suspension where everything has stuck, the ego is in the state of Yes and No, and there is the torture of arrested life and sterility. In such a moment the ego surrenders, saying that this is an insoluble conflict — one which *it*

44

cannot solve — and will submit to something objective, to a sign which will become evident. We say we will submit to what the dreams say. Neither analyst nor analysand can say anything further, but does the objective psyche produce any kind of material or signs which lead further? Only the dreams and fantasies are left, and they represent the dew, an objective living manifestation which comes from the depth of the psyche and can be studied, and which restores eyesight. If you can then understand the secret hints which are contained in a dream, your eyes are opened and you rediscover life and find it on a new level. Only the guidance of the unconscious can help at such a moment and provide the healing dew which falls upon us. That is why the tailor uses the dew and is able to go on again with his eyes cured and thanks God and goes to the king's city. In alchemy, the "divine" water is also the healing remedy for blindness.

Afterwards come the four tests where the tailor spares the horse by not riding him, the stork and the ducks by not eating them, and the bees by not taking away their nest. He then becomes the tailor at the king's court, where the shoemaker slanders him so that he is forced to find the golden crown, which the ducks bring up from the bottom of the lake; to make a well, which the horse stamps out of the ground; to build a copy of the royal castle, which the bees make from their wax; and then the stork brings a boy to the king who has only daughters. Four tasks, the typical number of totality. If you know many fairy tales you will know that this is not normal, for normally there are only three tasks, but in that case there is always a fourth thing which happens — an event and not a task. Here there are four tasks and no further event, the further event would be that the tailor becomes king.

The horse stamps out the water for the well. These are symbols of transformation. The horse renews a kind of domesticated vital libido which can bring forth the well of the unconscious. Only if we can invest our whole instinctive unconscious does it begin to produce its water of life. There are people who want to write on a theme but say it is dull and does not appeal to them, but after investing some libido in it they discover the water. Many lazy people wait for inspiration until they are eighty and none comes, but there are situations where one cannot wait, one has to make the first move and invest one's own vital strength in the task before it pays back, like the ducks which bring up the crown from the bottom of the lake.

45

The king has to be renewed, and the crown is the symbol of totality that has to be brought up. There are two ducks, two gallows, two eyes, and then two new eyes, there is always the duality. Because the tailor suffers the dualities and cooperates instead of fighting, he ends the suspension of the king's power; a renewed healthy relationship with the dualities of the unconscious allows vital life processes to flow again.

The motif of the model castle is a strange one (the model is probably put under a glass and shown to visitors), but if we consider it we must say that bees have always appealed to the human mind by their organized behavior, as evidenced also by the termites. Bees have an incredible unconscious cooperation of the whole group, though we think of them as completely unconscious and as having only the sympathetic nervous system. A book written by Karl von Frisch described most astonishing experiments made with bees. They can distinguish colors and can show each other where food is to be found. A bee will fly in a big circle and find honey, but does not have to fly back the same way, it can go straight and by certain movements of the back and wings can show and tell the others so that they can go straight to the honey. It has been discovered that their system of orientation has to do with the polarization of sunlight. The unconscious instinct of the bee is overwhelming and they therefore stand for a harmonious functioning without rational organization.

The more a system is educated, the more cooperation has to be forced and established by rational organization. So with the collective situation. Yet the same thing holds for the individual. As long as the conscious of the individual is carrying, it needs no forcing, it acts out of joy and impulse and does not need the help of the alarm clock. We have to have recourse to rationalization where we are not in tune. When life flows again all this discipline, now unnecessary once more, can be given up. Instinctual oneness with one's task and surroundings is an ideal state, the state where the archetype simply holds people together and they cooperate on a natural basis. This is a functioning which man has always lost and sought again — you find it in all youthful communities. In Zen Buddhism in late antiquity there were such groups gripped by the same living symbol; they were strong, social bodies which functioned without too many outer regulations. We know a little of the initiation of Apuleius into the Isis mysteries. He was to have been initiated into a higher degree but had not the money; then Osiris told him to go to the priest and ask to be initiated, and the priest had had a dream telling him to reduce the fees. The God therefore organized the group and both the priest and the organization submitted to archetypal functioning. As long as a community functions in that way there is real freedom of the human being and cultural life in a group.

So we can say that the building of the castle by the bees is a model of the rebuilding function in the state. And then the stork, the pious bird, as the old Jewish tradition says, brings the new child. In Jung's book *Alchemical Studies* there is a lot about the stork. He discusses the alchemical picture of the tree of life, on a high branch of which is the stork. The mysterious mythological meaning of the stork in Jewish tradition goes back to Jeremiah 8:7, "Yes, the stork in the heaven knoweth her appointed times: and the turtle and the crane and the swallow observe the time of their coming; but my people know not the judgment of the Lord." The stork stands for something which has its divine orientation from above from which it cannot deviate, like the wild geese who carry the same projection in Eastern mythology. The ancient pattern of this bird gives one the impression that it is obeying a secret order and has secret knowledge and knows how to behave. Storks live in North Africa in the winter. There are two types, one flies over Spain and the other over Yugoslavia. They fly as far as possible overland. Experiments have been made and eggs taken and hatched of the Spanish group: such a bird *sent off alone* at the proper time will instinctively take the Spanish route, and the bird hatched from the Yugoslav type will take that route. They will fly their right route, according to their pattern, even without companions, for they are guided by the urge from within. Such observations have given rise to the idea that they are pious birds which obey their own laws without ego judgment and they therefore stand for functioning in accordance with the inner truth and inner being. For this, and since it was believed to hate and kill snakes, the stork was taken as a symbol of Christ — as the transcendent function, that manifestation of the unconscious which tends to bring up the reconciling symbol, the bringer of the child and rebirth. It functions here by bringing a renewed form of dominant consciousness: the new king.

CHAPTER IV

THE ANIMA AND RENEWAL

In our next story, "The Loyal and the Disloyal Ferdinand," which picks up the same theme as "The Two Wanderers," the two people characterize the ethical opposites more definitely. A synopsis of the tale goes like this:

A very poor couple, she long barren, at last had a little boy but could not find any godparents for him. The man said he would go to another place and see if he could find someone there. On the way he met a poor old man who asked where he was going, and he replied that he was looking for godparents for his child, and that since they were so poor they could not find anybody. "Oh," said the man, "you are poor and so am I – I will be the godfather; but I am too poor to give the child a present." When they brought the child to the church to be baptized, the old man was already there and named the child Ferdinand the Loyal.

When they left the church, the beggar said he could not give a present, and they mustn't give him anything either, but he gave a key which the boy was to keep until he was fourteen and then he would see a castle in the meadow which the key would open, and the contents would be his. When the child was seven he played with other children who had had presents from their godparents and when he went home he asked his father if he had had nothing at all from his. "Oh, yes," said his father, "you received a key and when there is a castle in the meadow the key will open it." So the boy went to look but there was no castle. Seven years later he went again and there was a castle, and inside it a horse. And the boy was so delighted that he had a horse that he got on it and went to his father and said that now he would go on a journey.

On the way he saw a quill pen lying on the road, but he did not pick it up for he thought he could always get one if he wanted it. But as he rode away a voice called to him to pick it up, so he did. When he had ridden a little further he came to some water, and on the bank was a fish gasping for breath, so he threw it into the water. And the fish stuck its head out of the water and said that he would give him a flute as a reward

48

for having saved him, and that if ever he was in any difficulty
through having let something fall into the water, he should
play on his flute, and the fish would come and help him. So he
rode on and then a man came to him and asked where he was
going and what his name was, and he said he had almost the
same name for he was called Ferdinand the Disloyal. The two
went together to an inn in the next village.

But there things became bad, for Ferdinand the Disloyal
knew all that other people thought and wanted to do, and he
knew how to commit all kinds of evil. At the inn there was a
very pretty girl and she fell in love with Ferdinand the Loyal
and asked where he was going, and he told her that he was
riding around. The girl said he should stay there for there was
a king who was very glad to have servants, or defenders; and
she went to the king herself and told him about Ferdinand and
that he would be a good servant. So Ferdinand and his horse
were made servants of the king, and Ferdinand was appointed
head rider. But then the girl had to help Ferdinand the Disloyal,
who was also engaged by the king.

Learning that the king was unhappy because his beloved was
not with him, Ferdinand the Disloyal said the king should send
Ferdinand the Loyal to fetch her, and if he did not his head
should be cut off.

So Ferdinand the Loyal went to the stable where his horse
was and cried and said what an unhappy man he was and that
he would have to leave his horse and die. But a voice asked
him why he was crying. And Ferdinand said to his horse, "Can
you talk? I should go and fetch the bride, but how can I do
that?" And the horse told him he should go to the king and
tell him that if he would give him what was needed — a ship
full of meat and another full of bread — he, Ferdinand, would
fetch the bride. The horse told Ferdinand that there were
dreadful giants on the water and if he did not give them meat
they would tear him to pieces, and that there were birds who
would pick out his eyes if he didn't bring them bread.

The king gave him what he needed. Then the horse said
that they should go on board the ship, and when the giants
came Ferdinand should say to them, "Quiet, quiet, my dear
giants, I remembered you and have brought meat for you,"
and when the birds came he should say, "Quiet, quiet, my
dear birds, I remembered you and brought something for you."
Then they would not hurt him and when he came to the castle

49

the giants would help and he should take a couple of them to the castle with him where he would find the princess asleep. And he should not wake her but the giants should pick her up with the bed and carry her to the ship. Everything happened as the horse had said, and the giants carried the princess on her bed to the king. But the princess said she could not stay for she needed documents which had been left at the castle.

Again Ferdinand the Disloyal went to the king and said he should send Ferdinand the Loyal to fetch the papers or face death. So Ferdinand went to the stable and cried and said that once more he had to go. The same thing happened as before, and when they came to the castle Ferdinand went in and found the papers in the princess' bedroom in a chest. When they were on the water again, Ferdinand let his quill pen fall into the water and the horse said that this time he could not help. Then Ferdinand began to play on the flute, and the fish came and picked up the pen in his mouth and gave it to Ferdinand. So they brought the papers to the castle where the wedding was to take place.

Now the princess did not like the king because he had no nose, but she liked Ferdinand, and once when all the men were at court she said she could work magic — she could cut someone's head off and put it on again. Since nobody wanted to be the first, Ferdinand the Disloyal egged on Ferdinand the Loyal. The princess cut his head off and put it on again, and only a red thread was to be seen. The king asked where she had learned to do that. "Oh," said the princess, "I know how to do it; shall I try to cut your head off?" "Oh, yes!" he said. So she cut off his head but didn't put it on again! So the king was buried.

Then the horse said Ferdinand should ride on his back and gallop round the field three times. When he had done that the horse stood on his hind legs and was transformed into a prince.

It is a relatively incomplete story and there are some rather unsatisfactory motifs. For instance, the quill pen must have been taken over from another tale where it had a connection. It is a very old European story found in many versions which goes back to the Jewish Latin of Rabbi Johannan in the 12th century where the latter has to find the bride of King Solomon. In this story the destructive disloyal figure is not represented by a man, but by the rabbi's wife, who only wants money and who is finally killed. The king is also not beheaded in the end. Yet the basic idea of a loyal man who has to perform peculiar deeds for the king and is undermined by disloyal figures is found in this old manuscript. It must come from legendary material. Though our story is specifically German in form, it is also found in Italy, Spain, Russia and Scandinavia. In this context the motif of the quill pen seems rather meaningless.

Our main concern here is with the shadow problem where we again have the two men who wander about together, one slandering the other at the king's court. You may think that this is not such a good story and that it does not add anything new, and may wonder why I chose it, but it has some features which lead even beyond the first tale.

If you remember I made a diagram which we can use again here:

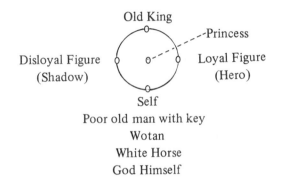

Old King

Princess

Disloyal Figure   Loyal Figure
(Shadow)   (Hero)

Self
Poor old man with key
Wotan
White Horse
God Himself

I said before that a renewal could come up only from the fourth factor, which is always the Self, and that would be the play of the opposites which the king should unite. In the other story the king was incomplete, since he was unable to produce a son, but all the same he remained king and was not deposed at the end of the story. This time we have a more classical and usual form in which the old king is deposed, but here he is incomplete because he has no nose, and is therefore unattractive to the princess.

The nose is the organ with which one smells and therefore has much to do with the function of intuition. One can say that a stockbroker has a "flair" for knowing the stock market, or that he "uses his nose" to scent out future possibilities. Also you can "smell a rat" in a situation, or something can "have a bad smell." There are many analogies to smelling, usually connected with intuitive perceptions which you cannot get through mere sensation. Therefore one could say that the king has lost his instinctive intuition; he can no longer instinctively smell out the right thing to do — that is, he is not in tune with his own unconscious. When we are not in tune we lose the capacity to notice what is wrong with ourselves or others.

As you know, most animals have a large lobe in the brain which concentrates on the function of smelling, and we must assume that they have a great sense of smell and that man is very much crippled in this respect. Apparently in order to build up one capacity in the brain others have to be sacrificed, and there is a theory that man's intelligence has been built up by the sacrifice of the sense of smell. Professor Vogt, a famous eye specialist, thought that short-sightedness was on the increase and that there was a tendency to build up man's brain at the expense of sight. People do not depend on sight and smell as much as formerly, and it is possible that these capacities will be sacrificed to produce other functions of the brain, for a capacity lost on one concrete level may return, so to speak, on a higher level; it may become a psychological function and be replaced by intuition, by psychological perception instead of physical perception. Therefore, if the king has no nose he has lost his natural capacity for distinguishing facts, and that fits in with the fact that he falls in with Disloyal Ferdinand's destructive suggestions and does not "smell a rat." Moreover, he has lost his beloved princess and apparently is unable to find her himself. Naturally the bride does not want to marry a man who has not the courage to come and fetch her.

In this story the symbol of the Self is personified by the poor old man and not by the king. This old man, whom nobody knows and who disappears after the baptism, gives the white horse, the speaking horse, which is also the unredeemed prince who has been bewitched. In other versions it turns out later that the poor old man who gave the horse is the horse himself.

J. Bolte and G. Polivka have written a five volume book entitled *Anmerkungen zu den Kinder- und Hausmärchen der Brüder Grimm*, 1913-32, which gives all the connections in all the Grimm's fairy tales of other countries, as well as the dates of the oldest manuscripts, etc. In this collection of parallels one says that the poor old man is the horse himself and another that the poor old man is God himself.

Fairy tales frequently speak of God wandering about the earth and some even start off, "In olden days when God was still wandering about on the earth..." The idea that God is a physical entity and walks about and can be met in ordinary form among us is contrary to our idea of God, but in folklore you often meet with the idea that he goes about in an unknown form, like an old man in the woods. There are interesting amplifications of the figure of the unknown old God-Father and the white horse. The old Germanic God Wotan is the God who wanders about among people and who goes to the king's court, his cap pulled down over his blind eye and wearing a gray or bluish-gray coat, and who asks for food and permission to stay the night, and then tells marvelous stories, after which he suddenly disappears and people know who it must have been. In another story Wotan goes to the smithy and has his horse shod and suddenly the smith sees the white horse jump high over the wall and disappear. Sometimes he is riding a white horse with eight legs called Sleipnir, who is the animal representation of the God himself. So we can see that there are definite connections with the old pagan image of God which turns up again here in the story as a compensation for the Christian figure of God.

There is another connection: this poor old man in our story has a key he gives to the child which unlocks everything. In another version the hero is not called Ferdinand the Loyal but Peter. St. Peter always had an attraction for the simple people because he is more understanding and closer to us than Christ. There are many stories in which St. Peter wanders about with Christ and in which he is always the damn fool who does stupid things and is told by God of his misdeeds. Also he is irascible and always making a fool of himself. In one story Jesus and Peter went about without money and got food without paying for it and Christ through some ruse arranges that Peter shall sleep on the outside of the bed so he would get the thrashing from the innkeeper when he discovers that he has not been paid. There are many variations of such stories in which St. Peter plays the shadow role: he is more human and more stupid than Christ. In a religion which has become too spiritualized human contact vanishes, there is no contact with the Godhead; consequently, the fantasies of simple people have brought up such themes again to make contact possible. St. Peter is a naive fellow, human in every sense of the word, a kind of duplicate figure of the figure of God but with the qualities which we do not dare to attribute to God, but the old paternal figure of God is now projected on to him. In the Bible St. Peter betrayed Christ at the crucial moment, but

53

compensated for it by his naive loyalty to his master. Then his irascible side was the cause of his cutting off Malchus' ear, the High Priest's servant, which Christ had to heal. So he represents qualities of the more primitive divine incarnation which are lacking in the Christ figure, but nevertheless Christ favors him, giving him the keys and the power to open the gates of heaven.

In the history of mythology St. Peter has inherited many of the qualities of the old Roman God Janus, from whom the month of January gets its name. He is also the doorkeeper and has in his hand the end and the beginning, and a head facing both ways. The month of January was dedicated to him for with it one year ends and the other begins. In Roman pre-Christian times he was the first God to create the world, a God in whom the beginning and the end are the opposites and completely together, and who had the keys. St. Peter has inherited certain qualities of this older archetypal figure for he could see both sides and also has the keys. One could say that in the naive name of Peter, there is an allusion to the fact that there is an old pagan figure of divinity behind this figure: the two figures have merged.

If the king is the representative of dominant collective consciousness, he must represent a dominant religious attitude and its symbolism, and if therefore the old man wanders about, building up the new king, he would be the more archaic figure of God who has qualities which have been lost in the dominant and are once more needed. This older God-image has the following qualities: he is irascible, just as the Old Testament Jahweh was before conversion in the New Testament; he has equally impulsive reactions; he is capable of contacting man by wandering about on the earth; and so on. He is closer to human incompleteness than the divine figure of the Christian religion, closer to our human feeling if we feel incomplete.

It is this incomplete and more archaic figure of God which has the secret power in this fairy tale to protect the hero and slowly build him up to become king. The beggar, then, is a representative of the transcendent function.

The Disloyal Ferdinand, the figure on the left of the diagram, is the slanderer who gets the conservative, aggressive tendency on his side with his plan to kill the new symbol of dominant consciousness, but he does not succeed. It is not the battle between the two Ferdinands, however, which is decisive. The primitive idea would be that there should be a fight and one would see which was the conqueror: that would be the solution of the shadow problem. But this is not true, the conflict is solved through another factor. It is also not the poor old man and the white horse which decides, for even the white horse has to be redeemed in the end. The figure which makes the new king is the fifth, the princess who refuses to marry the old king and prefers Ferdinand. She shifts the whole situation; she is the center of the story.

All the other motifs are relatively easy to interpret. The first problem is that he has to wait until he is fourteen, the age of puberty. A boy in those days was thought to be more or less grown up at that age. In the 16th century many boys of twelve were officers in the Dutch army: that is the magic age which should continue. In a dream series you may see that a change of personality is in preparation and then you have to wait for what is coming up from the unconscious, but before the time has come, either the outer event or the inner realization, nothing can be speeded up. The inner processes have their own time limit, their own rhythm, and cannot be hastened in any way. Thus the idea of the magic times and the moments of truth has been built up, and you have to wait till the time is ripe or completed, till the inner or outer change can take place.

The castle is an impersonal, feminine symbol, sometimes of the anima, but it is built by man and therefore is a specific aspect of the maternal image, the image of an anima-Goddess which has been worked on in former civilizations and in which you can find a new content. Castles are sometimes a system of fantasy building, such as children play at. People build themselves a castle or house in active imagination sometimes, and live inside it for a long time. They build up a framework of a specific attitude in which they can live; the castles provide the defense. The more unfavorable the outer conditions, the more a child tends to live in such a castle where behind the walls of the castle it can live its own life. Here the new image ripens, a new image of the God-Father. The hero is the new bringer of the sun. In the German poem "Heliand" Christ was represented as riding on a white horse. He was the bringer of a new light and the instinctive libido which tends towards a new consciousness. The horse can talk and turns out to be another prince.

The princess' lost papers and the idea of the lost feather we can take only as a just-so story; the figure of the anima is connected with the lost papers and the hero had something with which he should write. It therefore has to do with the capacity for poetical expression. Since the story has such a Wotanic background, we can remind ourselves that Wotan is the God of poetry and poetic writing, and it might be that the creative quality of the anima is lost with her and has to be found again through a renewal of attitude. I think there may be an historical background for this, but it is not important for our purpose. What we have to look at is the strange problem of why the difficult position with the shadow does not lead to a fight, the solution being brought about by another factor. This gives us a practical hint about the personal shadow problem of the individual. As far as I have seen, if the conscious personality is up against the shadow and takes the shadow seriously without cheating and double crossing, it ends with a complete suspension in the conflict. If the ego takes a one-sided ethical decision and a one-sided moral attitude and gets into real conflict with the shadow, there is no solution. That is one of the problems of our civilization.

In most primitive civilizations people never come to a serious shadow conflict because they can shift unthinkingly from one attitude to another and the right hand does not know what the left hand does. You can see this in missionaries' reports. They do something for the tribe which becomes quite attached to them, but then there is an epidemic and the missionary is blamed and killed: the counter movement comes up. Afterwards they regret it, but they are not really upset or depressed at what has happened and life goes on. This is an extreme case of something which happens to us all the time. The shadow conflict does not become too acute because we have a shifting attitude by which we live. We try to be good and commit all sorts of bad things which we do not notice, or, if we notice them, we have an excuse, a headache, or it was the other person's fault, or you forget about it, that is how the shadow problem is usually dealt with. I do not actually criticize this because it is the only way we can live. One has a shadow, a strong instinctive power, and if one does not want to get stuck in an insoluble problem one must ignore some things so as to be able to get through life. You get a certain amount of recognition and criticism, but if you do not go too far, you achieve a kind of in-between solution. If people are ethically sensitive and scrupulous the thing becomes more difficult, but as long as they know no psychology it is not such a problem.

Christian people, however, are no longer able to go along in this shifty way and do come up against insoluble problems. There is always a Yes and a No and the left hand plays all sorts of tricks and thus life gets stuck — one cannot go on living because one tries to be too perfect in a one-sided way. If we lived the Christian ideal consciously, it would mean having to be killed and die as martyrs, which is what the early church said. We would have to stand up for the imprisoned people in Russia and get killed for it, or something like that. Most people say that is foolishness and means that one has a saviour complex, so they wriggle out of it and say that as long as the problem of evil does not come too close they will leave it to others. An idealistic young man decided to go to the island where the Americans were to experiment with the atom bomb so as to prevent the experiment. Most people would say that he was just a fool, too idealistic, but actually he was trying to live the *imitatio Christi*, so there you see the conflict, either you live under the ethical obligation and so reach a dead end, or, if you do not want to be extreme, you regress and play with both ends. That is the conflict the Christian religion has set us: how far shall we go? If we go too far with the shadow problem we get stuck or we are martyrs, or we have to cheat a little and live the shadow and not look at it too closely in order to keep up a healthy defense. That is the question which the fairy tale answers in a specific way.

———

One question put to me during the interval was whether the nose had not to do with finding direction, and that certainly is one aspect. The hunting dog gets his direction by smell and so knows where to go, that is the capacity of orientation. The other question was, "What were the strange papers which were lost?" They must refer to a secret tradition because the anima has them in her faraway land, i. e., the unconscious, and they have to be brought back into the realm of consciousness. Within the history of the Christian era new writings crop up from time to time in the endeavor to reinterpret the Christian religion. We might assume that the documents refer to writings of the Albigenses and Cathars, or the legends of the Holy Grail

— attempts to revive the Christian truth in a poetical way — or a Gnostic aspect, for such secret traditions could not be taught officially but got repressed through the rigidity of the Christian religion. We may conclude that the documents may have to do with something of this kind and were kept in the realm of the anima who wants them to be fetched and insists that she cannot do without them. Also this princess must be a magician because she knows how to behead people and glue the head on again, so the documents may refer to her secret recipes for this. They represent unofficial and unrecognized knowledge. Magic is full of antique tradition and practices which still continue. Jung was once shown a book of magic incantations a Swiss peasant used for exorcisms, and in it was a perfect Latin prayer to the Goddess Venus, recopied by hand from medieval times and still used for such purposes. There are also traditions of the Germanic pagan past. We might assume that the documents have to do with established secret tradition, something with which the anima is often associated because, being a figure compensatory to consciousness, she always picks up what has been neglected and overlooked and not liked and which should still be kept alive and looked at.

Since the hero has a quill pen it looks as though he should one day write about possible new interpretations of the unconscious. All we do actually with fairy tales is re-interpret the religious and folklore traditions so that they may again be linked up with the conscious attitude. Fairy tales mean something and through hearing about them you can be linked again with those living traditions, which is why I talk about them. It is always a question of bringing up again the anima's secret documents. Men dream that their anima is a very learned woman and has a lot of books, and the theme can be developed in active imagination in which a kind of primitive religious teaching is given in a rather pompous style: "Hearken people of the earth and I will tell you a new truth." Consequently, men hate allowing the anima to write particularly because of her bad taste. It means a real act of courage to listen to her. If the animus figure turns up or the great medicine man, he will also talk like this. These pompous announcements of the great truth are awfully disgusting to sober-minded people. People with bad taste fall for it, and that is worse still, but most people get sickened. You must do neither: you must have the courage and objectivity to let the anima announce the truth in her own style and find out what she is aiming at.

It is the archaic form and annunciation of the great truth which does not correspond to our modern idea of writing, though certain modern poets have used it and Nietsche sometimes let Zarathustra talk in this way. I would imagine that the anima had such documents locked up in her castle.

Let us return to the problem of the shadow. I gave you the story of the young man who wanted to let himself be killed as a protest against the atom bomb as a typical example of someone whose fanatical and ethical convictions led to a cul-de-sac and to having to die for one's convictions — killed by the wickedness of the world. Everyday the analytical hour brings you up against such conflicts, people try to be decent and so get cut off from their roots and then don't know how to go on. A man may be tempted to have an affair with a woman outside marriage and comforts himself by saying that everybody does it and one must not make too much fuss about it and, making such excuses, does it behind his own back and is then sorry; but when his jealous wife makes a scene, he regresses again. Other people who have the same temptation try to exercize self-control and say it is not to be thought of, and thus repress and fight the shadow tendency. If it is a minor temptation they succeed but if it is very strong they get depressions and get tired and do not know how to go on in life, and the dreams show the shadow as furious because it did not get its way. That can lead to such a loss of libido that the whole life may get stuck. The man becomes neurotic because the other half of the personality won't accept the decision and is in a constant fury about it. He has hypochondriacal fantasies and depressions and bad moods and has no pleasure in his work. This can very often be observed with people who try to be too moral. Or the husband may be furious with his wife, which is the shadow's revenge because it lost out. In such a situation whatever the man does is wrong: it is disgusting to give in to the shadow and mean to reject it — if he gives in he is mean and if he does not he is hung for it; and that is what I would call the typical shadow conflict. No weighing of the pros and cons to a solution. If one cannot shift or cheat a little the basic shadow complex in human nature is insoluble, for it results in a situation where one cannot do the right thing. At such a time the weak person will use a crutch and either ask advice of someone else, or deny the conflict and say that there is none. That, unfortunately, is often done and with no good results, and then you have the old regression where the right hand does not know what the left hand does.

59

The fairy tale says that one stands such a conflict until the creative solution is found. The creative solution would be something unexpected which decides the conflict on another level. Here the image is this anima figure who suddenly switches the whole situation and makes someone else the king, i. e., a decision comes from the unconscious which is neither this or that, it simply switches the situation — the noseless king, the third party whom nobody thought of, has to go — and the situation is thus changed and everything looks different; that is the model of the creative solution in the shadow problem which is practically what we try to do: to suffer the conflict till something unexpected happens which puts the whole thing onto another level. Then, you might say, the conflict is not solved but different. In the other aspect it could never be solved. One has to be crucified and make no move with the ego against the Yes and No. It may last weeks or months, it is a tension of the opposites not to be decided by the ego, for such a creative solution of the shadow conflict means giving up the ego and its standards and conflicts, it means complete surrender to the unknown forces within one's psyche. As Christ says on the cross, "My God, my God, why hast Thou forsaken me? "

The fairy tale represents this in the third, the anima figure, which changes the whole thing. If Ferdinand the Loyal had played with the anima figure saying he loved her and what should they do with the old king, that would have been no solution; but the story shows that he had no intention of becoming king. He stayed in his place where he saw the opposites and, because he did not think of it, the princess was enabled to say, "I don't like this old king, let him remain beheaded." She made him lose his head.

If an anima wants to finish a man she beheads him, not concretely but psychologically, and then he is out of himself; that would mean anima possession, and that is the great danger and often happens when somebody cannot stand the clash of opposites. Knowing that the anima or some other figure of the unconscious will bring the solution is one of the greatest dangers with which students in Jungian psychology are faced. We know it through Jung's books or from lectures on psychology, or our own experience, and then comes the greatest devilish danger: when such a conflict comes we anticipate the solution intellectually and say, "I know the anima will bring me to the solution," and we do not accept the fact that first the ego conflict must be completely developed.

That happened to Lao-Tze's followers. He discovered the secret power or meaningfulness which he called Tao, and if one reads his life one sees that he really lived what he taught; but after his death Taoism completely degenerated and became black magic, and, since the Taoists always talked about it, their ego conflicts assimilated it and they misused the knowledge to escape the conflict. In analysis when people know a certain amount of psychology — which you cannot keep from them, for that would be another danger — the ego begins to misuse the psychological knowledge and again go into the shadow conflict and next time the thing becomes much more difficult. When the ego plots and speculates with the saving factor, the whole thing is ruined. The ego, the conscious personality, is confronted with the task of always keeping to its own limitation and of taking an ethical complex seriously as though there were no hope of a third factor, which means standing every ethical conflict till the autonomous psyche — the creative — begins to act, and not anticipating the solution by speculating what it might do should it appear. That is a very difficult attitude to reach but it seems to agree with the fairy tales and to be the only legitimate way of getting out of a shadow conflict without one side or the other, or the flow of life, being damaged until you have that *tertium quod non datur.*

CHAPTER V

THE SURRENDER OF EGO

Taking another Grimm European fairy tale because I wish to show how the problem of the shadow works in our civilization, I ask you to keep the fourth figure of "The Loyal and the Disloyal Ferdinand" in mind: the white horse which turned into a prince is the key to the whole problem, for the white horse always gave the right advice to the hero and then was transformed himself. The next fairy tale which seems to show this kind of figure in new light, is "Faithful John."

There was once an old king who was ill and, believing that he was on his deathbed, asked for Faithful John, his best loved servant so named for his faithfulness. When he came the king said that he felt his end approaching and was worried only about his son, who was still of an age in which he would not always listen to advice, and he therefore wanted Faithful John to promise that he would teach the young prince all that he should know and be a father to him so that the king could close his eyes in peace.

Faithful John promised not to forsake the boy and to serve him faithfully, even at the risk of losing his own life. So the king said he could die comforted and in peace, but then he added that after his death Faithful John should show the prince the whole castle, all rooms and the treasures they contained, but not the last room in the long corridor in which the picture of the Princess of the Golden Roof was hidden. If he saw that picture he would immediately fall madly in love, swoon, and be in great danger. When Faithful John gave the king his hand in pledge to do what was wished, the king laid his head back on the pillow and died.

When the old king was buried, Faithful John told the young king what he had promised his father on his deathbed and said that he would keep his promise and be faithful to him as he had been to the old king, even if it should cost him his life. When the period of mourning was over, Faithful John said to him, "Now it is time for you to see your inheritance; I will show you your father's castle." He took him all over it, up and down and round, and let him see all the riches and splendid rooms, but he did not open the room in which the dangerous picture was kept. Now the picture was so placed that it was the first thing one saw when the door was opened, and it was so beautiful that one loved it and thought it must be alive — there was nothing more loveable or beautiful in the whole world.

The young king noticed that Faithful John always passed this room by and asked why. Faithful John said there was something there which would frighten him. But the king answered that he had seen the whole castle and wanted to know what was in that room also and tried to open the door by force. Then Faithful John held him back by saying he had promised his father that he should not see what was in the room, for it might bring great unhappiness to both. But the young king insisted that it would not harm him to see it, for he would have no peace day or night until he had seen it with his own eyes; indeed, he refused to go away from the place until the door was unlocked.

Faithful John, with a heavy and foreboding heart, took out the key. When he had opened the door he stepped in first, hoping to hide the picture, but the king stood on tiptoe and saw over his shoulder. As he looked at the picture of the girl, shining with gold and precious stones, he fell to the ground in a dead faint. Faithful John lifted him, carried him to his bed, and thought unhappily that the misfortune had happened and wondered what would come of it. He gave the king some wine, and the first words he spoke were to ask whose the beautiful picture was. That was the Princess of the Golden Roof, Faithful John told him. Then the king said that he was so much in love with her that even if all the leaves on the trees were tongues they would not suffice to tell of it; that he would stake his life on having her; and that Faithful John must help him.

The faithful servant pondered for a long time as to how this could be accomplished and at last thought he had discovered a way. He told the king that the princess was surrounded with objects made of gold — tables, chairs, bowls, goblets, and basins and all household articles — and that as the king had five tons of gold in his castle, the goldsmiths should use it to make all kinds of vessels, utensils, birds, and wild and wonderful animals, since these would please the princess. They should take the things in a ship and try their luck. The king ordered this to be done, and the goldsmiths had to work day and night to get the beautiful things ready. When everything was on board, the king and Faithful John dressed as merchants so that no one would recognize them. It was a long way across the sea to the place where the princess lived.

Once there Faithful John left the king on board the ship, telling him to wait, saying that perhaps he would bring the princess back with him, and that the king should see that everything was in order and all the golden things exhibited and the whole ship clean. Then he collected a number of golden objects, put them in his apron, and went straight to the royal castle. In the courtyard there stood a beautiful girl holding two golden pails in which she was drawing water, and she asked Faithful John who he was. He replied that he was a merchant and showed what he had in his apron. The girl put down her pails, looked at the beautiful things, and said the princess, who loved things made of gold, must see them and would surely buy them all. She took him to the princess, who was delighted and said she would buy everything. But Faithful John said he was only the servant of a rich merchant and that what he had with him was nothing compared with what was on the ship, objects which were the most artistic and beautiful that had ever been made from gold. The princess wanted everything brought to her, but he said that would take many days and occupy so many rooms that there would be no room for the stuff in her house. This increased her curiosity and desire so much that she said she would go and look at the things herself.

Faithful John was very happy and conducted her to the ship; and when the king saw that she was even more beautiful than her picture, he thought his heart would break. When she came on board he took her below, but Faithful John stayed on deck and had the ship started, saying that all the sails should be unfurled so that it would fly like a bird. The king took many hours to show the lovely things, and in her pleasure the princess did not notice that the ship was moving. When she had seen everything she thanked the merchant and wanted to go home, but then she saw that they were far from land. She cried out that she had been deceived and was now in the power of a merchant, but the king took her hand and explained that he was not a merchant but a king as well born as she and that he had carried her off because he loved her so much. He told her how he had fainted when he had first seen her picture. So the princess was comforted and consented to marry him.

Now it happened while Faithful John sat on the deck that he saw three ravens; he stopped playing his music and listened to what they had to say. One said that the king was taking home the Princess of the Golden Roof, but the second said that that did not prove that he had her yet. The third said that he had her, since she was on the ship with him. The first said that that would not help him for when they got to land a red horse would run at him and when the king tried to get on it, the horse would run away with him and take him up into the air so that he would never see the girl again. The second asked if nothing could be done to save him, and a raven said that if somebody else jumped into the saddle, pulled the pistol out of the holster and shot the horse with it, the young king would be saved. But who knew that? And whoever did know it would turn to stone from his toes to his knees.

Then the second raven said that even if the horse were killed the young king would not get his bride for when they reached the castle, the wedding shirt would be in a basin and would look as though it were woven out of gold and silver, but that it was nothing but sulphur and pitch and when the king put it on it would burn him to his bones. Again the third asked if nothing could be done and the second said that if somebody wearing gloves took hold of the shirt and threw it into the fire, the young king would be saved, but what did that help, for whoever knew it and told the king would be turned to stone from his knees to his heart. Then the third said that he knew still more and that even if the wedding shirt were burnt, yet the king had not his bride for when they danced after the wedding the princess would suddenly turn white and fall down as though dead, and if someone did not pick her up and draw three drops of blood from her right breast, she would die. But if anyone knew that, he would turn to stone from the top of his head to his toes.

Then the ravens flew away and from that time on Faithful John was sad and silent for if he did not tell his master he would be unhappy, but if he told him he, Faithful John, would have to pay for it with his life. At last he decided to save his master even if he should die for it.

When they reached land a beautiful red horse leapt forward as the raven had said it would, and the king said he should carry him to his castle and wanted to mount, but Faithful John was quicker and shot the horse. The other servants said that was a dirty deed to kill the beautiful horse, but the king stood up for Faithful John. When they reached the castle, there was the bowl and the wedding shirt looking as though it were made of gold and silver. The king went to it and wanted to pick it up, but Faithful John pushed him away and with his gloved hand seized it and threw it into the fire where it burned. Again the other servants complained and again the king defended Faithful John.

When it came to the dance Faithful John watched the princess all the time, and suddenly she turned white and fell to the ground. Then Faithful John ran to her and carried her to a room, laid her down, and kneeling beside her sucked three drops of blood from her right breast and spat them out again. The princess soon recovered but the king had seen and did not understand why Faithful John had done that and was furious and said that he should be thrown into prison. Next morning Faithful John was condemned and led to the gallows and as he was about to be hanged he asked for the right to speak. The king gave it to him and Faithful John said that he had been unjustly condemned, that he had always been faithful; and he related what he had heard the ravens say and how his master could be saved. Then the king cried out to his most faithful John asking for mercy and saying that he should be taken down. But with his last word Faithful John had fallen dead to the ground, a stone.

The king and queen were unhappy. The king said he had rewarded great faithfulness with evil, and he had the stone carried to his bedchamber and stood beside his bed. Whenever he looked at it he cried and said if only he could bring him to life again. Time passed and the queen gave birth to twin sons who grew and were their pleasure. Once when the queen was in church and the two children were playing near their father, he looked again at the stone and wished he could make it come to life. Then the stone began to speak and said that he would come to life again if the king would sacrifice what he held most dear. The king said he would give anything he had in the world. The stone answered that if the king with his own hand would cut off the heads of the two children and smear the stone with their blood, he would come to life again. The king was horrified to hear that with his own hand he had to kill his dear children, but he thought of the great faithfulness of Faithful John and how he had died for the king, and he drew out his sword and cut off the children's heads. When he had painted the stone with their blood Faithful John stood in front of him and said that the king's good faith

66

should not go unrewarded. He took the heads of the two children and put them on their necks and smeared the wound with their blood and they were immediately alive and all well and played as though nothing had happened. The king was overjoyed, and when he saw the queen coming he hid Faithful John and the children in a big cupboard and asked her if she had prayed when in church. She said that she had, but that all the time she was thinking of Faithful John and how unhappy he had been because of them. The king answered, "Dear wife, we could give him back his life, but it would cost us our two little sons who would have to be sacrificed." The queen turned quite white and was terrified but she said that they owed Faithful John something for his faithfulness. The king was happy that she thought as he had and opening the cupboard brought out the children and Faithful John, and said that they should praise God that Faithful John had been freed and that they had their sons again. He told her what had happened, and they lived together happily for the rest of their lives.

Things came out as predicted in the story, and the young king at first does not understand why Faithful John does such horrible things, such as shooting the horse and throwing the wedding shirt into the fire. But when Faithful John sucks the three drops of blood from the bride's right breast, the king's jealousy is awakened and instead of standing up for him against the other servants as before, he has him thrown into prison. It is only when Faithful John, after being condemned, is led to the gallows, that he asks to be allowed to speak, since he is to die anyway. He then explains why he has acted as he did and says that he had heard what the ravens said. The king begs for forgiveness, but with his last word Faithful John drops down dead and turns to stone. The king and queen then realize what he has done for them and that they had had no faith in him, and the king has the stone statue put in his room by his bedside.

You have seen now that the word "shadow" has only a very relative and functional meaning in fairy tales. This time we can say that the hero and the shadow are both John and the prince — they are each other's shadows, as were the tailor and the shoemaker.

In the first story, the tailor and the shoemaker are also representatives of such an archetypal contrast. In that story the stork is the bringer of the new king. In the story of "The Loyal and the Disloyal Ferdinand," the beggarman influences the one figure (the loyal Ferdinand) so that he becomes king and the other figure (Disloyal Ferdinand) is cut out of the story. In the story of Faithful John the situation has progressed: since the old king does not need to be deposed (for he is already dying), the story would represent the stage of development where things have taken a step further and the king is dying naturally. The young king, the prince, is there, and Faithful John would be a parallel to the stork; John is the maker of the young king, and the shoemaker figure exists only in a very strange way, namely in the king's projections onto John whom he wrongly believes to be an evil doer. The poison in the story might in one way be considered as the king's projections, but it is also the poisonous blood in the bride, the red horse, and the wedding shirt. The poisonous element personified in other stories in the shoemaker this time is an element within the bride from which she has to be cleansed until she is the anima figure. Her poison is the cause of all the misunderstandings; it is responsible for the king's misunderstanding of his faithful servant.

The name "John" is revealing for it comes from the medieval Jewish legend of Rabbi Johannan, who helped King Solomon. In that story also there is a poisonous wife anima. If the name comes from that legend it reveals that John, the maker of the new king, is a kind of priest-medicine man personality.

This is a very interesting story. If I were to lecture about the anima in fairy tales, I would have here very typical amplifications. She is the Princess of the Golden Roof and is apparently possessed by evil magic which destroys anyone who wants to approach her, and this has to be exorcised before the king can marry her and remain unhurt. The theme is archetypal and the idea of a beautiful girl who in some way has been bewitched or has a poisonous body which kills anyone who comes near her unless he knows how to exorcise her seems to be a common element in oriental legends. In Northern European countries the poison in the bride often comes because she has a secret affair with a pagan demon living in the woods, and through this affair she becomes a destroyer of men; and until the king can cut the connection or kill the demon or evil spirit behind the anima he cannot win her.

If we try to interpret this motif psychologically, we might say that the anima has an influence which we define as a connection with the deeper layers of the unconscious. She represents an approach to the collective

68

unconscious; that is, if a man tries to make conscious moods and fantasies which get him from behind, if he meditates on them, then he can penetrate into the deeper layers of the unconscious. One has to ask oneself, "Why do I get so upset about this and that? " If a man asks that he will find what lies behind his anima and that she is the bride of the demon. Psychologically, you can say that she is contaminated with unconscious impulses which want to become conscious and, because they are not, they get at the man's emotional side and influence his moods instead, so he has to cross the bridge of his emotions to find out what the demonic powers are. Generally they are mainly religious ideas, figures of divinities, which have fallen into the unconscious and should be made conscious. We could say that they were religious connections which had remained unconscious, for what is not integrated falls into the realm of the anima, and therefore exorcising the anima generally means a re-discussion of religious problems. The anima, as a typical woman, picks up what is in the air and the needs of a new era, for being less rigid and prejudiced than man's consciousness she picks up possibilities of the new *Zeitgeist* and, becoming restless about these contents, brings the facts up into consciousness.

I once knew a scientist who, I think, had a rather rigid scientific *Weltanschauung* and was caught in the mechanics of the *Zeitgeist*. He allowed himself to a great extent to ignore the discoveries of modern physics and went along, mechanically and conscientiously, in his old ideas. In discussions I told him of psychological findings and impressed on him the findings of modern physics which had changed the image we had of matter, but he always became emotional and one day said that if those things proved to be true he would have to shoot himself. This seemed to me very foolish and I said why not look at such things objectively and see whether they are true? Why get so emotional about it? That is a wrong, feminine reaction, women judge like that. The world does not change if ideas do. But the man said that he considered that he should stand by what he had taught young students for generations, that he was responsible for teaching such ideas, and if he should discover that they were not right, it would be dishonorable for him to go on living, he would have to shoot himself.

This illustrates the typical logos attitude of men, unless they have developed enough spiritual attitude, and it explains why they are more conservative and do not like changing their ideas easily as women do. Women say,

"Why not? " It is just a question of the way you look at the facts, and then changing your ideas. But if you say to a woman, "Let's discuss a problem concerned with love instead of science. What about introducing polygamy?" Then there is an earthquake! A man might say, "Yes, why not try? " Women become emotional over changes in the forms of social life, for that is where her whole world is anchored, and changes in this field might make *her* want to shoot herself. Men and women should really know this about each other so that they can understand each other, which they cannot do otherwise. Women can toy with ideas for to them an idea is not a question of life and death, and that is why women have a positive effect on men's minds.

A woman can inspire a man's mental world by the lightness with which she can pick up new contents and present them to him. She inspires the man, but he has to do the work; it is just the opposite from the biological relationship where the man fertilizes the woman who has to carry the baby. That is why in outer reality often women are the inspiration of men, and the anima does the same thing within — she brings up seed ideas which are new contents and generally float in the air for a time before he has to deal with them. The tiresome thing about it, and what makes the anima so poisonous, is that she brings up these seed ideas, these creative hunches, in an unadapted, undigested way and in the strange style which she affects in speaking. Her new truth is presented in bad style, as evidenced in theosophical or popular religious magazines. If you read such literature, you see how new ideas are expressed in an undigested anima form, which is right away poisonous: it is a mixture of emotions and undigested ideas, and the worst of it is that you can neither accept or reject it. It is contaminated with absolute nonsense, but in it is a kernel of truth with something inspired. You find similar material in that of schizophrenic people who are not right over the border. They write inspired stuff, but if you check it you find that the footnotes are wrong, the material badly presented, and everything untidy. The evidence is full of lies. You are confronted with the typical ejaculations of the poison-filled anima, but there is something to it and it is inspiring. A truth-loving and responsible man would naturally hate such stuff, but he has to do something about it or he will sterilize his own development.

So it is a question of the critical mind, of exorcising the anima, and of getting to the feeling relationship in the unconscious; the inspiration of new ideas lies in a raw material form on the other side, raw material in which gold and dung are mixed and the man has to sieve it to extract the value. The poison in the anima is that she always tries to make the man think that he is the great announcer of the new truth, or the opposite. She is usually rather the type of the hysterical liar and exaggerates or twists things a little. The easiest way to watch a man influenced by his anima is by seeing where he begins to lie, for that is where the anima catches him, for she is full of lies and little twists and dissertations, that is her poison and that has to be exorcised in this princess before she can continue in a proper way. Every emotional state tends to exaggerate and twist facts and the anima has such qualities.

The dying king's situation is beautifully illustrated: the dominant principle of collective consciousness, the king, is fading away, is dying, and the female principle is not represented for there is no queen and no other female figure, except for the hidden picture of the Princess of the Golden Roof shut away in a room. So the beginning illustrates the state of affairs where the anima is completely repressed and the relationship to the queen is cut off and shut away. Moreover, the living woman is on the other side of the great sea, that is, far from consciousness.

It is clear that this fairy tale is a relatively late version and must represent a relatively late state of affairs within the Christian civilization of our countries, for here it is quite true that the female principle is excluded. In Catholicism the mother is represented by the Virgin Mary, but in Protestantism even that is cut out and the female principle is not represented at all; consequently, this higher image is repressed and shut away — it could be called a repressed complex.

A forbidden chamber in which there is a positive and luminous figure is a frequent theme in fairy tales, and the great trouble is the repressed complex, i. e., a living psychological factor which consciousness does not want to contact. On top of that, the Princess of the Golden Roof seems a lofty figure for she comes from the roof, not the cellar: the image is spiritual and high up. That fits in with the Christian civilization, where what is repressed out of existence is the female figure of the earth mother which appears in all pagan cults. Since the mother image is carried by the Virgin Mary, who represents everything beautiful and pure, but not what

71

is witchlike, destructive, and animal, we can say that Christianity has cut out the female principle completely in its lower representation, its shadow aspect, and has only accepted the upper, light part within the symbol of the Virgin Mary. Now there is an increasing tendency to give her back her dark side. The Pope has called her the *domina rerum*, the ruler of nature, so she is beginning to get back her shadow side, but naturally this is a dangerous revelation. Here you see the classical situation of our civilization: a ruling principle is losing its strength, even the *image* of the woman is shut away, and the reality still more so.

With the king is the strange figure of Faithful John, who is behind the whole story, and we first have to realize what he does and suffers. He opens the forbidden room, which you might say was unwise, for he disobeys the king as soon as he is dead — but he acts under compulsion. He has the keys, is the key figure; he is the representative of the transcendent function. These are the strange maneuvers of the unconscious, which always makes detours so that you never know where you are. The psychological pattern is beautifully represented in the 18th Sura of the Koran which Jung interprets in *Alchemical Studies*. Khidr is the first angel of the throne of Allah, a Messianic figure which has not incarnated, and in a certain way provides a parallel to the Gnostic Logos idea. He guides and helps people. In the Orient he is still a living figure, and simple people still believe in him. He is responsible for the sudden turns of good and bad luck. He appears in the dreams of modern Moslems; and, they say, if a stranger comes to your house, you are courteous to him because it may be Khidr. He is a Godhead who visits people on earth and he compensates the aloofness of Allah.

Khidr meets Moses, who asks him to take him with him on his wanderings. Khidr does not want to do this for he says Moses cannot live up to his standards and that there will be trouble, but Moses promises to accept everything that Khidr does. At a village Khidr drills a hole in all the fishing boats so that they will all sink and Moses expostulates. Khidr says that he had told him he would not be able to stand it, and Moses promises again to say nothing. Next they meet a beautiful youth whom Khidr kills, and again Moses complains and is reprimanded. Then Khidr makes the walls of a town fall so that the whole town is exposed, and once more Moses cannot hold his tongue. Khidr then says that they must part, but first explains to

72

Moses what he has done. He sank the boats because he knew that a fleet of robbers intended to attack and steal them and, as it was, the boats could be repaired. The youth was on his way to commit a murder and Khidr prevented his losing his soul by committing such a deed. He let the walls of the town fall because under them there was a hidden treasure which would now be found and which belonged to some poor people. So Moses is obliged to see how badly he has misunderstood and misinterpreted Khidr's ways. This can be looked at as a symbol of the strange higher wisdom of the unconscious which our rational consciousness can never reach. Ego consciousness perpetually fights and rationally rejects the greater wisdom of the unconscious which is snake-like with detours and takes into consideration the things which we do not know so that we always revolt against it.

Faithful John is like Khidr: he is a representative of the divine principle of the unconscious which has great knowledge, and therefore he is misunderstood by the new principle of consciousness represented by the prince.

The figure of John provides a striking parallel to the alchemical figure of Mercurius, the friend of the king, the near friend of the alchemist, who is represented sometimes as servant and sometimes as master; Mercurius also exasperates the alchemist by his strange ideas and paradoxical behavior so that when the alchemist tries to deal with Mercurius, he feels a fool, for Mercurius always plays tricks — and that is similar to the personification of the unconscious in the figure of the servant John. I have drawn this parallel to Mercurius because Faithful John's advice seems very alchemical: he tells the prince to make the golden animals, birds and fishes, vessels and tools, which will attract the princess. What would that mean?

In primitive tribes, ghost traps are often made by which to catch the ghosts of those who have recently died and prevent them from spooking. The ghosts, the natives say, have lost their sense of perspective, and therefore the natives make little models of the houses in which the deceased persons formerly lived and put them between the grave and the former home; this model the ghost enters, not noticing that it is not the real house. By a similar kind of magic the Princess of the Golden Roof is to be attracted. In the relativity of time and space, contents of the unconscious can be followed up by these methods, but that is on the level of black magic. And this is also a kind of magical action by which the Princess of the Golden Roof is attracted.

73

The modern psychological parallel would be active imagination, through which one can literally attract the contents of the unconscious. If you succeed in producing either by drawing, or conversation, or imagination the right kind of symbol, you can, to a certain extent, constellate your own unconscious. The achievement of the connection between conscious and unconscious is a relatively slow process. For instance, an individual with a certain conscious attitude has a dream which we interpret and, if the interpretation is correct, there is a reaction and the conscious changes its attitude or ideas. The fact that consciousness has changed affects the next dream, and there results a slow interconnection. If for certain reasons the process must be speeded up, or the pressure of the unconscious is so great that something more has to be done to save the conscious from inundation, or if consciousness is blocked off, we then try consciously, while remaining within the fringe of consciousness, to let things happen in a waking state, representing and dealing with them in that state; and this effort has a constellating effect on unconscious processes. I was much struck when I first observed how much more could be done through active imagination than by dreams.

I had a patient who drank and was in a dangerous situation inwardly and outwardly. He dreamt again and again of a dead school friend whom he described as a man who had been very intelligent, but neurotic, if not schizophrenic — the type of schizophrenia which you could describe as moral insanity. His mental functions were not affected but the ethical personality was destroyed. He got into difficulties with the law and tried to commit suicide, and after internment succeeded. Since this figure appeared almost every night in the patient's dreams, I said that he must somewhere have such a figure within him (for he also did not believe in life), that it must have to do with his drinking, and that he should take up the shadow figure. The man agreed, but did nothing. When we counted up the number of times he had dreamt of this same man it averaged about three times a week.

After some time of this I had enough and said that the patient must have it out with the figure in active imagination and, being naive and gifted in that way, he succeeded. He asked his friend why he was annoying and disturbing him, and the friend replied that the whole psychological business was a fake, that the patient was afraid of cancer of the liver and wanted to save his skin, there was nothing else behind it, he was just a coward. The

74

patient defended himself, but he was not nearly as intelligent as his friend and after a time did not know how to argue and gave it up and said the friend was right. That was about five p. m. in the afternoon. He went to bed that night and about eight a. m. woke up with a horrible heart attack. He telephoned to a doctor but nearly died. The doctor looked after him and a cardiogram was made, but it was a purely psychological attack which nearly killed him!

We went through the active imagination again and I said that he had forgotten the arguments of the heart. The friend had got him through arguing on an intellectual basis in which there are always pros and cons, but there is the possibility of *choice*, and that implies the heart, or feeling. I said he should begin again. He did so and said to the friend, "Look here, I have thought it over." "Oh, no," said the friend, "you have talked it over with your soul governess in Zürich!" The friend had this kind of destructive wit. But the patient said that the *heart attack* was his own, in spite of the discussion in Zürich, and that it was the conversation with his friend that his heart had not been able to stand. So this time he was on the spot and the conversation ended by the other not having anything more to say. The same night he dreamt that he was at the friend's funeral: for him the friend was buried only then.

In the ensuing analysis, which lasted a year and a half, this figure appeared only once, instead of three times a week, the previous average. Thus active imagination, if done in the right way, really has an impact on the unconscious. It has a much stronger effect than only dream interpretation, and the above case shows how creating the right symbolical figure in a symbolical dialogue caught the cynical shadow and exerted an actual influence on the unconscious. Naturally, this is on the same level as age-old magic which has always been used to influence the psychological situation — it is really the same practice — but magic has an outer purpose. If this man had been a person of medieval mentality, I would have said that to dream so much about this cynical friend meant that he was haunting him; but as he was a modern man, he had it from within.

The difference between white and black magic would be that the latter is used for egotistical purposes. A woman in love uses a love potion, but that is the ego trying to push through egotistical demands. There is also white magic in the form of exorcism, but that serves a religious aim.

Active imagination is produced entirely from within and is looked at in the same way, though it has sometimes an outer effect; indeed, one should only do it for one's own inner sake. We have experienced that if done with living people the other person is affected, though we cannot explain how it works, but that is why it is dangerous, and we try to keep away from it. You can talk to your *projection* on the living person, but not directly *to* the living person. If you hate someone very intensely and want to work on that you can personify your hate.

I had an analysand who had a kind of admiration transference for a couple with whom she was first friendly, but then began to hate intensely. She always went to see them and always returned poisoned and upset. It was clearly a projection: they had a lot of shadow in common. Then she heard vaguely about active imagination, but what she thought was active imagination was to imagine the man was there and then to insult and fight and in the end kill him. Afterwards she felt quite relieved and went to bed and then dreamt that a witch had caught and imprisoned her. I asked her what she had done and said that something must have happened during the day, and she told me of the active imagination; her dream showed that she had practiced witchcraft and not active imagination. She could have personified her hate or affect and then it would have been all right, for she would have had the two figures of herself and "a woman who hates" and she could have asked the latter why she wanted to kill the man and that would have worked. To deal with the outer person is a mistake which has bad results and can act like a boomerang. The analysand did not rid herself of her hate, but fell into the archetype and even deeper into the unconscious. If you wish to work on a relationship with a real person and don't want to fall into magic, then talk to your own personified affect; but you must keep it within the vessel of your own personality and not exteriorize the person in any form.

In cases where you can watch the effect of witchcraft, you can see that there are exteriorized destructive effects, but more than that: it harms the person who does it, making him even more unconscious, and it has no curative effect. In active imagination the ego must empty itself and be an objective onlooker. The ego should say, "Now, let's look at my affect," so the first step is that of disidentification when the ego becomes an objective onlooker. The analysand identified where she should have disidentified.

76

That is what we call an *"Auseinandersetzung,"* namely to "sit apart and have it out with each other," and the first thing is to "sit apart." That is a wonderful description of active imagination. I sit apart from my hatred, or my great love, and then I discuss *with that factor*, but I leave out the object because otherwise I am practising black magic. The object of your hatred or love is something on which your unconscious greed fastens and by that you produce *wishful thinking*, just the opposite of active imagination. People think of what they love, or what they would like to do, and believe that that is active imagination, but that is magic, and has all the effects of an *abaissement du niveau mental*; it can even release a psychosis.

If we are upset about something, a discussion goes on all the time within us, but that is passive imagination and completely different from the difficult art of sitting apart and disidentifying and looking at something objective. If people can do active imagination for hours, then it is wrong; if done rightly one is exhausted after ten minutes for it is a real effort and not a "letting go" — that is passive imagination.

You ask how the other person could be affected by the black magic method described above? Well, the other person might have an open place, so to speak, and that would be affected; that is how all such things work among primitive people — someone has a photograph and puts a pin in it, etc. If you do witchcraft imagination, you can become an addict and go on and on — the thing that was started involuntarily cannot be stopped.

Dr. Baelz, in Tokyo, described the case of a Japanese schizophrenic woman who had a fox ghost. She came from a little village. She was in a catatonic state and was stupid and heavy. She would sit in a corner by herself and after a time would say, "Now it is coming!" and from her chest a voice would begin to bark, becoming louder and louder. Then her eyes would become brilliant and shining and she would become very amusing and witty and would tell every doctor off; she would bring out all sorts of home truths which were absolutely correct. Everybody hated her. Then after a time the barking would begin again and the thing would die down and she would become the stupid person she was before.

This is a classic case. Schizophrenic people swim so much in the collective unconscious that they are in everybody else's unconscious and see through things in a most amazing way. I once visited a man who had been put into the hospital. He said he had become double, and would I please come.   I went because I thought it might be interesting, and he was at once quiet, reasonable, and calm, and could say what had happened. And then he said, "These doctors are the most amazing fools! They gave intravenous injections to one catatonic man who would not eat, but I saw at once what was the matter and told them they could give the man all the stuff he needed, if they would only give it in a bottle." Most of the doctors ignored him, saying what could another poor lunatic know! But a young Jewish doctor said why not try it, and the man took the food in a bottle! In *Wisdom, Madness and Folly* John Custance tells of a similar case where one patient knew "telepathically" what another had dreamt in that same night. Such people swim in the same kind of embryonic liquid and therefore will have an immediate contact. In the lower layers there is complete contamination.

CHAPTER VI

THE ANIMA AND THE RETURN

Last time we discussed the motif of Faithful John and how he attracted the princess: we compared his actions and manipulations with the technique of active imagination, a new, and in some ways very different, form of magic, but on a psychologically higher level, for it has the same basic idea in that it produces certain symbols or symbolical creations by which the unconscious gets constellated and "attracted." Thus one can affect the unconscious to a certain extent, one can use the magic influence, with the difference that magic is generally used for external purposes, i. e., in the form of projection, whereas in the other form the conscious part of the personality plays a definite role — it is the creator of the symbol; but there is actually a cyclical process, for the symbol by which we can influence the unconscious is inspired by the unconscious itself. You might say that the unconscious produces a symbol, and that the conscious is inspired by it, reproduces it, forms it, and gives it expression, which in turn influences the unconscious. The same thing happens less dynamically in dream interpretation.

Faithful John is a kind of personification of that part of the unconscious which has a tendency to build up a new conscious position; we might call him the creative spirit in the unconscious — and that would make him analogous to the alchemical idea of the spirit Mercurius, who is a creative spirit in the depth of nature, or, as we would say, in the depth of the unconscious. We could call him a personification of what Jung calls the transcendent function, that which can unite the opposite positions.

After they have abducted the princess, and the king and his bride are on the boat together, everything seems all right; but Faithful John then hears the conversation between the three ravens which predicts the dangers and the steps which can be taken against them, and which also states that if the person who saves the king tells what he knows he will be petrified. Consequently, complete trust in Faithful John is required, just the same blind faith that Khidr asked of Moses, with no questions as to the why and wherefore or dotting of the "i." Faithful John, who suspects that the king will not accept the situation and trust him in regard to his actions, all the same decides to save the king. I could skip the conversation of the three ravens because it is similar to that of the two crows on the gallows, but I cannot skip the ravens themselves. Here we have a triad of ravens, birds which belong to the sun God and birds used for divination. Thus they have a connection with parapsychological facts and telepathy; they can see into the future and into secret thoughts. They represent more the male principle than the crows which represent the female principle.

Here we have a triad which alludes to all the triadic Godheads which there were in the pre-Christian times in the Germanic and Celtic traditions, and which later became merged into the Christian Trinity. If you remember, in Dante's "Inferno" the devil has three heads going in three directions, which Jung interprets as the mirroring of the upper three, i. e., of the Trinity. The double triangle would be the symbol of the totality. If you cut it into two, you have the Christian tradition as the upper Trinity and the infernal trio as the lower. That is why the underworld in folklore, which compensates the Christian position in consciousness, appears as a pagan triad, which has to do with the pagan God Wotan who often appears with two other Gods.

The ravens have a more general quality of being neither good nor bad, but pure nature; they express the truth in a way similar to expression by the unconscious. Naturally, it is anthropomorphic to say that the unconscious is benevolent, for it is up to the conscious to make decisions. Since the ravens talk to each other, and not to Faithful John, there is no plan to make consciousness understand. They simply converse together and you can eavesdrop; it is as though the unconscious was indifferent as to whether the king was saved.

But Faithful John makes up his mind to save him. The three dangers are: 1) the red horse, which would induce the king to jump on it and then would go up into the air and disappear, and which has to be shot down with the pistol in the holster on the horse itself; 2) the wedding shirt, which if put on would burn the king; and 3) the three drops of poison in the bride's breast. All the dangers are connected with the return to the original place. Often in fairy tales a man or a woman goes to a faraway realm — a deeper level of the unconscious — and then when he returns to the place he left there are dangers; although there are dangers on the way toward the goal, those on the return journey are generally of a different character. We have to see what these different layers of the unconscious mean.

Most people who interpret fairy tales loosely take crossing the ocean to the Princess of the Golden Roof as going to the unconscious, but this cannot be correct, for the characters are in the unconscious from the beginning. Since the king and Faithful John and the new king are all in the unconscious from our standpoint, we cannot simply skip this fact but must ask ourselves what the different realms mean. In some fairy tales we have more than three — the king goes to one kingdom after another; consequently we must reckon not only with two, but with three or four or five kingdoms, stations on the way. I would say the starting realm, the realm where the action of the tale begins, has to do with consciousness; it has to do with the conscious situation, but *as seen from the unconscious.*

Let us understand, here, consciousness as the layer of collective consciousness represented in newspapers and publications concerned with the spirit and problems of our time — collective consciousness as it looks at itself. We always try to realize our conscious situation by talking about it, etc., within this realm itself. But if we begin to look at dreams, or the works of artists who draw their inspiration genuinely from the unconscious without much reflection, then we get another image of the situation; we get the mirrored image, a kind of photograph of how the unconscious looks at the conscious situation. All dreams, you could say, have this aspect. In a dream situation you may behave like a fool or a hero, and then you might say that that is not the way you see yourself, but how the unconscious sees you — it is the photograph of your ego taken from the unconscious. That is one aspect where this photograph is generally the opening situation in fairy tales: it depicts the conscious situation, but as seen from the unconscious. In the first photograph the principle of collective consciousness is ageing or dying. There might be a gloomy newspaper article saying that our civilization is in need of renewal, and that might be so or not; but here the photograph says it is so, the old king is dying and the image of the anima is rejected and removed to a distance, and so on. Then there is the other realm of consciousness, namely the kingdom of the anima, to which people go over the ocean in their ship. In this situation the image of the anima is seen only as an image (the portrait) in three dimensional reality; and since it is no longer alive as a psychological reality, it is further removed from the conscious into the

81

kingdom of the anima. The return dangers are, then, an attempt at union of the two fields.

This movement might be compared with a person's development in an analysis: often when people begin analysis their dreams bring up a completely strange other world with anima and shadow, and in the analysis one discusses these facts, which creates the situation of the inner retort; therefore one says that analysis is not a relationship as in ordinary life but is a specific relationship between two people whose concentration is fixed on the unconscious and where other facts of life are left out. The analysand may say he has difficulties with his wife, or profession, etc., but you ignore the situation from the outside and look at it from within with a kind of relative exclusion of the outer situation. This exclusion is comparable to the alchemical process in a retort or vessel. It is a rather artificial situation in which the problems are seen as an inner dream within the individual; and this perspective forces the thing into a vessel. We create this artificial situation for the purpose of introversion.

People have sometimes tried to interpret fairy tales as timeless phenomena with eternal events in which the collective unconscious ages and dies, but I do not believe in this. After analyzing many European, Japanese, Chinese, and African fairy tales, you come to see that the basic construction, so to speak, of the fairy tale is eternal. There is always the wizard, the prince and the king, the witch and the helpful animal, and the specific set-up or situation is an answer to a specific conscious situation. Therefore, if you compare the European with the Japanese you have the same figures but in a different architecture, and if you go further into that you realize that you cannot interpret a Japanese fairy tale without knowing about Japanese civilization and the conscious situation in Japan, or without knowing about Zen-Buddhism and the Samurai, and not only from the outer situation but from the collective conscious of the Japanese people, and only then can you understand the fairy tale. I even go so far as to say that we should be able to date fairy tales, but I must confess that I cannot always succeed and cannot date more accurately than within about two or three hundred years, for they depict a relatively slow process as compared with the rate of conscious development. Since the slow decay of Christian symbolism has been going on for nearly a thousand years, from then on there have been unconscious changes. Naturally, therefore, if you have a

82

fairy tale which compensates the Christian consciousness it would be difficult to place it exactly into that process as to time, though I think we can date this fairy tale pretty accurately, which I shall do later. So, in one way, the unconscious taking a photograph of the conscious situation puts it into a more eternal general situation, that of the old king dying, and quite naturally, for one can see that civilizations have always decayed and come to an end, *sub specie eternitatis*. The old king dying is a classical situation in human life; and then specific changes are proposed which can guarantee a change.

In a personal analysis dreams partly react in a specific way, and then the unconscious reveals the unconscious situation and shows it as an eternal problem yet one which bears the structural makeup of the time. The personal mother is the family drama and beyond that are the archetypal dreams which say this is the general problem of the young male, the pulling away from the mother which every man has in some specific form; so it may be said that these productions are partly timeless and partly topical, for neither a dream nor a fairy tale is quite unconscious. One can correctly call dreams products of the unconscious, but they are a phenomenon on the fringe of consciousness — only those which you cannot remember are unconscious. Fairy tales share the timelessness of the unconscious with the relative time of the conscious because they are not completely in the unconscious. In personal analysis interpretations which click will be accepted, but if they do not click there is stagnation; then the analysis may propose this or that step and the analysand will agree, but nothing will happen.

Fairy tales "written" by an author are not genuine fairy tales, for they contain to some extent the problem of the writer. Andersen's mirror the specific religious problem of his country. He had a gift for showing what was going on underneath and produced almost genuine fairy tales, but he was highly neurotic, he never got away from his mother, and he never married. His stories have a constant tragic atmosphere: the connection with the anima cannot be made, just as it was not made in Andersen's own life. He could not quite free himself from his personal problem. Though they would be interesting to study, I keep away from poetical fairy tales because as far as I can see practically no artist is able to disidentify completely from his personal problem, and that results in a different category. In folklore we have the actual bones which dramatize a more general phenomenon.

83

The problem on the return journey is to get at the more distant problem of the unconscious: though people at such a time insist on outer solutions and say that they are relevant — should they marry, or should they change their profession — that is not the point. We have to make conscious the unconscious process, and we cannot pin it down prematurely to the outer situation. The very rational person will always press for dream interpretation to be accurate and one-sided and will be shocked if it is vague and remains in the symbolic. He wants to know in a few words what is meant, for he wants to bring the situation into the intellectual realm.

In such a case you must insist on your interpretation, leave the thing in its own realm, and not be forced into outer solutions. In this way you can reach the other layer and live in that; but then comes the "red horse difficulty," which is that naturally   the outer realm has not been changed and there remains the problem of the practical meaning. This occurs with the foreign analysand who comes here and discusses the family situation and works it out on a psychological level; but then he has to go back and wonders if the whole thing will not collapse when he gets home. Because of the analysand's change, however, the situation is different. Sometimes an analysand, on returning home, says, "My mother must have changed in the meantime," not seeing that he has changed and that this changes the whole situation. Yet the same thing arises with people who live in the same place, for the artificial situation is made and then there is the return difficulty — and the question arises as to how the link is made with the outer life. Although it is useful to look at the psychological situation purely as psychological, after a time you have to confront the two, and then there is the danger that new crises and new problems come up. In this specific situation, in the realm which mirrors the conscious situation, the anima was recognized only as an image, not as a three-dimensional living reality.

Now the king and Faithful John come and meet the living reality. This means they meet it in the in-between realm, in the timeless, stateless realm of the unconscious; for example, in a personal situation, when a man has no relationship to his deeper feeling and emotional layers, the anima does not live for him, he has only ethical views. One often comes across men who have an image relationship to the unconscious. They can accept the fact that the unconscious is full of symbolism and motifs, but if you try to convey to them that it influences life and does things to the conscious, that it has a life of its own, and that the anima can fall ill if you don't do the right thing, then rationalism crops up, for they cannot accept that the unconscious can make them ill, or make them run into a car. Let us say that a person in a borderline situation hears voices. If you say these are manifestations of the unconscious, that they can accept, for that is quite a good thing since they can pretend that it is not a pathological phenomenon peculiar to them; but if you tell them that the voice must be taken as a great authority to be obeyed, often an illness or an accident is required before they give in, because that is a step further.

Artists are often willing to accept the idea that there is an unconscious which provides the inspiration which they project into their painting or writing, but they are awfully shy of analysis. They pretend that it would destroy their creativeness. The real fear, however, is that they might have to take what they have painted as a reality, and they fear that the statue of the Goddess Venus might come down from the pedestal and embrace them. They think *they* have produced it and that therefore it has no right to move, for it is *their* product and has no right to come alive and grip them. They recognize the image, but do not allow it living reality, which might break into their lives. All this gives us a hint for the data of the fairy story. In such a situation the "return problem" arises when one begins to ask, how does that link up with actual reality, with life? Here the anima has been recognized as an image of the anima in the Golden Roof, high up, whilst the red horse is the other aspect; the anima exists and has a sexual attraction, but at the other end she represents something divine. Dante's Beatrice would be the Princess of the Golden Roof at the upper end, and the witch dancing with the devil would be the lower end. Mary the saint and Mary the prostitute are both images of the anima. As the prostitute she is the attraction to the other sex, the emotional attraction, the drive, and at the upper end she is all the things Dante says about Beatrice. There is Venus *ourania* (the heavenly Venus) and Venus *pandemos* (the profane Venus), the divine and the vulgar. The symbol of one is the dove, and of the other, the sparrow. The anima which contains this duality is neither intellectual nor physical, but, by its own essence, something between the opposites. A man gets torn between the two aspects, between the common well-known attraction to the other sex and all its emotional mechanisms, and the inner experience of the highest order.

In his lecture on Gérard de Nerval, Jung tells how Nerval fell passionately in love with a Parisian *midinette*. He wished to write poems (like Dante) for she seemed the Goddess. But French realism and Nerval's rather cynical and vulgar ideas about love caught him at the same time and he termed her *"une personne ordinaire de notre siècle"* and could not grasp the paradox that the ordinary little woman could be the Goddess. He did something to the girl — he must have hurt her feelings in some way — but he only suggests that he did something terrible because he could not stand the paradox. He ran away from her, and in his work "Aurélia" he describes how he dreamt that he went into a garden where a statue of a woman had broken apart: that is, his soul had petrified and fallen apart because of what he had done to the girl by running away.

Another woman tried to save the situation. She thought the love affair had to do with his trouble and had the two meet again; the girl came towards him, they shook hands, and he got a terrible shock from the look of sad reproach in her eyes — but they could not be reconciled. The girl died soon and he hung himself. Here is an illustration of someone who becomes the tragic victim of his inability to stand the anima's paradoxical aspect: it is a living soul which lives between the two worlds, it is neither Goddess nor "femme ordinaire," it is a living force which appears in different layers of reality. We might say, that is the anima and she has to be taken as such, but the man might then reply, "All right, but must I go to bed with her, or must I worship her and keep away from her? ", for consciousness always wants to pin down what is what, and one has to keep out of this issue and not answer the question but say that it is a living power which has to be worshipped as it is, and one must wait to see what other angle comes in. But the conscious says, "Shall I telephone her, or shall I take it only on the other side? " That is the rational problem, for the other situation always comes up again because consciousness says it must be an "either — or" and then people go mad because the conscious situation has pinned it to this one-sidedness and cannot let in the other.

In our story the first approach to finding the anima is made appropriately through the golden images. If Faithful John had tried to rape her, that would not have worked — she had to be approached with the adequate means to attract her aloofness — but on shore the red horse will get loose and will carry the king away: that is the outbreak of the sexual instinctive drive, which here is imaged by the stable, not by the golden roof. Naturally, though this is not said in the story, the red horse is an aspect of the princess herself: she now constellates the animal underworld, but we must not overlook the fact that it is a horse; it does not take the rider into a swamp, which would be a sexual drive, but up into the air — a kind of Pegasus which takes one away from the earth, reality. Physical passion if really carried by the anima does not lead to reality because the anima is an image and because the divine quality of the anima leads to possession and unreality. It is a well-known fact that young couples are completely unreal if their sex life works all right because then their passion carries them away into the air, away from the rather subtle in-between attitude by which consciousness stays on the earth.

Since Christian prejudice is against the instinctual end of the anima projection, the tendency has been in the other direction, to become inhuman, especially, for instance, in the case of the parsons' daughters and sons who have been too prudishly brought up and are apt to become very unreal; they are as though driven by the dark horse as compensation for the aloofness of the Princess of the Golden Roof. This danger arises when one touches the anima, for this aspect may carry one away and can be suppressed only by brutal intervention. Here is a specific situation, and in this story the only solution is to shoot the horse down — a radical operation which in analysis would correspond to saying, "This or that does not come into question!" Although the young king does not have to shoot the horse, Faithful John must, and consequently he represents the transcendent function, the urge to bring up a higher consciousness; that is, consciousness does not decide, rather, the unconscious stops it itself.

The horse interestingly carries the gun itself. Freud thought that the instinctual drives were unilateral and that consciousness had to deal with them, or sublimate them; Jung believes that the unconscious drive contains its own possibility of sacrifice in itself. The chapter on sacrifice in *Symbols of Transformation* (p. 394 of Chapter 8) explains this phenomenon. (When Jung wrote that, he separated from Freud.) If we look at animal nature it seems so obvious, for animals do not overdo sexuality, or eating, or fighting, except under disturbed conditions, which means that in nature the instinctual drives have their own brakes. All drives do not become one-sided, they contain their inner possibility of being sacrificed; and the same applies to human drives, for they get braked and only become manic when consciousness in its devilish one-sidedness interferes wrongly. Take the parson's son who runs wild in a university town, i. e., his red horse gets loose. If he is not an intellectual and not liable to neurosis, after a time he will get tired of that kind of life and want a more permanent relationship and time for his studies; the first outbreak will stop. But if he should become an advocate of free sexuality, then he will overdo it and go far beyond his nature. Such people may realize the first indications towards curbing their sexuality, but yet persist, and nature may then make them impotent. I have seen that happen several times. It is like shooting down the horse from the unconscious, which says, if you will not listen I will shoot down the horse. Sexuality braked by itself is something very brutal, it may be halted by disease of some kind. Analysis would have shown that nature wished to put on the brakes and that the situation demanding sacrifice had not been attended to: the urge towards individuation through sacrifice can brake the one-sided instinctual drive which deviates too much from the middle way.

Instinct is of the nature of the "all or nothing" reaction, and consciousness has to interfere by adapting to a normal (moderated) use of instinct. Apart from the sexual angle we could exemplify it also by aggression. Very aggressive people generally knock their own heads against a wall. They get hit over the head by parents and teachers and so learn repression. They learn the destructive nature of aggression and so repress it, but later, analysis shows that they should somehow liberate it again. Such people also do not know how to hit back; they confess that if they hit back they go too far, so they prefer to do nothing, and then naturally they become the underdog and build up resentment since they are living below their own level, or they develop persecution ideas. Or these people may become aggressive again, go too far, and they say that they should not have tried, for trying always leads to a catastrophe; they need to learn the art of letting the thing out consciously, a little at a time. If you take the lid off, all the steam rushes out; to let it out little by little requires more self-control than the "all or nothing" reaction, for consciousness has then participated in bringing out the adequate amount for civilized behavior — the middle way that lies between the all or nothing of the instinctive way, and that harmonizes with the unconscious urge towards individuation.

CHAPTER VII

THE GREAT MOTHER AND ONENESS

In "Faithful John" one matter remains a mystery until the end: Why
must Faithful John be petrified? One feels that a curse lies at the bottom
of it, but since the reason does not come out until the end, I intend to introduce another story — "The Two Brothers" — in which the responsible
figure is revealingly petrified well before the end.

If we take Faithful John as the principle, or urge, in the collective unconscious towards building up a new dominant of collective consciousness,
the "maker of the new king," and therefore the representative of the transcendent function or the Self, it seems strange that he should become
petrified while fulfilling this task. But if in the conscious there is a wrong
attitude, then the messages from the unconscious, whether heard or seen,
become misunderstood, and the conscious has a petrifying effect on them.
If we think of the developments which have taken place in our Christian
civilization, then the fact that the young king and queen took the statue
of Faithful John into their bedroom is typical: it stands there as a reproach-
ful figure, and the king and queen are depressed and unhappy whenever they
look at it.

One might say that Sigmund Freud rediscovered the petrified Faithful
John in the bedroom of our civilization, for the living principle of the unconscious was discovered first as a fact in the form of something petrified,
something not alive, not assimilated there. Thus, in the bedroom of the
king and queen, remains an unsolved problem. Freud himself never saw
the creative living principle in the unconscious, but thought of it as of
something not lived, something rejected by the conscious. He was the
first to discern that within our civilization a stumbling block manifests
itself mainly in the relationship between the sexes, but he could not get
beyond asserting the existence of such a blockage — he saw it only in its
negative and destructive aspect and as a reason for the sadness of a king
and queen. That was the situation in which he met it first and that, in
a way, is what happened at the end of the Christian era: we discovered a
principle which was a stumbling block in the sexual realm.

Jung discovered then that the petrification, the block, was the personification of a dynamic principle — a principle which can come alive again and show itself as a living religious principle, but only if one sacrifices the child to it. The relationship between the sexes is in a way a seismograph which shows other disturbances as well. Most disturbances in sexual life and in the relationship between the sexes are, from our standpoint, not so much a difficulty in themselves, but rather indications of a much deeper problem. Usually in cases of frigidity in women, for instance, the real problem is animus possession; if one treats the thing on its sexual level only, one does not reach its much deeper roots. Every kind of psychological disturbance shows mainly either in problems of social adaptation, or in the attitude to death, or in situations such as sexual relations, i. e., wherever an instinctive reaction is needed, because such reactions require the help of the vital and important archetypal patterns. There are archetypal situations in which the human being needs his total personality; if he has a neurotic split, he will show it in such a situation. The king and queen cannot meet completely, then, because between them a petrified figure always watches reproachfully and gives them such feelings of guilt that they cannot enjoy their life together.

The petrification of Faithful John can also be seen wherever the dominating principle of consciousness does not recognize the ever-changing aspect of the unconscious, for this failure of vision has a petrifying effect on the unconscious: the failure creates a non-elastic and rigid point of view. Whenever we theorize about the unconscious and treat words as more than descriptive terms, we petrify it and make it impossible for it to manifest as a living force. Every kind of theory can affect it as a static thing not allowed to manifest on its own.

In our story, Faithful John can still be saved after petrification, and he advises the king, while the queen is absent, to cut off the heads of the two children and to smear the blood on his statue, after which Faithful John can come to life and restore life to the sacrificed children. The latter must have to do with those conscious activities which keep Faithful John in a state of petrification and which should therefore be killed, but we have to bear in mind that children and not any other figures are concerned and see what the child means from the king's standpoint. The child is the king's future possibility and also what he loves best in the world. The archetypal idea of the sacrifice is the same as that in the Abraham and Isaac story, for Abraham would surely have preferred to kill himself: the sacrifice of Isaac typifies the greatest possible sacrifice.

We can say that at this point Faithful John reveals what he really is — an image of God — for we know that only to God does one sacrifice one's own child. On the other hand, the child has always a double meaning: mythologically, it can represent the Self, and, depending on the context and the nuance, the infantile shadow. It is of course the same thing, because you might say that the realization of the Self always brings with it the restoration of the naiveté, the genuineness and totality of the reaction of the child. But the question is, "Am I still too childish, or have I again to become a child? " As Christ said, "Whosoever shall not receive the kingdom of God as a little child, he shall not enter therein." But one has to first become adult, and then a child. Sometimes one sees that Christian civilization has preferred to believe that one should stay as the little lamb of Jesus in order to reach the Kingdom of Heaven, but actually what is required is the restoration of the unreflecting capacity for total living reaction, backed, so to speak, by the Self.

In this connection we have to recognize an aspect of the infantile shadow and see that behind this conscious attitude there is an immature and childish attitude. It is a tendency or inability to see the paradox — the opposites — due to one's own conscious behavior, a tendency towards one-sidedness in saying this is right and that wrong; thus one keeps oneself infantile and outside the conflict. The duality of the child can be understood for the child has the double aspect of childishness and spontaneity. A Freudian analysis tends to kill any kind of spontaneity with the idea of wanting to kill infantilism: all mistakes and slips of the tongue are linked up with the Oedipus or Electra complex. This way of interpretation can be destructive, for while it kills any kind of infantile behavior, it also exorcises any kind of spontaneity — and creativity — and leads to a dull unspontaneous attitude, a cramped kind of consciousness in which one is perpetually questioning oneself as to whether one's behavior is not betraying an Oedipus or Electra complex.

If the fairy tale had not worked out as it did, one feels that the same old situation would have been repeated with the king and a friend, the same problem would have continued *ad infinitum* — a sterile continuation of the same conflict. Previously the king had only given expression to his desires: he wanted to see the contents of the locked room, he wanted to have the original of the picture; and Faithful John had done everything for him. But the king himself made no contribution to his own happiness. If one looks at the story from his aspect, one might say that he had been lucky to have this old servant to manage his life for him and that the one thing he could have done, namely to trust Faithful John, he did not do. Perhaps that was also lucky because there he begins to awaken. He says, "Why do these things happen? " And then he atones for his former passivity by sacrificing the children.

Psychologically, that would mean the sacrifice of the conscious principle and the sacrifice of oneself, which means sacrificing one's own immaturity and infantility. The ego is always engaged in some kind of nonsense: to give up what the ego thinks is right and wants, to submit to what is happening, is the great deed. The ego does not really sacrifice *itself,* but its infantility. That this is a real sacrifice is proved by the fact that the king gets frightened when he hears he has to kill his beloved children. Fairy tales are extraordinarily economical in the use of feeling adjectives, and there are few psychological or feeling comments, but the story says that at first he was frightened at the thought of killing the children but then, remembering the great loyalty of Faithful John who had died for him, he took his sword and killed them. One could therefore say that he had developed since the petrification of Faithful John. He must have suffered all the years of the children's life, while the statue stood in his bedroom, for every time he saw it, he cried and wished he could bring it to life, and that, probably, had the maturing effect — when at last Faithful John asked for the sacrifice he was ready to make it. The king is roasted in his suffering while the children are growing, and then when the magic time comes and the statue talks, the king comes to the conclusion that Faithful John's return to earth matters more than anything else in the world. This conclusion corresponds to this problem: if one has lost contact with the meaning of the unconscious, nothing else really matters any longer for nothing except renewed contact can replace that which is lost.

The queen was in church while the sacrifice took place. The king checks on her, and, on her return, asks what she would have done. She accepts his deed. That she was in church would mean that she was still in the service

92

of a really religious attitude; for her, apparently, this is still a living principle. (The congregations in churches nowadays are 90% women; the husband stays at home and smokes a pipe while his wife goes to church, which
shows how modern the fairy tale is!) She is contained in the arms of the
church, the anima is Christiana; consciousness has the problem. If you
analyze modern men who say that they do not believe in the Christian
dogma, you see that their anima still goes to church because all those figures of the unconscious are still going back in time. We have all the layers
within us, figures which are not as modern as consciousness; parts of us
are in the Middle Ages, parts in antiquity, and parts naked on the trees.
It is implied that the anima has not the same problem because she is contained in the teaching of the church.

Another aspect of this problem concerns the *king*: *he* has received
everything from Faithful John, *he* has to pay the debt, *he* got what he
wanted through Faithful John, *he* was the recipient of the gifts. Naturally he should be the one to pay, and not the queen. The story of the
queen is normal and undramatic, her life is not involved in the message of
the fairy tale. Women are not generally so aware of the opposites, they
can slip through and therefore, unless a woman has a father complex and
a very strong animus, this problem does not generally present itself so
strongly. A woman lives more in terms of the continuity of life and
"never mind about the opposites."

You might say, therefore, that the woman within the man is the same,
the anima is interested in life, but not in the problem of good and evil, or
truth and its opposite, the Logos principle to which man is more devoted
and which makes the problem of the opposite acute. In the Jewish civilization there is no female Goddess, the law was the God; either you followed
it or not, and *that* creates the problem of ethical response. In the Greek
religion there are as many Goddesses as Gods, and the ethical problem is
not so acute because the anima is interested in life, as is the mother principle, and the problem of the opposites is not similarly constellated. But we
will come to the female in the next stories.

———

Next I will study two Grimm fairy tales which run parallel to each
other, "The Two Brothers" and "The Golden Children." In both stories

the pairs concerned are of equal rank, there is no servant and no king; but one marries and the other remains a lonely figure, just as Faithful John did. Here, where it is even more likely that a marriage quaternity might be established, it does not take place. We must discuss what that could mean.

THE TWO BROTHERS

Once upon a time there were two brothers, one rich and one poor. The rich brother, a goldsmith, was bad-hearted; the poor brother, who made brooms, was a talkative good man. The poor brother had two boys, twins, as like to each other as two drops of water. The boys went in and out of the rich uncle's house and sometimes found a scrap to eat. The poor man went to the forest to fetch twigs for his brooms, and there saw a golden bird, more beautiful than anything he had ever seen. He picked up a stone, threw it at the bird, and luckily hit it; but only a golden feather fell to the ground. The bird flew away. The man took the feather to his brother, who said it was real gold and gave him money for it.

The next day the broom maker climbed a beach tree to cut off a few branches, and the same bird flew by. When the man looked he found a nest with a golden egg in it. He took the egg home and brought it to his brother, who again said that it was real gold and gave his brother its value in money. Then the goldsmith said he wanted the bird itself. The poor man went a third time into the wood and again saw the golden bird sitting on the tree. He threw a stone at it, brought it to the ground, and took it to his brother, who did as before. The poor man went home quite contented, thinking that now he could help himself.

But the goldsmith, clever and cunning, knew very well the kind of bird he had. He called his wife and told her to roast the bird and be careful that no part was lost, for he wanted to eat it all himself. It was a magic bird and whoever ate its heart and liver would find a piece of gold every morning under his pillow. His wife prepared the bird and put it on the spit to roast. Now it happened that the woman had to go out of the kitchen to do other work, and the two children of the poor broom maker came in, stood in front of the spit, and turned it round a couple of times. And as two little pieces fell out of the bird into the pan, one said to the other, "We'll eat those two little bits, I am so hungry and nobody will notice."

94

The woman came back and noticed that they were eating something and asked them what it was. "A couple of little bits that fell out of the bird," they answered. "That must have been the liver and heart," said the terrified woman, and in order that her husband should not notice anything she quickly killed a chicken and put the liver and heart with the rest of the golden bird. When it was done she took it to the goldsmith, who ate it all up by himself, leaving nothing over. Next morning when he put his hand under his pillow nothing was there.

The two children had no idea what a piece of luck had happened to them. Next morning when they got up something rolled onto the floor, and they saw it was two pieces of gold. They brought them to their father, who wondered how that had happened. But when this happened everyday, he went to his brother and told him the strange story. The goldsmith saw at once what had happened and in revenge, since he was mean and hard-hearted, told his brother that the children were in league with something evil and that he should not take the gold nor let the children remain any longer in his house, for the devil would ruin him. The brother was afraid of the devil, so, though it made him very unhappy, he took the two boys into the woods and with a heavy heart left them there.

The children ran about trying to find their way home, but could not. At last they met a hunter who asked them who they were, and they told him what their father had done and about the piece of gold they each found under their pillows every morning. "That's nothing bad," said the huntsman, "as long as you remain honest and don't turn lazy." Since the good man liked the children and had none of his own, he took them home with him, saying he would be a father to them. He taught them how to hunt and he put the money by for them so that they would have it if they wanted it later on.

When they were grown, the huntsman said he would test their shooting, but for a long time nothing came by. At last the huntsman saw some snow geese flying in the shape of a triangle and told them to shoot down the end geese, which they did. Afterwards more geese came by in the form of the figure two, and again the boys were successful in shooting down the corner geese. Whereupon the hunter said that they were now trained huntsmen. That evening the two brothers refused to touch their food until the hunter had granted them their request: to let them go out into the world.

Their request granted, on the appointed day the huntsman gave each a gun and a dog and let them take as much of the money that had been saved as they wished. On parting he gave them a knife, saying that if ever they separated, at the dividing of the ways they should stick the knife into a tree; when either came back he would see how things went with his brother for in the direction in which the other had gone the knife would be rusty if he were dead and bright if he lived.

The two brothers came into a vast forest and since it was impossible to get out of it during the day, they spent the night there and ate what they had in their knapsack. The same thing happened the next day. With nothing left to eat, they said they must shoot something, and one loaded his gun. An old hare came by, and begged for his life, saying that in exchange he would give two young ones; but when the two little hares came out they played so happily together that the brothers hadn't the heart to kill them, and the hares followed them. The same thing happened with a fox, a wolf, a bear, and a lion, so that in the end the hunters had two hares, two foxes, two wolves, two bears and two lions — and increased hunger. The fox thereupon led them to a village where they bought food. After having fed their animals they went on further.

Since they could not find any work, they decided they must separate; they divided the animals between them, swore brotherly love to each other until death, stuck the knife into a tree, and then one brother went east and the other west.

The youngest came with his animals to a town that was covered with black crepe. He went to an inn and asked if he could put up his animals. The innkeeper gave him a stall which had a hole in the wall through which the hare went out and brought in a cabbage and the fox a chicken and a cock; but the wolf, bear, and lion, too big to get out, were fed by the innkeeper. Afterwards the brother asked why the town was draped in black and was told that the next day the king's daughter was to die, for she had to be given to a dragon who every year had to have a young girl; the princess was the last girl left, and if he didn't have her he would destroy the whole land. Many young men had tried to kill the dragon but all had been killed themselves, and the king had promised his daughter and his kingdom to whoever should kill the dragon.

The next morning the huntsman went up the dragon's hill

with his animals. On the altar of a little church he found three beakers on which was written that whoever drank their contents would be the strongest man in the world and should have the sword which stood at the doorway. The huntsman first tried to pull up the sword but couldn't until he had emptied the beakers; then he could do it easily. When the princess, the king, and the courtiers came out, they saw the huntsman on the mountain and took him for the dragon.

The princess came up the mountain and found the young man instead of the dragon. He comforted her and locked her up in the church. Soon out came the seven-headed dragon and asked the young man what he was doing there. The young man said he was going to fight him. Out of his seven mouths the dragon spewed fire, which should have ignited the dry grass and so burnt up the young man, but the animals trod it out. Then the dragon went for the young man, who promptly cut off three of his heads. In a rage the dragon spewed fire over the man, but the huntsman cut off another three heads and finally the last head, after which his animals tore the rest of the dragon to pieces. When the man opened the church door he found the princess senseless on the ground, terrified by the fight. When she came to, he showed her the remains of the dragon and told her she was free. She was very happy and said that now he should be her dear husband as her father had promised. Thereupon she took the coral chain she was wearing off her neck and divided it up among the animals as a reward; she gave her hand-kerchief to the man, who cut out the seven tongues from the seven dragon heads and wrapped them up in it.

Since he was so tired after the battle, he proposed that they should sleep for a little while, and he told the lion to watch over them while they slept. But the lion asked the bear to watch, and the bear asked the wolf, the wolf the fox, and the fox the hare. Since the poor hare was also tired and couldn't hand the watch over to anyone else, they all went to sleep.

But the marshall had watched everything from far off and when he saw what had happened, being a bad man, he took the sword and cut off the huntsman's head with it, seized the girl, and brought her down the mountain. She woke up and was terrified, but the marshall said she was now in his power and should say he had killed the dragon. When she refused, he threatened to kill her, so she promised. The marshall then went home with her, said he had killed the dragon, and demanded the princess as his wife. The king asked the girl if it was true, and she said, "Oh yes, it must be true, but the wedding must not take place until a year and a day have gone by" — for she thought during that time she might hear something of her dear huntsman.

Meanwhile the animals still slept. Three times a bumble bee came and sat on the hare's nose and the third time he stung him and woke him up. As soon as he was awake he woke the others, and when the lion saw that the girl was gone and the man dead, he roared and cried out, "Who has done this? " All blamed a different animal for not having woken the other up; only the poor hare had no one to blame, so he was the guilty party. To save his skin he said he knew of a root that would heal any illness, and in twenty-four hours he fetched it from far away. The lion put the young man's head on again (backwards) and when he saw that the girl was gone he thought she had run away from him. At noon when he wanted to eat he noticed that his head was on the wrong way round and asked what had happened to him. So the lion pulled off his head again and turned it round, and the hare healed the wound.

The sad huntsman wandered from town to town making his animals dance, and just a year later he came to a town all decked out in red. When he asked why, he was told that the king's daughter was to be married to the marshall who had saved her from the dragon by killing him. And then all the animals had to help. The hare had to fetch bread from the king's table. the fox roast meat, the wolf vegetables, the bear sweetstuff, and the lion wine; and each time an animal went to the princess, who knew it by the corals on its neck, she gave it what it wanted. The huntsman and his animals ate the food together and were happy because the huntsman realized that the princess loved him.

Then the huntsman went himself to the court and took with him the princess' handkerchief with the seven dragon tongues in it, for the king had sent somebody to fetch him when his daughter would not tell him about the five animals which had come to her in the palace and gone away again. But the huntsman first asked the king to send him royal clothes in which to come and a carriage with six horses and servants, which his daughter said he should do. And the king went out to meet the huntsman whose animals all followed him, and he sat at the table by the king and his daughter, with the unsuspecting marshall opposite. Then the seven heads of the dragon were brought out and the king said that because the marshall had killed the

dragon he was giving him his daughter, but the huntsman opened
their mouths and asked where the tongues were? Then the marshall went very white and said that dragons had no tongues. The
huntsman replied that liars should have no tongues and that the
dragon tongues were the sign of the victor. Then he opened the
handkerchief and put each tongue back in the proper mouth and
showed the handkerchief with the princess' name embroidered
on it to the princess and asked to whom she had given it, and she
answered, "To the man who killed the dragon." Then he called
his animals to him, took the collars off each of them, showed
them to the princess, and asked to whom the corals belonged.
She told what had happened. And then the huntsman explained
that when he was tired and slept after the battle, the marshall had
come and cut off his head and carried away the king's daughter,
pretending that he had killed the dragon. And the princess said
that, since the truth had come out independently of her, she
could confirm it, though she had promised the marshall not to
say anything.

So the marshall was torn to pieces by four oxen, the marriage
was celebrated, and everyone was happy. But one day the huntsman, now king, wanted to go hunting. He followed a white doe
so far into the woods that he got lost. He made a fire and with
his animals round him prepared to spend the night there. Then
he heard voices coming from the tree and saw an old woman
sitting up above him who complained that she was cold. He told
her to come down and warm herself, but she, afraid of the animals,
threw down a stick saying he should touch the animals with it so
that they should not hurt her. He did so, they turned to stone,
and when she came down she turned the man into stone too.

When the other brother went to look at the knife, he saw it
was half rusted over on one side and knew some misfortune had
befallen his brother. When he came to the city gates, the guards
asked if they should announce him; he thought he must be taken
for his brother and that he should accept that, so that he might
know better how to help him. Consequently, he was taken to
the palace and everybody, even the princess, thought he was the
right king. He had to explain that he had lost his way in a wood.
At night when he was brought to the royal bed he laid a naked
sword between them; the princess, not knowing what it meant,
did not dare to ask.

After a few days, when the brother had found out all he
wanted to know, he said he must go hunting again. They all

99

tried to dissuade him, but he insisted. Again the white doe came to him. Later, like his brother, he made a fire. The same old witch sat up in the tree, but when she threw him the stick, he refused to touch his animals with it and told her she could come down or he would fetch her down. Then he shot at her, but she was proof against that; so he took three silver buttons from his coat and shot with them, and she fell to the ground with a loud cry. He then put his foot on her neck and threatened to throw her into the fire if she did not say where his brother and his animals were. So she told him he lay in a ditch and was turned to stone along with all his animals. He forced her then to bring him to the place and to deliver his brother and the animals under peril of being burnt to death. So the brother and the animals and many other people also were brought back to life. Then they bound the witch and burnt her, whereupon the whole wood lighted up and they could see the royal palace three hours' distance from where they were.

As they went towards the palace the brother told the king how he had been taken for him and how he had eaten and drunk as the king and even lain in the king's bed. But the king, when he heard that, became angry and jealous and cut off his brother's head. Soon, however, he regretted his deed and cried, and the hare had to go and fetch the root again and heal the huntsman, who noticed nothing at all of his wound. Then the two separated and entered the town from two different sides so that the guard from each gate come to the old king and announced the young king's arrival. The king knew that the gates were an hour's distance from each other, and said it was not possible; but when the two brothers appeared, the old king told his daughter to say which was her husband, which she was able to do by the collars which the king's animals wore. When they went to bed that night the queen asked the king why he had put the sword between them the night before, since she thought he wanted to kill her. And that was how the king knew his brother had been faithful to him.

THE GOLDEN CHILDREN

A poor man and woman had nothing but a little hut and the meager food they got from catching fish. But it happened one day that the man sat by the water and threw out his net and caught a golden fish. As he looked at it in amazement, the fish

100

began to talk and said, "Listen Fisherman, if you will throw me back into the water I will turn your hut into a beautiful castle." But the fisherman answered, "What would be the good of that to me when I have nothing to eat!" But the fish said that that also should be attended to for there would be a cupboard in the castle in which all the drawers were full of the most wonderful food, as much as he wanted. "If that's so," said the man, "I can certainly do you a favor." "Yes," said the fish, "but on condition that you tell nobody in the world, whoever it may be, how your good luck came about; if you say one single word, everything will be lost."

So the man threw the magic fish back into the water and went home. But where his hut had been there was now a large castle. He stared at it, went in, and found his wife dressed in beautiful clothes and sitting in a beautiful room. She was delighted and said, "Husband, how has this happened? I am very pleased about it!" "Yes," said the man, "I like it too, but I'm very hungry; give me something to eat." But the wife answered, "I have nothing and don't know how to do anything in the new house." "That doesn't matter," said the man, "there's a big cupboard over there, open that." When they opened the cupboard they found in it cakes, meat, fruit, and wine. Delighted, they sat down and ate and drank together. When they had eaten all they wanted, the woman said, "But where do all these riches come from? " "Oh," said he, "don't ask me that, I mustn't tell you; if I tell anyone our luck will be over." "Good," said she, "if I shouldn't know, then I don't want to." But she didn't mean that for she was tormented night and day and bothered him so much that in his impatience he blurted out that it all came through the magic golden fish he had caught and freed again. And as soon as he had said that the beautiful castle with the cupboard disappeared and they were back again in the old fisherman's hut.

So the man had to begin all over again. As luck would have it, he caught the golden fish, and the fish said if he would give him his freedom he would once again give him the castle with the cupboard full of food, but this time he should be strong and not tell anyone. But the same thing happened. The woman said she would rather not have the riches, for if she didn't know where they came from, she would have no peace.

Again the man went fishing, and for the third time caught the golden fish. "Listen," said the fish, "I see that I shall always

101

fall into your hands, so take me home and cut me into six pieces. Give two to your wife to eat, two to your horse, and put two in the ground, and you will receive a blessing." The man did as he had been told: the two pieces he put into the earth produced two golden lilies, the horse bore two golden foals, and the fisherman's wife two golden children.

The children grew big and beautiful, and the lilies and foals grew marvelously too. The children said that they wanted to ride out into the world on their two golden horses. But their father said, How could he bear it if they went away and he didn't know what was happening to them? They answered that the two golden lilies would remain and by them he could tell whether all went well with his sons, for if the lilies remained fresh the children would be well, if they faded they were sick, and if they died the children would be dead. So they rode away and came to an inn where there were many people, who when they saw the two golden children began to laugh and mock them. One of the children was ashamed and wouldn't go out into the world but turned back and went home to his father. The other went on and came to a big forest, and when he wanted to go through it the people said that he couldn't because the forest was full of robbers who would do him harm and that when they saw that he and his horse were golden they would kill them both. But he wouldn't be frightened and insisted on going on. He took a bearskin and covered himself and his horse with it, and rode into the forest. After he had gone a little way he heard noises and voices in the bushes. One cried, "There goes one"; but the other answered, "Let him go, he's only got an old bearskin and is as poor as a church mouse. What should we do with him!" So the golden child rode happily through the forest.

One day he came to a village where he saw a girl so beautiful that he thought she must be the most beautiful in the world. He was so much in love with her that he went to her and said, "I love you with all my heart! Will you marry me? " As the girl liked him too, she agreed and said she would be his wife and would be true to him as long as she lived. So they got married and were very happy together. But when the bride's father came home and saw that his daughter was married, he was very much surprised and asked where the bridegroom was. She showed him the golden child, who, however, still wore his bearskin. Then the father waxed angry and said his daughter should never marry a man in a bearskin. He wanted to kill the bride-

102

groom. However, when the bride said that he was her husband and she loved him, her father quieted down. But, unable to rid himself of the thought, he got up early the next morning to see whether his daughter's husband was an ordinary ragged beggar. When he looked, he saw a beautiful golden man in the bed and the bearskin on the floor. So he went away and thought what a good thing it was that he had controlled his anger for he would have committed a great crime.

The golden child dreamt that he went to the hunt on a beautiful stag, and when he woke in the morning told his wife that he wanted to go hunting. But she was afraid and begged him not to go, saying that he could easily meet with misfortune; but he insisted, got up, and went into the forest, and before long a beautiful stag stood in front of him, exactly as in his dream. He wanted to shoot it, but the stag ran off. He went after it through the bushes and over ditches all through the day, but in the evening the stag disappeared. And when the golden child looked around he saw a little house — and in it was a witch. He knocked at the door and the old woman came out and asked what he wanted so late in the middle of the forest. He asked if she had seen a stag. "Yes," she said, "I know the stag well." Then a little dog which came out of the house with her barked at the golden child furiously, and he said, "Be quiet, you little beast, or I'll shoot you dead!" "What," said the old witch furiously, "You'd kill my little dog, would you? " And she changed him into a stone so that his bride waited for him in vain and thought that, as she had feared, something must have happened to him.

But at home the other brother stood by the golden lilies when suddenly one fell over. "Oh," he thought, "something must have happened to my brother; I must go, and perhaps I can save him."

His father, however, thought he should stay at home for if he lost him as well, what would he do? But the other insisted and got on his golden horse. He came to the great forest where his brother lay like a stone. The old witch came out of her house and called to him and wanted to tempt him in, but he didn't go near her. Instead, he said he would shoot her dead if she didn't bring his brother back to life. Unwillingly she touched the stone with her finger, and he immediately returned to life. The two children were happy to see each other again and rode out of the wood together, the one to his bride and the

103

other to his father. The father said he knew that one son had
freed the other for the lily had suddenly stood up and blossom-
ed again. So they all lived happily together until the end of
their days.

We will use these stories only to throw some light on the tale of Faithful
John and on the problem of the shadow. We have the interesting motif of
the golden bird (or fish) which is responsible for the birth of the brothers,
or which turns them into magic figures. The bird (or fish) is a single principle, and not a duality; it is a genuine symbol of the Self which comes
from the depths of the unconscious, rather like the intuitive idea of wholeness, and this principle is responsible for the origin of the dual situation in
the conscious world.

The principle of evil in the story of Faithful John is in the background
only: it is the poison in the Princess of the Golden Roof, which Faithful
John has to suck out. The old king in this story died without making further difficulties, but evil is still so active that in the end Faithful John is
petrified; in the story of the shoemaker and the tailor, the former is thrown
out in the end – he is rejected and lands under the gallows; but in the story
of Faithful John, evil is in the poison and acts like a curse. I have therefore
taken another story in which evil is personified in the form of a witch.

In comparing the stories and looking at the symbol of the witch, we
might ask how and why this old woman is responsible for the destruction
of the one principle. It is easy to believe that the unconscious cannot
manifest itself when evil comes from a wrong attitude in consciousness:
that is what we tell people all the time – that they have a wrong attitude
in their conscious and that therefore the unconscious cannot involve itself
in helpful ways and is reduced to inactivity; the unconscious, reduced to
complete inactivity, can only produce feelings of guilt and neurotic symptoms. But if we look more closely at the situation we sometimes see that
it is more complicated: as shown in this story of the golden children, evil
does not come from the principle of consciousness, but from a neglected
archetype of the unconscious, from the witch.

The witch is an archetypal figure of the Great Mother. She is the neglected mother Goddess, the Goddess of the earth, the mother Goddess in

her destructive aspect. The Egyptian mother Goddess, Isis, is called the great magician and the great witch: when angry she is the witch, and when benevolent the redeeming all-bestowing mother who gives birth to the Gods. In such a figure you have both aspects of the archetype of the mother for she has a light and dark side — the witch, and the benevolent and maternal. Kali also can appear as the life giver or the bringer of great destruction.

In fairy tales which, in the main, are under the influence of Christian civilization, the archetype of the Great Mother, like all others, is split into two aspects. The Virgin Mary, for example, is cut off from her shadow side and represents only the light side of the mother image; consequently, as Jung points out, the moment when the figure of the Virgin Mary became more important was also the time of the witch persecutions. Since the symbol of the Great Mother was too one-sided, the dark side got projected onto women, which gave rise to the persecution of witches; since the shadow of the Great Mother was not contained in any officially worshipped symbol of the Goddess, the figure of the mother became split into the positive mother and the destructive witch. In fairy tales innumerable witches and even the Great Mother appear in many stories, as Albert Dietrich proved in his book *Mutter Erde*. There is, for instance, the figure of the devil's *grand*mother — or, *great* mother; and in fairy tales the devil therefore lives with the old woman, i. e., his own mother, the Great Mother Earth.

Behind the popularity of the Black Madonnas is the same problem, for they too have to do with the black Goddess of Isis. The legend concerning the Black Madonna in Einsiedeln holds that once the monastery was burned down, and since then the statue has remained blackened. But one can see that this is not so: she is black, and she is black because she is more potent and magical and effective than she would be as an ordinary white woman. Here the archetype of the Great Mother Earth comes in through the back door, for if the archetype is excluded by dogmatic teaching it necessarily returns by the back door. Being despised by the ruling collective consciousness, the archetype here does something horrible, for the witch does not attack the king directly, but hits at another figure, e. g., Faithful John. Faithful John gets attacked by evil and the king is then hit secondarily, for he has to sacrifice his children. Yet here is a typical archetypal event which one also has to keep in mind in the treatment of individual cases: when the neurotic complexes in an individual are not simple and something in the unconscious is rejected, the disturbance goes round the corner and the rejected thing lames something else.

A man with a negative mother complex is caught by a tremendous but half unconscious ambition and power drive which apparently makes him very successful in life — but he has a dim feeling that something is wrong, especially in his relationship to women. In analysis you discover that the power drive sits like an evil animal on his sex; within the unconscious it harms the sex instinct but does not directly harm consciousness. Through dream analysis you see that there are two factors in the unconscious which collide, for within the dream the two unconscious principles fight and you feel that consciousness cannot be made responsible; but, indirectly, it is responsible for the battle in the unconscious because of a certain wrong attitude.

In the field of consciousness people have an indirect conflict: they say that they want to marry but are always unlucky, something in the unconscious stops them. It is not they who have the projections, they say, but something goes wrong, and they do not know why. You can then see that Eros is attacked by another unconscious factor and that the destruction goes on mechanically in the unconscious, consciousness being only indirectly responsible; consequently, you have to make a detour and follow the dreams. In such a situation consciousness has not explicitly done any harm — the old king never harmed Faithful John but treated him rightly — yet obviously some force was neglected in the kingdom which first hit Faithful John and then the young king.

Hence you have the double situation. And in the story of the golden children you see that it is the archetype of the Great Mother who avenges herself by attacking the transcendent function, the process of becoming conscious, the process towards individuation; and that is worse than if she attacked the conscious part directly.

The theory of repression does not always work; often omission or unawareness of a factor has a directly destructive effect on the whole process of individuation. On the other hand it can be said that in the worst neurosis the climax is also the healing place. One must look for the healing fact in the worst spot because there lies the trouble *and* the urge towards individuation. It may be the archetype of the mother which is hit, but, even so, it comes via the Self. The neglected archetype of the mother in Christian civilization destroys the whole process of individuation, and the whole problem has to be rediscussed from those angles.

The story of the golden children points to another problem. In the previous story we had the figures of the new king and Faithful John, but now there are brothers of the same age and rank. Here is the new principle of consciousness in the making and the urge towards individuation, which stands behind the new symbol. They are again each others' shadows (a shadow, it must not be forgotten, is only relative), but they are here twin figures, characterized in two ways, for one stays at home disgusted by the world's stupidity and the other goes out into the world. There are similar stories in Old Egypt: Anub and Bata, brothers, have the same fate, one is caught in the world and the other is a hermit. The twin who goes out into the world marries, for he is that part of consciousness which tends towards living life and getting involved in it. And as the anima is the great entangler and the Maya who involves him in good and evil, naturally he should be the one to marry the princess and also fall for the evil behind the anima, the Goddess of life and death, the witch, the tendency towards getting involved in the process of life and death. He risks himself in life, the condition for becoming conscious.

If you analyze elderly people who have escaped life, you realize how much an unlived life mutilates the possibility of becoming conscious; you realize how much not having lived and risked by throwing yourself into the hopeless conflict is really a mutilation of the possibility of individuation. On the other hand, the one who throws himself into the conflict and tries to swim in life ends up petrified, is petrified in a deeper sense by the life principle itself, the Great Mother, for she turns into a death-bringing principle. So just the one who takes the risk is the one petrified — and at that moment the one who stayed out of life and did not get involved physically or spiritually in the life process is the great redeemer who can finish off the witch, who can see through her and put an end to her destructiveness, to the destructiveness in the anima.

In the light of our civilization this has happened in the following way. Christian civilization is relatively an extraverted civilization compared with that of the East, and therefore the official symbolism involves the brother who married. In the chapter on the king and queen in *Mysterium Coniunctionis*, Jung discusses the text of an English 15th century alchemist (Ripley) in which there comes first the genuine union of the king and queen who give birth to the philosopher's child, the philosopher's stone; but, being a churchman, Ripley then brings in an unusual second *coniunctio*. Jung says that Ripley introduces this second *coniunctio* because he has in mind the marriage of the Lamb with the Church, and this, Jung says, brings to light a divergence between the alchemical archetype and the Christian symbolism. It is difficult to understand, after the first *coniunctio* (the union of the conscious with the unconscious principle), why there has to be a second union unless one sees that the new dominant of consciousness has to unite with the *corpus mysticum* of mankind, or with the Ecclesia-Luna.

The lonely alchemists have not the motif of the marriage of the Lamb because in this is contained the idea of the final sacrifice of the king – an idea lacking in alchemy. The alchemical philosopher's stone is the hermit's idea, the goal for the lonely individual. The stone represents the union of opposites, of the male and female within. But for the community, the stone does not belong to any; it is rather like the treasure in the field which the man took and hid again. So the one wonderful pearl, the philosopher's stone, remains the marvelous secret of the individual, though the old masters said they did not hide the secret. That the stone is kept secret and not kept secret can be explained this way: these are two opposites in which the process of individuation culminates. When a new symbol of the divinity is built up during the process, the divinity is either sacrificed to strengthen a community or kept secret within the individual.

If Jung had founded a sect of Jungians, then one might say that the king was sacrificed in a second *coniunctio*. That event would build up a new community and would revitalize an organization as secret mystical clubs did. This possibility raises a very urgent problem. People say, "What you are doing is wonderful, but what does it do for Europe? How does it help in our situation and time? Here and there a lonely individual is helped, but that should be altered and the masses enriched." People say that we should make a collective recipe, easily understood, and feed it to the masses to save the Christian civilization. But the second marriage would kill the original symbol, for then the esoteric symbol marries the community. That was the Christian idea: Christ married the Church and will do so till the end of days – ultimately, then, the process of individuation is sacrificed to establish a new community. The counter idea – that the found symbol is

again hidden and does not marry this world and the community but remains
the secret of the lonely person, the alchemist-hermit — cryptically imaged
in the Mundaka Upanishad:

> Two birds, inseparable friends, cling to
> the same tree. One of them eats the
> sweet fruit, the other looks on without
> eating [without entering reality].

In a Hawaian myth a man (parallel to our Adam) was whole in the Beyond, but then was called to earth; only one half of him came down, however, and that is why the Adam of this civilization is called the half-man.
At the end of the world, the myth intimates, he will reach his other half.
In many primitive civilizations every person born is believed to have a
twin brother, his placenta. Rather than enter the world, this twin is
dried and wound round the neck; and at the moment of death the two
halves meet.

The Upanishad continues:

> On the same tree man sits grieving, im-
> mersed, bewildered by his own impotence.
> But when he sees the other lord contented,
> and knows his glory, then his grief passes
> away.
>
> When the seer sees the brilliant maker and
> lord [of the world] as the Person who has
> his source in Brahman, then he is wise, and
> shaking off good and evil, he reaches the
> highest oneness, free from passions.

In the Svetâs Vatara-Upanishad it is said:

> There is one unborn being [female], red,
> white, and black, uniform, but producing
> manifold offspring. There is one unborn
> being [male] who loves her and lies by her;
> there is another who leaves her, [the sword
> which the brother placed between himself
> and his brother's wife] while she is eating
> what has to be eaten.

109

In life one eats what has to be eaten.   All these quotations are amplified in the Maitraya-Brahmana-Upanishad:

> He who sees this does not see death, nor
> disease, nor misery, for seeing he sees all
> [objectively, not as affecting him subjec-
> tively]; he becomes all everywhere [he be-
> comes Brahman].

> There is the person in the eye, there is he
> who walks as in sleep, he who is sound
> asleep, and he who is above the sleeper,
> these are the four conditions [of the
> Self], and the fourth is greater than all.

> Brahman with one foot moves in the
> three, and Brahman with three feet is
> in the last.

> It is that both the true [in the fourth
> condition] and the untrue [in the three
> conditions] may have their desert, that
> the Great Self [seems to] become two, yes,
> that he [*seems to*] *become two.*

These two brothers in the fairy tale, then, are the figures of these *seemingly* two aspects of the Self. They are secretly one, just as the golden children in our story are secretly one because they are of the same flesh of the one fish. The conflict exists only as long as consciousness exists, and as long as consciousness exists, the conflict is inevitable — but it is a *seeming* conflict. One should remember their secret oneness and all that it implies:

> Two birds, inseparable friends, cling to
> the same tree. One of them eats the sweet
> fruit, the other looks on without eating.

PART TWO

DEALING WITH EVIL IN
FAIRY TALES

CHAPTER I

PRIMITIVE LEVELS OF EVIL

Without trying to prove it again, I take as my starting point the fact that fairy tales mirror collective unconscious material — which leads us, before we enter into details, to a further general question: if it is collective unconscious material, are there ethical problems in fairy tales? If there are, that would mean that the unconscious has an ethical moralistic feature or trend, which is something we cannot assume out of hand. Before we go into this, it is better to turn first to personal and collective unconscious material as it can be observed in individual people, for there one finds all the information: and for this I can refer you to Dr. C. G. Jung's article on "The Conscience." I do not know whether this has already been translated into English, but it has appeared in German in the *Studien des C. G. Jung Institutes* entitled "Das Gewissen"; in the last paper Dr. Jung discusses his standpoint on conscience. He raises that same question which I have now put to you, and answers it in the following way:

Certainly human society as a whole shows a basically ethical tendency. Except for a few abnormal cases, it can be assumed that everywhere, in every nation, the human psyche includes in its structure a certain proneness to what Jung calls man's ethical reaction towards his own acts. Man is not indifferent, but everywhere tends to have an evaluating judgment towards his own activities and motives. Such judgment may differ from one nation to another, but the fact that one has such a feeling reaction is a generally human feature. Closer analysis, however, shows a separation between unconscious motivations, and a conscious super-structure of reflections, conscious thoughts about one's own motives, and subjective evaluating judgments. Thus conscience, when we analyze it in detail in human beings, is a very complex phenomenon which has led to the world-wide question known to theologians as the problem of the wrong, bad conscience, and the wrong, good conscience, with all the falsifications of conscience and pseudo-guilt feelings. Other observers contend that all these complications are not guilt problems, for this complex situation of an unconscious and a conscious part already existed in the basic structure of the whole phenomenon.

Jung then discusses at length the problem of the Freudian concept of the super-ego, i. e., the Freudian explanation of the reactions of feelings of guilt, bad conscience, and ethical tendencies in man, and he finds that this coincides with what he calls the collective moral code which, in our society, is combined with our Judeo-Christian patriarchal religious tradition. In individual cases this code can function partly unconsciously, and can lead to all sorts of feelings of guilt and complications, inhibitions, or motivations to act, summed up by the Freudians as the phenomenon of the super-ego.

In this sense, we Jungians do not deny the phenomenon, for it exists and is the collective moral code which can either be recognized consciously by an individual or can exert an unconscious or semi-unconscious pressure on his motivations. But on closer examination this super-ego is seen to be an historical formation and therefore not responsible for the whole ethical problem, but only a part of it.

In other words, what Jung calls the ethical reaction of the human psyche is not identical with the Freudian super-ego. On the contrary, the two concepts can even clash and be opposed. Jung expresses his view that we are under the pressure of two factors: that of the collective ethical code which differs from nation to nation and generally dictates our ethical behavior, and that of a personal moral urge, which is individual and does not coincide with the collective code. Naturally if both coincide, they are difficult to differentiate.

Let us assume, for instance, that you are furious with someone whom you feel like killing, but you realize that normally and personally that is not something you could or would do. Is that the general collective code speaking within you, or is it your own personal, more ethical side, your feeling relatedness, which stops you? In such a case one cannot make a distinction. Personally, one could say that even if there were no observer, no police or moral code, one would not do such a thing, but that would be hard to prove; the fact is that you *can't* do it, because something within you prohibits it, and that is all there is to it. That these factors, the personal urge towards an ethical reaction and the moral code, are not identical, is obvious only when there is a so-called collision of duties.

114

As you know, Jung says that it is not really difficult to know what one has to do as long as there is no collision of duty. The difficulty arises in a situation where whatever you do is half right and half wrong, where whatever you do has a partly wrong aspect. A typical problem is that which confronts a doctor who has to tell, or not tell, a patient that he has a carcinoma. If he doesn't tell the truth he lies, but if he gives the patient a mortal shock he may do him great harm, so what is he to do? The moral code does not answer such a question. Some of his colleagues may say one must never tell, while others will say that one must tell the truth, that even such a shock is better in the long run. But there is no general ethical rule and that is a collision of duties; the duty to tell the truth, and the duty to spare the patient.

With endless such, and much more complicated examples, we suddenly realize that the ethical code is not the only rule for our behavior. In certain cases, even if there is a clear answer as to what you should do, you may yet have a strong feeling that to do it would be immoral *for you.* Then you are in the soup, and then you realize that really there are two things which dictate human behavior: the collective ethical code, which we can also call the Freudian super-ego, and the personal moral individual reaction. The latter, which sometimes coincides with the collective code, is generally referred to as the voice of God: the Romans would call it the genius, Socrates would say "my daimonion" and the Naskapi Indians of the Labrador Peninsula would call it Mistap'eo, the great man who lives in everybody's heart. In other words, it is a figure which we would call an archetype of the Self, the Divine center of the psyche which naturally, in different cultures, has different names and connotations. If this phenomenon arises within oneself, one generally has a strange feeling of certainty as to what is the right thing to do, no matter what the collective code may say about it, and generally the voice not only tells one what to do but imparts a conviction which even can enable an individual to die for it, as did Socrates and many Christian martyrs.

If this inner voice dictates something exceedingly noble, something which is on the line of the collective ethical code, then nobody will get upset but will think it wonderful, right, heroic, and what not. But unfortunately, in practical life, as we see every day in analytical work, this voice of God, or inner instinct can sometimes dictate something

115

absolutely shocking. This occurs even in the Bible: imagine Hosea being told by God that he should marry a prostitute! I am sure that if he had gone to any Protestant, or Anglican, or Catholic, or Jewish clergyman, they would all have said, my dear man, this is a psychological delusion, God *can not* tell you to do such a thing, for theologians tend to think they know what God can and cannot do, and therefore one must be wrong and it is the Devil or one's own shadow or one's repressed sex problem — nowadays they would say it was his own repressed sex anima problem which spoke within Hosea, but it was not God!

How they would know this, God knows, but they would seem to know it. They have perhaps dined with God and discussed it over black coffee and therefore know for sure! But someone not willing to submit to such knowledge, which is the traditional moral code, gets into terrible difficulties, for naturally, if he is honest, he will not know! He may say, yes, perhaps it is my foul anima which makes me feel I have to marry a prostitute, who can prove that this is the voice of God? And then the problem becomes difficult. One could say that there is no answer to it, except that Jung has observed that if one stews long enough in the agonies of such a conflict, then somehow an inner line, an inner development, becomes clear, which gives the individual enough certainty to continue on his way, even at the risk of committing an error. Naturally, one is never sure, but from the Jungian standpoint it is better always to remain in an attitude of doubt towards one's own behavior, which means to do the best one can, but always to be ready to assume that one has made a mistake. You can interpret your dream one way and make a big mistake; then, looking at it again, you can think that it might have been interpreted differently, and there you are! This we must risk, there is no remedy. But according to the Jungian standpoint, this is a grown-up attitude which has given up clinging to infantile kindergarten rules.

All these are higher and more differentiated problems which naturally are not visible in the collective unconscious material of fairy tales. In this material there are only references to what Jung mentions first in his article, i. e., a basic ethical reaction inborn in the human psyche, which is strangely impersonal and very different from what one would call a conscious ethical reaction. The following example will give you a feeling of the atmosphere of this phenomenon.

116

An international criminal who had already murdered ten or twelve people, a kind of pathological creature who committed cold-blooded murder without the slightest reaction of conscience, killed an unknown old man in the street in Zürich, took his money, and got caught. Dr. Guggenbühl-Craig had to give the court the psychiatric expert's opinion and ascertain whether or not the man was responsible for his deeds. Dr. Guggenbühl had the intelligent idea of investigating the dreams of this man, and he told Dr. Riklin and me the dreams without telling us the whole story. He simply asked us what we thought of a man of forty who had such dreams. Naturally I did not know that the dreamer was a pathological murderer, but I said literally, "Hands off, leave that man alone, he is a lost soul!" The dream in question was very simple. It was one which was repeated frequently and in which the murderer went to an amusement park where there were big swings. He was on such a swing, swinging up and down, higher and higher, when suddenly the swing went too high and he fell into empty space. That was the end of the dream.

I thought, "My God, swinging between the opposites and taking it as a pleasure with no reaction towards it, taking it as fun!" And the lysis in the end sentence of the dream was, "falling into empty space," without even the reaction of "I woke up with a cry." There was no emotional reaction. I could only say that this was a lost soul. I felt, to put it into pictorial language, as if God had written off this soul. In the dream there is no attempt by nature to save the man by giving him a shock. We assume that dreams come from the unconscious instinct towards nature. His unconscious tells him, just as cold-bloodedly as he murders, that he is lost! It speaks with his own cold-bloodedness, talking to him on his own level.

I tell you this story to give you an example of a moral reaction of the unconscious. It is not like an aunt who says, "You shouldn't do this or that." It is not an ethical super-ego which gives rules of behavior. It is a nature reaction, and cruelly objective in an uncanny way, but one cannot help feel that it is an ethical reaction, for the unconscious somehow reacts towards the immense inhumanity of this murderer.

So the so-called ethical reactions of the unconscious psyche are sometimes very objective, and different from our conscious ethical standards. However, Dr. Jung in his paper also tells of another example which might

117

lead one to conclude that the unconscious can be moralistic, even in the old aunt and school-teacher manner. He mentions a businessman who had an offer to join in a crooked business affair. The man had not consciously realized how shady it was, but wanted to sign a document by which he would join the business. In the night he dreamt that his hand, when he was about to sign the paper, became black with dirt. He told this dream in analysis and Jung warned him not to become involved. It transpired that it was a very crooked business in which he would have been caught. In this specific case it can be said that the unconscious coincided with the collective moral code; it gave one a clear ethical warning in the conventional sense of the word, for it said, you will make your hands dirty if you go into this business. So the unconscious shows that it has many ways of reacting. Sometimes it reacts as though there were an ethical reaction, but sometimes it is also just cruel nature as in the case of the murderer. Nevertheless, with the feeling function, one can realize that basically there is something like a moral reaction, though it can be difficult to grasp it in detail.

Thus one can say that an ethical reaction, even if it comes from the layers of the collective unconscious of the human psyche, seems to be something highly individual and highly specific. One could even say that each individual has his own ethical level and form of reaction. There are, for instance, thick-skinned people who can afford a lot of what we would call sins. They can walk happily on other people's corns without the slightest repercussion. Other people cannot afford anything, as soon as they side-step a bit from their own inner law they get the most awful dreams and inner reactions. So along with all the other problems there is that of ethically and the not-ethically gifted people. Naturally the ethically sensitive individuals have trouble in finding their own individual inner way, but one can also say that to be ethically sensitive is one of the great incentives in the process of individuation. Whenever I see that somebody in analysis has this sensitivity, I know that is all right, for a lot of problems are already solved. The thick-skinned sometimes give one a lot of trouble because they can repress more easily. People in analysis sometimes do the most incredible things, and you think that now it will be possible to catch them on their shadow. But naturally, as an analyst, one has to wait until they themselves have a dream. Then they have no dream!

The unconscious has pardoned them. And then you just put your own moral indignation in your pocket and say nothing, because that would be a waste of breath.

Here, however, our main concern is not with all these super-structures of ethical problems. I only mention them to clarify that the collective material I am now going to talk about is on a much more simple basis than all the complications which belong to the problem of individuality. I have looked at collective fairy tale material for many years, wondering whether it would be possible to find a few general rules of human behavior which would always be valid. I was fascinated by the idea of finding some generally human code, simple, but beyond national and individual differentiations, some kind of basic rules of human behavior. I have to confess that I have not found a standard basic rule, or rather, I have found it and I have not found it, for there is always a contradiction!

I can tell you stories which say that if you meet evil you must fight it, but there are just as many which say that you must run away and not try to fight it. Some say to suffer without hitting back, others say don't be a fool, hit back! There are stories which say that if you are confronted with evil the only thing to do is to lie your way out of it; others say no, be honest, even towards the devil, don't become involved with lying. For all these I will give you examples, but it is always a Yes and a No, there are just as many stories which say the one as the other. It is a complete *complexio oppositorum,* which simply means that, *post eventum,* I disappointedly came to the conclusion that really it *should* be like that, because it is *collective* material! How, otherwise, could there be individual action? For if collective material is completely contradictory, if our basic ethical disposition is completely contradictory, only then is it possible for us to have an individual, responsible, free *conscious* super-structure over those basic opposites. Then we can say that in human nature it would be right to do this, or that, but *I* am going to do this, the *tertium,* the third thing, which is my individuality. There would be no individuality if the basic material were not contradictory. That was my comfort after having discovered the terrible truth of the contradictory structure!

The one exception to the rule of contradiction, however, seems to be that one must never hurt the helpful animal in fairy tales. I have found a few cases where disobedience leads to trouble, but in the long run does not

lead to disaster; you may temporarily disobey the advice of the helpful fox
or wolf or cat. But if basically you go against it, if you do not listen to the
helpful animal or bird, or whatever it is, if any animal gives you advice and
you don't follow it, then you are finished. In the hundreds and hundreds
of stories that is the one rule which seems to have no exception. However,
when we analyze what the animals say, again it is completely contradictory: one says to run away, another says to fight, another to lie and another always to tell the truth. The animal plays it this way and that, from
an ethical standpoint, but if you go against it you are lost. This would
mean that obedience to one's most basic inner being, one's instinctual
inner being, is the one thing which is more essential than anything else. In
all nations and all fairy tale material I have never found a different statement.

There is another factor which I want to mention briefly, which we can
see when we look at the ethical problems posed by fairy tales, and that is
the function of compensation. Jung has observed this as being one of the
typical features of the functioning of the unconscious in individuals in
general. In his paper on "The Conscience" Jung mentions a lady who
thought of herself as a pure saint and who every night dreamt the dirtiest
sexual obscenities. That is a coarse example of what we call the law of
compensation. We know also that sometimes people who live their darkest
side and repress their better ego have all sorts of dreams of Christ, redeem-
ers of mankind, and so on. Hedwig Boyé has written a book entitled
Menschen mit grossen Schatten (People with a big Shadow). It has not yet
been translated into English. The author is an analyst who specializes
in working with prisoners and is principally interested in big fish. The
more people a prisoner has killed, the more interesting he is to her. She
has analyzed several such people and it is striking how many of these
black sheep have an amazingly white shadow. At the end of the book she
quotes the sentimental, idealistic, and touching letters which such big
fellows write to their mothers at Christmas. There you can see that they
have an infantile, goody-goody boy shadow which is typically compensatory to the fact that they are reckless murderers in their conscious lives.
Sometimes she could make good use of this fact, and would succeed, with
tears and much drama, in converting the murderers to their positive
shadow. Then they could be let out of prison and they behaved.

These generally compensatory tendencies in the unconscious are mirrored in fairy tales. There is a Japanese fairy tale where the positive solution is that a man has to beat up an official and then can find hidden treasures. This, I would say, is typically compensatory for the ethical set-up of that country, where it is specifically unthinkable that anyone could beat a Government official over the head with a stick. But the fairy tale says that that is what must be done and then you will find treasure — under your kitchen floor, so to speak. Such a fairy tale would not have much value for Swiss democrats, for we don't need to be told that it is good to beat officials over the head from time to time, so that they do not get too big and too inflated, but in other countries where the social hierarchy is severe, such a fairy tale contains a shocking truth which has to be recalled to consciousness. Such compensatory tendencies are to be found in fairy tales everywhere, so before I finish an analysis or interpretation I always say to myself: to whom has such a story to be told? Who needs that? And generally it is just perfect for the nation where the story originated, which is why people tell it to each other there with such pleasure.

I want now to begin with what I would call evil met with on a primitive level. By this I do not mean that the level is sociologically primitive, nor does it imply a primitive nation or particular person, but that the situation is primitive, in the sense of original man who is still living in nature. For us this is the past, and it has partly become a sociological problem. For instance we find stone age features nowadays in peasants who live in the mountains or in obscure mountain valleys, so there it is also a sociological and historical problem. But here I mean primitive man in the sense of man in his original condition, man still living in nature at a time when certain historically built-up sociological and religious super-structures did not yet exist. I will try to show you fairy tales which mirror this basic layer of what was then probably originally evil for man.

You may say I have not yet defined what evil is — I talk about the problem of evil as if we knew what it was. I prefer first to present you with some practical material illustrating how it looks on different levels. We can discuss it better if we have as facts in hand the problems of evil in fairy tales or in the ethnological and folklore material of primitive man.

I would also like to call your attention to something else. Zoologist Professor Konrad Lorenz has published a book on "so-called" evil, the

121

word "so-called" inferring that it is not really evil. He does not intend to imply that in his own opinion it should not be called evil, but that the subject matter is represented from a purely zoological standpoint. He discusses the problems of self-defense and aggression and what he calls intra-specific aggression, which means the aggressive tendencies in the patterns of behavior of different animals, fish, and birds both among each other and towards other types of animals. Most animal species have their specific enemy types; they don't bother about other animals but just ignore them. Also Lorenz speaks of intra-specific enemies, meaning the battles over feeding grounds and territories, which are carried out by strong males of the same species among each other. For instance, a blackbird will not react towards a mouse on its territory, but will react towards another blackbird and will carry out such an intra-specific fight even to death.

Lorenz feels that man has over-differentiated, or over-developed this intra-specific fighting tendency and in that way is an abnormal animal. He says that if we do not want mass suicide of our species we had better become conscious of this fact, and he then proposes simple animal level remedies, which, he says, are not supposed to solve the world problem, but are only his contribution towards it. One suggestion is to get to know each other better, because as soon as animals know each other well, their intra-specific aggressions are braked. When one animal is accustomed to the smell of another animal, it can't kill any more. Lorenz performed such experiments with rats. He took a rat out of its tribe and put it into a hostile rat tribe. When he re-introduced it to its own tribe, it had the smell of the others and was torn into bits instantly. But if the rat was first put into a cage so that the others couldn't tear it to pieces at once but could sniff at it for a few days they then would not kill it, which shows — put into plain words — that we should sniff at each other a bit more!

That is certainly a constructive proposition but, as Lorenz himself admits, it only comments on a certain instinctual level of the whole problem. I warmly recommend the book for it illustrates well much of the problem we are now going to discuss, especially in connection with what comprised evil for primitive man and his reactions to it.

As far as I know, the phenomenon of evil in a primitive set-up is simply the appearance of something demonic or abnormal, a kind of overpowering nature phenomenon, which does not pose any ethical problem but the purely practical one of how to either overcome or successfully escape it. It becomes a question as to whether one can overpower the phenomenon or whether one simply has to save one's own life. Subjective questioning as to whether one has made a mistake in letting the other thing attack, or as to personal responsibility for the phenomenon does not exist on this level.

I will give you an example of such a story. I generally base my material on the collection *Die Märchen der Weltliteratur,* published by Diederichs, Jena, in which there is a volume for practically every country. It is arbitrarily chosen material, but the themes are repeated so frequently that it gives enough examples of what we want to illustrate. In the Chinese volume there is a story, number forty-eight, called "The Horse Mountain Ghost." It comes from oral peasant tradition and from the country of Kiautschou.

At the bottom of the Horse Mountain is a village where a peasant lived by selling corn. To do so he always rode to the next little town. One day slightly drunk, he returned from the market on his mule, and coming round a bend he saw a monster. Its enormous face was blue and its eyes, which popped out of its head like a crab's, were bright and shining. Its mouth stretched from one ear to the other and looked like a bowl of blood in which was a chaotic mass of very long pointed teeth. It was sitting near the river and had just bent down to drink. One could hear it soughing up the water quite plainly.

The peasant was terribly frightened, but thank God the monster had not yet seen him, so he quickly took a slightly smaller path which people sometimes used, and galloped away as fast as he could. But when he turned the corner he heard someone behind him calling out. He looked back and saw his neighbor's son, so he stopped. The man said, "Old Li is very ill and won't last very long so his son asked me to go to the market to get a coffin and I am just on my way back. Can I come with you? "

The peasant agreed, and the man asked why he was going this unusual way. The peasant replied, rather uneasily, that he had wanted to go the other way, but had seen a monster which was absolutely awful, so he ran away.

The neighbor said, "When I hear you talk like that I get frightened myself and am afraid to go home alone. How would it be if I were to sit on the mule with you? "

The peasant agreed and the neighbor got up on the mule with him. After a while the neighbor asked what the monster looked like, but the peasant answered that he felt much too uneasy to say and that he would do that when he got home.

"If you don't want to talk," the other said, "then turn round and look at me and see if I look anything like the monster."

The peasant replied that he should not make such silly jokes, a human being did not look like a devil.

But the other man insisted and said, "But look at me!" And he pulled the peasant's arm and the latter looked round and there sat the monster he had seen at the stream, and he got such a fright that he fell unconscious from the mule and remained there. The mule knew the way home and when people saw it return riderless they suspected that something bad had happened. They split up and hunted for the missing peasant and found him at the bottom of the cliff and brought him home, but it was midnight before he recovered consciousness and could tell them what had happened to him.

This is a classical story. I could tell you any number of the same type from Eskimos, from Swiss peasants, and from African and South American countries. It is a completely international story and is in a Chinese volume just by chance. What seems striking to us is that the story does not seem to have any point! It is just exciting and makes you feel shivery, and if you tell it or read it in the evening before you go to bed you suddenly don't want to go upstairs, and you look all around and are afraid. You know how those ghost stories make you feel in a way terrible and in a way wonderful; it is a gruesome wonder which many of you must have experienced in your childhood. Man has a certain pleasure in that; I have often watched children and noticed that if one keeps them away from such stories, they invent and enjoy them themselves.

Some friends of my childhood had a big park garden and every evening the children played the same game. My friend, her brother and two of her cousins would line up in the dark garden and talk about the yellow dwarf who was sitting on the manure heap at the end of the garden, and one of them had to go quite alone, as far as he dared, in the dark, towards the invented figure of the yellow dwarf. Generally they would manage eight or nine steps and then would rush back, and the one who got closest to the dwarf won. So you see it was not only terrible but also exciting. For instance, people run when there is a really dreadful car accident and afterwards bathe in recounting all the details. They will tell it once or even twice at the table and turn quite white and say they feel so sick, they can't eat anything. That is the primitive peasant in man! They will describe the condition of a body which has been under an avalanche for twenty years, or a corpse which has lain in the water for a week, saying that you could only see the teeth and that the dentist had to identify the body, giving all the details! They can never spare you, but bathe in it. Dr. Jung said that in Africa whenever something awful happened, everybody would sit around the corpse for hours, palavering about it and feeding on that terrible sight.

If we take the monster of this story as a personification of such a phenomenon of evil in nature, then we can say that it is super-natural. It is highly numinous and therefore highly fascinating, which is why one has all this pleasurable excitement about it. And it is frightening! It is as terrifying as it is attractive, and it is an absolutely non-personal and non-human phenomenon. It is like an avalanche, or lightning, or a terrible enemy animal. There are things like this: illness and death, and spirits in nature, monsters, ogres which appear to be as real as other destructive phenomena in nature, and you have to deal with them. If there is an avalanche, you either erect an obstruction, or run from it; it would be foolish to do anything else. If the river overflows its banks you either put up a barricade or, if you are too weak to pile up stones against this evil, you retire onto a higher level or a mountain.

There is no ethical problem, it is simply a question of fighting if one can, or running away if one can't. But it is nature and — an important factor — it has about it something divine, which is shown in its attractive numinosity and our desire to hear about it. It is also archetypal, for figures such as this Horse Mountain ghost exist all over the world; that is, the human psyche is structured to produce such fantasies everywhere. Wherever man has lived in nature there were such Horse Mountain ghosts around, which, though slightly different, all have that same feature of being unnatural, super-human, gruesome and overwhelming.

125

That is how evil looks on this level. This Horse Mountain ghost is not a human being but one could call it a nature divinity. Now I will give you the same phenomenon when it appears in or through a human being. This is a South American Indian story from the Warrau tribe and it is in the volume of the South American Indian fairy tales. It is called "The Spear Legs."

There were two brothers who liked to go hunting in the loneliness of the forest. One day they heard a noise as of a drinking feast and the elder brother said, "Let's go and see!" But the younger said that they couldn't be real people, they were far too far away in the woods for such a feast, they must be ghosts. But the other brother insisted on investigating.

So they followed the sound of the voices and found a number of human beings having a big festival and the brothers joined them. The elder brother in particular drank a lot, but the younger brother rather nervously refused to drink anything and felt suspicious and had the feeling that they had got among the Warekki, the great rain frogs who had taken on human form. His suspicion proved to be well founded.

After a while the brothers went on their way. As night was approaching they built a roof under a tree to protect themselves and the elder brother sent the younger to fetch wood, and they put up hammocks and made a fire. And the elder brother always made the younger put more and more wood on the fire and make it bigger and bigger, but the younger brother suddenly noticed a strange smell of burning flesh, and he noticed that his brother's legs were hanging out of the hammock over the fire and he called out to him to look out. But the other brother only said, "Akka! Akka!" which is an expression of astonishment in the Warrau language, but is also very much like the rainfrog's croak. The elder brother pulled his legs in, but then forgot again and let them hang over and the younger brother thought that was a very bad sign.

After a while the elder brother himself noticed that his legs were burnt completely away, right up to the knees, and had become like charcoal. So he took a knife and cut away the flesh and the feet and made points at the bottom of the bones of the legs, making them into spears. Then he lay in his hammock and tried to catch the squirrels and birds which came along. After a while he became very proficient in this sport.

Naturally he had to stay in his hammock all the time and the younger brother had to get his food and serve him. But the elder brother became more and more tyrannical and finally would not even let the younger leave the hut for any length of time, so the latter felt he must get help and he ran away. When the elder brother noticed that the younger no longer came when called, he jumped out of the hammock and ran after him and found that he could run quicker on his spear legs than on his feet. By mistake he followed the footmarks of a deer, thinking they were those of his brother, and when he came up to the deer he jumped on it and speared it to the ground. He then said to the deer, "I am sorry, brother, that I have killed you, but it is your own fault, you shouldn't have run away from me." Then he turned the deer over and saw the animal's black mouth and thought that was funny, had he got it from eating fruit? Then he noticed the four legs and thought that was very funny, and then he began to count the fingers. This took him a long time, but he finally discovered that it couldn't possibly be his brother that he had killed, but that he had killed a deer. So he went back to his hut and lay on his hammock.

In the meantime the younger brother had gone home and said that something had happened to his elder brother, that he couldn't be his friend any longer and that he must be killed. So he led the villagers back into the wood where they surrounded the hut in which the elder brother was lying. They were afraid to attack because of the spear legs, but tried to lure him out of the hammock into the open. First they sent a bird to entice him, but the elder brother was so quick with his spear legs that he killed it. Finally they got Hura, the little squirrel, the quickest animal they knew, to lure him out. The squirrel always ran past him and he tried to spear it, but at last he followed Hura out of his hut and the people made a circle round him and killed him. (That is the end of the story.)

In a way, there is not much difference between the two stories because again you see that evil is brought about by a ghost. Obviously the big rain frog ghosts are responsible for the elder brother's transformation and illness so that it is they, behind the scenes, who are the real problem of evil. Though there is no direct fight with the rain frog

127

ghosts, the problem is that they alter the human being in the form of *possession,* so that the man is no longer human but himself behaves exactly like a demon.

This is to illustrate the problem of the phenomenon of possession, which ethnologists consider the greatest problem in primitive society. We psychologists believe that it is so in every society. Possession means being assimilated by these numinous archetypal images, and this story shows wonderfully the slow, horrible dehumanization of the elder brother, beginning when he joins the drinking party and has no instinctual warning. The other brother has something which tells him to look out, but the elder brother says not to mind, that they must have a good time. That is a pardonable mistake, but from then on the elder brother is possessed. The next thing, which is still relatively harmless, is when he puts too much wood on the fire, but that shows a lack of judgment. In primitive society, where collecting wood and food means hard work, nobody uses too much wood. In a peasant society it is a great sin before the Lord to throw away bread, and, in a similar way, it is an abnormality if you throw too much wood on the fire.

Where the hardships of life are great, one learns to do everything to save effort and to respect other people's effort as much as possible. All rules are kept meticulously and to break such rules is very bad. For instance, where I go in the holidays there is an unwritten rule which I would never dare go against. If you find a nice block of wood lying round you may take it, but if you have already as much as you can carry, then you can put it upright against a tree and nobody may ever touch that. You have taken possession of the wood by that sign. It would be the greatest sin to touch it, much worse than going inside somebody's house to take wood. That is how the primitive feels and if you know how hard it is to carry wood home then you know why. If the next day the wood is gone you get into an absolutely murderous rage.

It is absolutely paramount for living together in human society that such rules are kept and they are kept, strangely enough, even by the evil doers of the country around. The elder brother throws too much wood on the fire and that is a terrible thing to do, if you know the set-up of such a situation. Then, when he burns his legs, he says, "Akka!" and goes on doing it. He has lost the instinct of self-preservation and now there is a very bad change in his personality. From then on he is a demon and behaves exactly like the Horse Mountain demon, and what is interesting is that by falling into evil he gets supernatural power, super-human gifts and qualities. Imagine being able to lie in a hammock and spear squirrels and birds with your legs!

Analyzed psychologically, this is exactly what happens if a human being identifies with an archetypal figure. He gets the life energy and even certain parapsychological gifts, clairvoyance and so on, connected with the archetype. Psychotic borderline cases often have parapsychological gifts — knowing through the unconscious things which they couldn't otherwise know. As soon as you fall into an archetype, or identify with the powers of the unconscious, you get those supernatural gifts and that is one reason why people do not like to be exorcised or re-humanized again. The loss of those gifts accounts for one of the resistances against therapy.

In this primitive set-up there seems to be no idea of therapy, or the exorcism of this poor hunter by a ritual. They simply say he has become a devil and has to be removed. Again there is no ethical problem. The phenomenon is treated like an avalanche, or a wild beast, or an earthquake. You do something against it if you can, and run away from it if you can't. The same treatment is accorded to the evil ghost in the Chinese story as to the man possessed by the evil ghost. It is a practical problem and nothing else.

I think that is something very important to know, because naturally one has such a basic primitive reaction in oneself too. We have not got away from it, it is still one of the basic realities.

In the volume of the South American Indian tribes there is another demon story called "The Rolling Skull" which is another example of this gruesome problem. It is not what you would describe as possession, but as alteration of a human being.

A group of hunters camped in the forest and collected a quantity of meat. Many apes were on the spit near the fire and the skins of the apes that had been killed lay all around the camp. The hunters had all gone off hunting, leaving only

129

one boy in the camp to overlook the cooking of the meat. Suddenly there appeared a man in the camp. With a grim face he inspected all the booty and counted the hammocks and then left. When the hunters returned to the camp in the evening the boy told them of this strange visitor, but nobody took any notice. But when the men had all gone to bed he repeated the story to his father, who got upset, and he and the boy took their hammocks into the darkness and put them up in another place away from the camp. Before long they heard owls and tigers, and other nocturnal animals, and the groans of human beings and the breaking of bones. "On," the man said to his son, "this is Kurupira (the spirit of the woods) who, with his followers kills the hunters."

In the morning they returned to the camp and found empty bloodstained hammocks and the remains of broken human bones. Among these lay the head of one of the hunters. When the man and the boy turned to leave, the head cried out, "Take me with you, brother." The man looked astonished and the skull repeated, "Take me home, brother!" Then the man sent the boy ahead on the way back to the village and he himself took a rope and tied it onto the skull and dragged it behind him. After a while it began to seem uncanny and he left it behind. But the skull ran after him, like a gourd, crying, "Brother, brother, wait a bit. Take me with you!" So the man had to go slowly so that the skull could roll along behind him and he always pondered as to how to get rid of his uncanny companion. He asked it to wait a minute, saying he had to go into the forest. Then he did not return to the skull but rejoined the path a good bit further on. There he made a trench which he covered with small twigs so as to trap the skull, and he hid himself to watch. Meanwhile the skull kept calling out, "Brother, haven't you finished yet? " And the man's excrement replied, "Not yet, brother, not yet." But the skull said, "What! In my time, when I was a man, excrement couldn't talk!" So he rolled along on the path and soon fell into the trap. The man then came out and covered the place over and stamped it down hard and then went on to his village.

But when night fell, cries came from the wood, getting nearer and nearer to the village. "That's the skull which has got out of the trap," the man said to the other villagers.

Meanwhile the skull had acquired wings and claws like a

big falcon. It flew towards the village and threw itself on
the first man who came across his path and ate him up. But
the next evening a medicine man hid on the path which led
out of the wood, and waited for the monster with his bow
and arrow. When darkness fell it came, uttering cries, and it
settled itself on a tree at the edge of the forest. It now
looked like an enormous falcon. Then the medicine man
shot it between the eyes with his arrow and the monster fell
to the ground dead.

There is a parallel story about such an uncanny skull in which the
medicine man throws it into the sky, where it turns into the moon and
from then on it is the moonlight in the night.

This type of uncanny and evil phenomenon, seen from a primitive
standpoint, is a phenomenon which is still to be found in Greek and
Egyptian civilizations and which survived in the magical practices of antiquity. It still exists nowadays in our folklore and concerns people who
have committed suicide, or have been killed or who died before their
time. Such people turn hostile after death and turn into evil demons.
The primitive explanation for this is that they feel frustrated, for there
is a certain amount of life energy in them which has not been exhausted
but has been unnaturally blocked before the proper time. The clock's
spring has broken instead of running down, and that unexhausted life
energy turns hostile. The dead person is jealous of the living and has
not had time to detach naturally from the living and therefore now has
a destructive and dangerous effect in the world of the living. Therefore
even people who during their lifetime were really good people and not
possessed by evil, can, out of resentment at having been robbed of life,
turn into such a thing if they are killed before their time.

That is why late antique invocations of black magic always begin:
"Oh, you Gods of the Netherworld, Hades, Proserpina, and you the
nameless enormous army of those who killed themselves, or who were
murdered, or died before their time." That is a classical late Greek invo-
cation to be found in most of the magical papyri of antiquity. This belief existed not only in late antiquity, but all over the world. Normal
life energy which has not been used up turns a human being into an evil
ghost and there is this slow transformation; what was only a human skull,
becomes a real ghost-like falcon, for it grows wings, becoming more and

131

more numinous and supernatural. First there is an unhappy hunter, resentful that he has been killed, but then he himself becomes like one of the Kurupira mob of owls and tigers and ghost animals.

Now we have to try to look at this problem from a psychological standpoint. I have too often seen the bad effects of sudden deaths of my own relatives and those of my analysands not to know that there might be, besides the problem of projection, a very objective basis for these beliefs. The problem really needs more explanation. It often happens that people who have lost a close relative have, after some days, a car accident. One might use the rationalistic explanation that it is because one is tired and unhappy after the funeral, or one might say that the dead person is pulling one into the grave. No one can say which is the true explanation, but psychologically, there is the phenomenon of a death pull. Where it comes from we cannot say, but it is there, and after the death of a close relative it is a phenomenon which can clearly be seen. Rationally, it might be said that the amount of psychic libido which is invested in the relationship goes back into us and has no other outlet.

This is especially the case if you lose someone with whom you have lived closely, for an enormous amount of psychic energy went into the adaptation and relationship with that person and suddenly that is all cut off. So the energy now flows back on you, but it has no use, and any unparked energy is liable to have a dangerous effect. These forces make you unconscious, they dissociate the personality until new objects of adaptation and canalization are found, and things go better. That this is so I am absolutely convinced; one can really see how it works and it can be seen in detail. If you have lost somebody with whom you lived closely, when you wake in the morning and have forgotten that the person is dead, you want to say "Oh, hullo, Good Morning" — but the person is no longer there! Or you have a pleasant experience and want to tell it to that someone — but you can't! To whom can you tell it now? You always fall into the same terrible hole! Everybody who has lost someone they loved has had the terrible experience of wanting to move to the other person, and then they fall into the black hole in the ground. And if that happens to someone who is not very conscious and does not realize what is happening, if the personality is not strong, that person

132

can be dissociated, or the energy flows into inappropriate objects. In primitive society, and I have even seen it in our country, it may then take the form of a black rage and you find a scapegoat; it gives birth to the idea that the man has not died naturally, that there has been black magic and someone must now be killed to satisfy this feeling of revenge. In our society it can be an accusation of the doctor, or there can be terrible quarrels over the distribution of the inheritance, not because people are really so greedy, wanting to get this or that carpet, or something from their departed father, but because they have to abreact this plus of libido which they do not know where to place. So they have to find that the doctor, or the nurse, has been the devil itself, and there are always these post mortem devilries going around. A certain amount can certainly be explained in this way. An analysand's dream material, however, is often formulated differently, saying that it is really the dead person who is creating mischief. So, take it or leave it, you can choose your hypothesis.

CHAPTER II

POSSESSION BY EVIL

In my last chapter I tried to define briefly the psychological area in which the problem of evil arises, that is, on the level of the archetypal constellations of the collective unconscious, and told you a few stories which, to my mind, mirror primitive mentality in the sense of the original experience of evil by man still living close to nature and not cut off from it by civilization or technical evolution. As you saw in these stories, on this level man has no problem; evil is simply a fact of nature which has either to be overcome or escaped.

In the story of "The Spear Legs" the younger brother watched his older brother getting slowly possessed and destructive and then mobilized the other villagers to kill him. Out of such material one could, in modern literature, write a beautiful novel or tragedy showing the younger brother's terrific conflict and the collision of duties between his attachment to and former love of his older brother, and the collective necessity of having to destroy this murderous creature. But we hear nothing of the kind! The younger brother has no problem. When his older brother gets possessed and completely evil he quite rightly concentrates on escaping from him, because otherwise he would have been killed. Afterwards there is no conflict about killing him; he simply tells the villagers to eliminate this possessed murderer and shows them the way back to the camp. So that which on a higher level of awareness of motivations and ethical problems would afford a collision of obligations is no tragedy on this level, but a simple, matter-of-fact affair.

On this level evil not only appears as the nature demons living in the woods, in the snow, on mountains or in lakes, but can also originate from dead people. The souls of the dead, mainly the ghosts of murderers or murdered people, and of those who died in battle, of people who died before their time turn into demonic powers. One has the feeling that their lives did not come to a natural and harmonious end, but had been cut off in some violent way. A primitive explanation is that in the ghost of the dead is resentment because of frustration, which turns him into an evil demon.

To show you that this is not only the case with the South American Indians, I will tell you a similar gruesome Chinese ghost story (*Chinesische Volksmärchen*, No. 66: "Die Geister der Erhängten"), in which you can see another element of the same fact.

It was said that the poet Su Dung Po always liked to tell ghost stories, although he had never seen a ghost himself. Another man, Yüan Dschan, had written a paper contending that there were no ghosts. One day when he was writing about this, another scholar came to visit him and said, "From oldest times there have always been true stories about Gods and ghosts, how comes it that you deny this? " Yüan Dschan then tried to explain in terms of modern reason why there couldn't be any ghosts, and the other scholar became very angry and said, "But I am a ghost myself," and before he had finished his sentence he turned into a terrible looking devil with a green face and red hair and disappeared into the ground. Soon afterwards Yüan Dschan died.

That was only a prelude to get you into the right attitude for what is to come, for now the story changes and says that there are many types of ghosts, but the worst are those of people who hang themselves. Generally these are the ghosts of women of poor peasant families who, if ill-treated by their mothers-in-law, or if hungry, or over-worked, get discontented. If they quarrel with their sisters-in-law, or are scolded by their husbands, if they don't see any way out of their trouble, often in despair they put an end to their lives. They take poison, or jump into a well, but most hang themselves, and such people make those awful ghosts. Our grandfathers say that the ghost of a woman who has committed suicide always tries to seduce other women, for only thus can it go to the Beyond and be reborn and re-enter the wheel of existence and return to life. Until they have found a substitute they have to wander around in an in-between realm of life and death, which is why they look for a substitute and try to seduce others.

> In Tsing Schoufu was a man who had passed his first military exam and was now travelling to the capital to continue his military career. It was the rainy season and he had to go through a lot of muddy wet roads. He progressed very slowly and in the evening had not reached the capital and had to stay

in a village where there were only poor families and nobody could give him shelter. But the villagers told him to go to the nearby temple and stay there with his donkey for the night.

The pictures of the Gods in the temple were in complete ruin and it was not possible to distinguish them any more, and everywhere there were spiders' webs and dust. He tied up his donkey to an old tree of life and drank something out of his gourd. The day had been very hot and now he felt a bit better and he shut his eyes to sleep.

Suddenly he heard the rustling of leaves near the temple and a cool wind passed over his face (the famous wind which announces ghosts). He saw a woman sneaking out of the temple, dressed in old and dirty red clothing and with a face as white as a whitewashed wall. Carefully she sneaked past him so that he should not see her, but the soldier did not lack courage and pretended to be asleep. He did not move and then he saw a cord hanging out of the woman's sleeve and knew at once that this was the ghost of someone who had committed suicide, so he got up cautiously and followed her.

The ghost went to a poor villager's hut where the soldier looked through the window and saw a woman of about twenty sitting by her little child's cradle, sometimes stroking the child, and crying. And then he saw the ghost, who was sitting on one of the rafters and making movements with the rope which she had hung around her neck, inviting the woman, intimating that this was the solution. And he heard the woman say to the ghost, "You say that it is best to die! I will, but I can't give up my child," and she began to cry again, and the ghost laughed and continued to swing the rope in front of her face.

Finally the woman said, "All right, I have made up my mind, I'll die!" She opened the door of her wardrobe and dressed herself in new clothes and made herself up in front of the glass. She then got onto a stool and took her belt and tied it onto the rafters. She had already put her neck in and was going to jump down when the soldier banged on the window and finally even broke it and jumped into the room shouting, and so rescued the woman. The ghost disappeared. But the soldier saw that the rope was still hanging down from the rafters and he quickly seized it and then lectured the woman, telling her not to be so stupid, that she should rather look after her child and that she had only one life, and he went back to the temple.

On the way, the ghost suddenly appeared in front of him, bowed, and said very politely, "For years I have been looking for a substitute and today just when I found one you ruined my business, and that can't be helped; but in my hurry I left something behind which you certainly found. Could you please give it back to me, for without it I cannot find another substitute."

But the soldier just showed her the rope, saying, "This is it, and if I give it back to you, you will hang someone else, but I shan't let you." And so he wound it round his arm and said, "Now get out of my way!"

Then the ghost woman was furious, her face became a greenish-black, her hair hung all tangled round her neck, her eyes turned bloodshot and her tongue stuck far out of her mouth and she stretched out her hands and tried to seize the soldier. He hit back with his fist, but somehow hit his own nose which began to bleed. He threw a few drops of blood at her and, as ghosts do not like human blood, she ran a few steps away from him and began cursing him. That went on until the cock crowed and she disappeared.

The next morning the villagers came to thank the soldier for saving the woman's life. They found him in the temple, still flinging his fists in the air and shouting, but when they talked to him he told them what had happened, and on his bare arm could be seen the mark of the cord, which had grown into his flesh and become a red ring there. And when the sun rose, he jumped on his donkey and rode away.

This is like the South American story of "The Rolling Skull", for there is a kind of after-effect of a suicide or murder. So it is not only that the skull of the actually murdered man turns into an evil ghost, but, according to this story, the thing goes on for generations, for one suicide triggers off another. Psychologically this is true, for we know that suicide is infectious. In schools and colleges if there is one suicide there will be two or three more, because of the destructive infectious effect, which is probably why it is explained as the ghost of the dead luring others to death.

Suicides can continue for generations in a family. Put pictorially, one could say that the grandfather who committed suicide was trying to lure his grandson into following suit; in that way it is really a slaying without end, as the noose is described in the text of one of our tales, for it goes on from one generation to another until some courageous man, in this case the soldier, interferes and puts an end to the destructive effect.

Here the ghost does not act purely out of wickedness, but in order to free herself from her in-between existence, in which she can neither go back into life nor definitely into the Beyond. What that means psychologically we will discuss later. I want first to give you a few more of these horrible stories so that we can later discuss the details and types.

I will now tell you a very short story (No. 20 in the South American Indian stories) which brings in another motif. It is called "The Outwitted Wood Spirit."

A whole family was invited to a drinking feast and all went except the daughter who stayed at home alone. In the late afternoon a girl friend came to visit her whom she had not seen for a long time. At least she thought it was her girl friend Dai-adalla, but actually it was a wood spirit who had taken on her friend's form in order to carry out his evil intentions more easily. As the girls were very good friends, the wood spirit, in the form of Dai-adalla, asked her what she was doing alone at home. When the girl explained that she had not wanted to go to the party, the spirit said that it would stay the night with her and keep her company.

When evening came and they could hear the frogs croaking, the girl suggested that, as they liked eating frogs, they might go and catch some.

So they went out into the dark and after a time began to call out to each other to ask how many frogs the other had caught. The wood spirit when asked answered that he had caught a lot, but that he always ate them directly he caught them. This strange answer, that he ate the animals raw, frightened the girl and she realized the real nature of her supposed girl friend. So when the wood spirit called out again asking how many she had caught, she answered that she had caught a lot, but that she had put them in her calabash. All the time she was wondering how she could

get away safely. She told the wood spirit to be quiet and
not talk, saying that he frightened away the frogs, because
she knew that from her voice he could tell where she was
standing. Then she crept quietly home and turned over all
the pots in the house without making any noise, threw away
the frogs, and climbed up onto the roof and waited to see
what would happen.

Soon afterwards, the wood spirit, not getting any answer
to his questions, realized that he had been outwitted and
hurried back to the house. In the dark he stumbled around
among the pots trying to find his prey. At last he cried out,
loud enough for the girl to hear, that if he had only known
she was going to try to get away he would have eaten her
with the frogs.

He hunted fruitlessly, looking in all the pots, until dawn
came and then he had to leave. The girl then came down
and waited for her parents and when they came she told
them that the wood spirit had visited her in the form of
her friend. Then her father said that the next time they
told her to come with them, she would obey.

This story is important because we will later discuss what kind of
people and what kind of behavior invites possession by, or attracts, evil
spirits. Don't think that this type of story is either specifically Chinese
or South American Indian; I picked it at random because I wanted a
certain type of story, not a definite story, but a type which is to be
found all over the world. To emphasize the one little point about the
girl who doesn't go to the party and is thus exposed to a wood spirit I
will give you a relatively close European parallel, a Grimm story (No. 43)
called "Frau Trude" ("Mrs. Trude").

There was once a little girl who was obstinate and prying
and rather impertinent, and she didn't always do what her
parents told her. One day she said to her parents that she had
heard so much about Mrs. Trude she would go to see what
she was like. People said that she looked so funny and that
everything she had looked so wonderful, and that there were
such strange things in her house, and the girl was very curious
and wanted to see it. Her parents forbade her to do this and
said that Mrs. Trude was a very bad woman who did evil things
and that she would not be their child any longer if she went

139

there. But the girl paid no attention to what her parents
said and went all the same. When she got there Mrs. Trude
asked her why she was so white.

"Oh," said the child, trembling all over, "What I saw
frightened me so!"

"What did you see? "

"I saw a black man on your staircase."

"That was the charcoal burner, who burns charcoal in the forest."

"And then I saw a green man!"

"Oh, that was the hunter!"

"And afterwards I saw a blood-red man."

"That was the butcher!"

"Oh, Mrs. Trude, I am shivering with fear! I looked through the
window and I didn't see you, but the devil with a fiery head!"

"Ah-ha," she said, "you saw the witch in her true make-up!
I've waited for you for long and now you shall give me light!"

And then she turned the girl into a block of wood which
she threw onto the fire and when it was glowing red she
warmed herself by it and said, "That gives a good light!"

So you see it is not simply a problem in South America, it is with us
as well, and this story hints at the similar features which attract such
things. To show you a case of possession similar to that in "The Spear
Legs," I will give you an Icelandic parallel which is in the volume of
Icelandic Fairy Tales, No. 37, and is entitled "Trunt, Trunt, and the
Trolls in the Mountains." (Trunt is a name.)

Two men once went to the mountains to collect herbs.
One night they both lay in their tent, but one slept and the
other lay awake. The one who was awake saw how the one
who slept went out. He followed him but could hardly walk
fast enough and the distance between them always grew
greater. The man was going towards the glaciers. On the top
of a glacier the other saw an enormous giantess. She gestured
by holding out her hand and then drawing it back towards her
breast, and like that she bewitched the man, drawing him to
her. The man ran straight into her arms and she ran away
with him. (That is like "The Spear Legs" where of the two
brothers in the woods one is bewitched.)

A year later the people of that district went to collect
herbs again at the same place and the man who had been
bewitched came to them, but he was so quiet and reserved
and incommunicative that one could hardly get a word out

140

of him. The people asked him who he believed in, and he said that he believed in God.

The second year he again came to the herb people, but this time he had become so hobgoblinish that they were afraid of him. And when they asked him who he believed in, he did not answer. And this time he stayed with them a shorter time. The third year he came again, but had become a real troll and he looked awful. But one of the people ventured to ask him what he believed in and he said that he believed in Trunt, Trunt, and the Trolls in the Mountains, and he disappeared. Since then he has never been seen again and for many years nobody ventured to collect herbs at that place.

This is an assimilation into an evil ghost similar to that in "The Spear Legs," only the man does not become destructive, but just becomes a mountain troll. He does not harm the other villagers as the Spear Legs man did.

If we ask ourselves to what type these powers of evil belong in these primitive stories, we see that some are definite, known spirits, like Kurupira, the spirit of the woods, who after the wholesale killing of the hunters eats them all, or like this giantess of the Icelandic mountains. These are known figures in folklore who are called evil spirits and live in that part of nature which is somehow uncanny or dangerous to that sociological group of people. For people who live near the sea they would be sea-demons, for people who live near the primeval forests, they would be spirits of the forest, and for mountain people they would be spirits of the mountains and the glaciers. This has caused people to believe that these spirits are simply personifications of evil in nature, which is what you will read in practically every philological and ethnological work. But we shall see that this is a superficial judgment. Certainly these powers of evil in this original form have to do with evil in nature and are closely connected with the destructive natural powers of devouring animals, the dangers of forests, snow, water, landslides, and so on, but they are not just that.

Then there is another type where human beings have been assimilated by those demonic nature powers, such as the Spear Legs man, and the troll man, where an originally normal human being slowly becomes transformed into something destructive and demonic by being completely possessed by evil powers. This I think is very important, because if you were to ask me what, in my experience, is the most terrible evil I know, I would say the phenomenon of possession. The worst thing one can meet, or which I have met in my life, is people who have been assimilated by these archetypes of evil power.

Then there is a third category which is closely related, that of the spirits of the dead, people who have not turned evil but who have been killed innocently and, because of this, after death turn into evil spirits. This has to do in part with the energy which frees itself, and in part with the mystery of death, about which we do not know much more than natural man knew.

If you look at the conditions under which these people fall into evil, you will see certain features which are common to practically all the stories. In several, drinking played a role in some form or another, so drinking is for the primitive one of the simplest and easiest ways by which he opens the door to being possessed by evil. Another is loneliness, being alone, being separated from the village group or the tribal group to which he belongs. Most of the people who get into such adventures are lonely, or go out only two together in the woods collecting herbs or collecting in the mountains, which means being alone with nature, or as did our girl with the wood spirit, staying alone at home. She hadn't committed any sin other than not wanting to join the drinking party. In this case drinking is the other way round. You see how you get into contradictions! She wanted to stay alone and that gave the wood spirit the idea that she was somebody he could come and eat, and he sneaked in disguised as her girl friend.

So loneliness, especially loneliness in nature, opens the door to the powers of evil, as does being in a foreign country. Our soldier, for instance, gets into his ghost adventure because of that. He doesn't have his family and his people around him. That also belongs in the category of loneliness, being among people with whom you have no emotional feeling ties. In the case of Mrs. Trude, it is a kind of infantile curiosity, a lack of respect for the powers of evil which opens the door, and that also seems to be a typical feature. In many stories all over the world there is this kind of infantile daring which is not courage. It looks like it, but it isn't. This pseudo-courage, which is infantile daring out of unawareness or lack of respect, is a common feature through which man steps suddenly into the area of the

142

archetype of evil. In our mountain sagas this infantile daring is generally called *Frevel*.

Frevel belongs in the same word group as the English word frivolous. It has the same nuance, but means much more than just a frivolous attitude. In modern German, *Frevel* means transcending certain not so much legal but common rules of behavior. We mostly use it now in connection with hunting. *Jagdfrevel* is the usual word, and there it means transgressing the hunting rules: shooting pregnant deer or hunting in the closed season, for instance, or shooting badly and wounding without killing, and then not bothering about the wounded animal afterwards. That is how our technical language sums *Frevel*.

In former times it had a more religious connotation and approached the meaning of blasphemy (sacrilege); spitting in the church or such things could be called *frevlerisch*. In still more primitive conditions *Frevel* meant stepping over the border, going beyond a respectful attitude towards the numinous powers. There is a famous story in the Canton of Uri which illustrates this.

Two men were herding the cattle high up on the mountains. It is the custom in Switzerland that peasants who own cattle in the valley have their own Alp, or the community owns Alps in the mountains, and in the summer generally two together drive up all the cattle, stay there the whole summer, and with the first snow come down again for the winter. Sometimes there are even grades of Alps: high mountains, half-way mountains, and so on. That is our system for cattle herding. Generally two or three men go up without women. They live a lonely life in the mountains and have a pretty hard time.

In this Uri story, two men, an older cattle herder and a young boy, were on such an Alp. In order to protect himself and his herds, the Senn (herdsman) as one calls him, has to go out in the evening and recite the evening benediction over the cattle and the Alp in the four directions of the horizon. This is still done. This prayer is called the evening prayer of benediction. The custom is practiced so that God may protect the cattle, the Alp and the men on it.

One evening the cattle herder came out of the hut and looked around, and a voice up in the mountains called out, "Shall I let it go? " And he, instead of getting unduly frightened said, "Oh, you can hold it still longer!"

143

And nothing happened. The next day passed and the next evening the voice said, "Shall I let it go? " The herder called out, "Oh you can hold it longer!" But the boy got nervous and thought that was not the right way to behave and that it was getting very dangerous so he started running away. Then he suddenly heard a cry from the top of the mountain, "I can't hold it any longer!" And with an awful roar the whole mountain collapsed, burying cattle and huts and the older herdsman, but the boy just escaped at the edge of the valley.

That is a famous story related in Müller's "Sagas of Uri." There you see that this older cowherd was a *Frevler*. He had that infantile daring, as I would call it, that infantile impertinence towards the spirit of the moun-tain. In German there is a very good book entitled: *Goldener Ring über Uri*, written on this kind of mentality by an Uri medical doctor, Ludwig Renner. This man lived in such a primitive country and had to assist at deaths and births under miserable conditions in the Swiss mountains, and he said that our Swiss mountain peasants seem very modern and enlightened as long as you don't know them well, but when they are shaken by a birth, or death, or something like that, they suddenly open up and tell you what they really feel and what their real attitude is, as he tries to show. I fully believe what he says. Superficially, these peasants are Catholic, but that is not more than skin deep; underneath, their attitude is completely prehis-toric. For them nature is populated by something to which they do not even give a name! Cattle herders in our mountains are even more primitive than those South American Indians, because they don't have a Kurupira, a definite spirit with a definite shape and name; they talk about the "IT."

You see, it was "IT" which called, "Shall I let it go? " Who is that "IT," which holds the mountain boulders and then just lets them go? Renner amplifies with many stories and, strangely enough, "IT" is some-times good, sometimes bad and sometimes neutral. It sometimes behaves like a human being and sometimes is completely impersonal, and nobody knows what it looks like, it just does things. It lets the mountain fall on you.

Another story says that if at Seelisberg you go round the corner, there "IT" likes to sit and take the cattle away, and if it does, for God's sake, don't get frightened, because if you get into a panic the cattle will fall into the abyss, or you will take a wrong step and break your leg. The one thing to do is to go on with your whip, or your stick, calling to the cattle as

144

though the cows were still there, and when you come round the next corner there they are! The "IT" needs quite special treatment. You must not be impressed by it, you must not get into a panic, but you must also not have this kind of frivolous daring — *Frevel*. With any kind of *Frevel* it gets very nasty and destructive. So it is not really a definite personification of evil. It is even more primitive, it is that uncanny thing which is sometimes good and sometimes bad. But the attitude shown in the Mrs. Trude story and the attitude of this cowherd show the same thing: there must be no infantile daring. I don't think I need to give a psychological interpretation because all of you, if you have had some experience in life, know that this is still the way to get possessed and fall into evil.

These rules of behavior and phenomena still exist and are completely valid. The one moment when I feel really bad in analysis is when I see in one of my analysands that infantile, daring curiosity about evil. An analysand may say, "Oh I like going to a place where there are murderers!" Or, "I like to experiment with this woman, I know she is an evil woman, but I must have some experience of life and I shall try out sleeping with her, I must explore that!" If you explore this because it is you, that is, if there is a reason, if your dreams say you must do it, then it is all right, because you can say that this is *your* evil, that this is your own abyss which you carry within you and sooner or later you will have to meet it. But when you act out of a kind of frivolous attitude, or just out of intellectual curiosity, just to find out about it and with a lack of respect toward the infection and destructiveness of the phenomena, then one feels very uneasy.

Once I had a very intellectual analysand who fell for a girl who was pretty but had a heavy psychosis. He got very much involved with her and was always telling me that he intended to marry her. I went through agonies as to whether or not I should give him warning; after all, if he married a girl with a psychosis that might have meant meeting his fate — but it would be no fun, to say the least! So I battled with myself as to how and when I should put in a word of warning. Then he had dreams about the girl which spoke in plain language. But talking seemed to have no effect. Finally, with cold hands and a red face, I made up my mind, thinking that I must clear my conscience, and I said, "Now listen, to tell you the truth, I think So-and-So has a heavy psychosis." I thought that would give him

145

an awful shock and might destroy our rapport, but he calmly said, "Oh, yes, I saw that long ago," and went on telling me his dreams. Obviously he had not realized what it meant other than intellectually. He had read some psychiatric books and could label the woman as psychotic, but he did not know what that meant; he did not know the emotional weight of the statement, and that is like the girl who went to see Mrs. Trude.

This attitude one finds very frequently among intellectual people in modern life, as well as among primitive and young people. In grown-ups it is usually among intellectual people, which simply means that they are infantile as far as ethical and feeling problems are concerned, babies as soon as there is an ethical or feeling or relationship problem. They behave exactly as the girl in the Mrs. Trude story does, stepping inadvertently into the most horrible evil without even noticing what they are doing.

Now we have to go into the problem of what these different personifications of evil look like. There is a book by Rasmussen on Greenland sagas in which evil and semi-evil spirits and ghosts of the type of the South American Kurupira and the type of the "IT," the thing which holds up the mountains, were drawn by Eskimos. They are authentic Eskimo drawings of different types of spirits and I think they are most revealing. One among them is an enormous ice bear called the bear of the sea which sometimes destroys people by overturning their boats. It would certainly personify nature power and therefore confirm the theory held by so many people that it is just the evil forces in nature which man personifies in this form. I do not deny this theory, but I think that is not the whole thing. The evil forces of nature, which simply mean evil to man, disagreeable and destructive to his life, belong to the archetypal experience of evil: hunger, cold, fire, landslides and avalanches, snowstorms, drowning, storms at sea, being lost in the forest, the big enemy animals, the ice bear in the North, the lion or crocodile in Africa, etc. These can be the symbols or the personification of evil. But it is striking that there is a strong tendency to represent such creatures as half human and half inhuman. For instance, one giant is built out of blocks of stone and crushes everything, but his outlines are human. Another demon is a dog with a disagreeable-looking human head. There are many mixed figures, half animal and half human, as well as misshapen human forms. One spirit of evil is terribly thin and people say that his wickedness makes him look like that.

146

In a comparative study of evil spirits one often finds crippled creatures, something in which only the upper part of the body is human, or where there is only a rolling head and nothing else, or something which walks without feet, or has no hands, or hops along on one leg. All sorts of — one can't avoid the word — schizophrenic distortions show in those demons. This has led to the widespread theory among ethnologists that evil spirits are the fantasy product of schizophrenic individuals, the people who see and cope with evil spirits, like the medicine men and the Shaman, who are simply the psychotic individuals of the tribe who terrorize the rest of the tribe with their psychotic fantasies.

If you have treated psychotic people you will know that this is quite true. If you ask them to draw the evil demons who haunt them, they will draw things very similar to those the Eskimos drew for Rasmussen. But from our viewpoint the explanation is the other way round. Many people who disappear in a psychotic episode, or who live in a chronic psychotic state, disappear at the same time in the archetypal experience and expression of evil. In former days one would have said in colloquial terms that the devil had got them. If such people draw such evil spirits, the distortion of the evil spirits does not come from the schizophrenia but from the fact that evil spirits always look like that. In the archetypal experience of evil, evil powers are seen as a crippled human, or as a distorted thing, and I think we should therefore understand it symbolically and see in that the projection of a human psychological fact, namely that evil entails being swept away by one-sidedness, by only *one single* pattern of behavior.

The lives of all animals, even in the very early level of evolution, are shaped by what the behaviorists would call patterns, a certain mode of fighting, or courting, of looking after the young, of mating, and so on, which differs for each animal species, and already on the animal level such patterns can collide or become confused. One can see this in a normal manner among certain fish, for instance, in the "Stichlinge" (Latin Cichlidae), where male sexual behavior is closely linked with aggression. The Cichlidae are very short-sighted, so if a male fish sees another small fish approach he gets into an aggressive fighting mood. If later he notices that it is a female, it is all right and he can mate her. But if he sees a bigger fish, then he gets into the fear mood, turns pale and displays flight behavior. Then, even if he recognizes that it is a beautiful lady, he cannot mate any

147

more because he has already turned into flight behavior. So among the Cichlidae only a bigger male can marry a smaller female, and not the other way round.

That still happens to a certain extent on the human level, for if a man is frightened of a woman he becomes impotent, he has turned pale and there is nothing doing any longer! With women it is the other way round, they can combine turning pale and getting into a running-away mood with mating. But if they feel aggressive, if they are in the animus, then love is not possible.

So sometimes patterns of behavior overlap, get close to each other and collide, or get the animal into difficulties where they are not adapted. Though such patterns are meant by nature to adapt the animal to life situations, sometimes they work the wrong way round and collide with each other. If he interferes with nature, man can make an animal have conflicts and can transform such patterns of behavior in the funniest ways. Therefore already on the animal level one can speak of conflict, meaning conflict in the literal sense of the word, the collision or banging together of two patterns of behavior. For example, if you approach a broody hen with your hand outstretched, you will see how she gets into a conflict. She would like to run away and not let herself be touched by a human being, but her mother instinct keeps her on the eggs and she becomes more and more tense. Then suddenly either the flight behavior collapses and she puts up with being touched by a human being, or she will suddenly fly off screeching as the flight pattern wins and she gives up the mother instinct. But in between there is a moment of suspense when you don't know which will win out.

Thus patterns of behavior even on the animal level are not a nicely regulated affair; there is no central office where there is a reasonable switch-over from one behavior to another. It is even possible that for that reason nature invented our higher forms of consciousness to create such a central office and avoid the inadaptability which is to be found on the animal level. But whatever the reason, we display these same features, for a woman can get into a conflict between self-preservation and the protection of her children, exactly the same conflict as the hen, and we constantly get into other life situations where patterns of behavior collide.

It can be said that whenever someone is completely one-sidedly swept

148

away by a pattern of behavior, adaptation is disturbed. Certain animals, probably because of early imprints in their upbringing, overdo one pattern. Certain stags or wolves become unusually aggressive and get carried away by the pattern of aggressivity, causing great disturbance in the tribe or pack to which they belong. Usually they meet with an early death because of it. So to be completely swept away by one of the behavioral patterns always contains a certain danger. In our present civilization, wild animals such as deer and foxes have a very good and intelligent adaptation to man, avoiding him at all costs; but if, for example, a male deer is caught up in sexual passion he will practically run into the gun of the hunter and will not be able to control himself. One can read of instances where a stag has overrun a hunter and knocked the gun out of his hands. To use anthropomorphic language, they are blind to any kind of danger, being swept away by sexual passion. Or a cat, if she has kittens, will attack the biggest Alsatian wolf dog and get herself killed, the mother instinct sweeping away any other "reasonable" reaction.

This probably is the natural root in man, for he, too, tends to be swept away by certain patterns of behavior, that is, by archetypal patterns, by affects and fantasies. And, as in animal life, if anyone is overcome by these patterns, we speak of his being possessed. Possession for us is still just as bad as in primitive society, for it means being swept away by one tune in the melody of one's inner possibilities, and in that there is already a great amount of evil. Now you see why and how that links with pure evil in nature, because if you are swept away by an affect it is exactly like a landslide, but one within you rather than outside. The boulders of your affect roll over you and you are completely overcome; anything like reason or relatedness or any other mode of behavior is gone.

In analysis, people who are threatened with being swept away by a pathological rage may dream of a landslide or an avalanche, and there the unconscious uses an apt symbolic image to predict not an outer but an inner landslide, where the cultural behavior built up within the personality is completely covered up and swept away by one single mode of behavior — aggression or fear, or anything of that kind, by a powerful primitive reaction, pure nature, you could call it. Thus we would not deny that the evil spirits in nature have reference not only to actual evil in nature, but just as much to pure nature within us which contains these same phenomena. If

149

you look at it from that angle, the fact that these creatures are so often represented as cripples is very adequate, because that implies distorted one-sided human nature; there is only one leg. If, for instance, you get so angry with your wife that you hit her, then you are walking on one leg; you remember only your rage, and not that you also love her. You forget the opposite, so to speak, forget the other side of your behavior. You behave in a "one-legged way," in a "crippled way," being swept away in the one-sidedness of a momentary affect, and therefore have only one leg, or are only a head rolling along.

Many modern scientists are like skulls rolling along, lacking any heart or other normal human reactions. That is an apt picture for this kind of psychological one-sidedness, and the analogy to schizophrenic material becomes understandable in that way too, because in our definition, schizophrenia is a very strong dissociation into the complexes of the unconscious personality. Therefore drawings of such people resemble the drawings of evil spirits which the Eskimos and the South American Indians and other primitive people have always drawn. They are not abnormal drawings but very normal primitive pictures of evil; if a schizophrenic person draws such a demon it is in order to convey that this is the thing which has him, the thing in which he is caught.

Now we come to the other problem, for my intention is not so much to lecture on evil as to concentrate on how man copes with it. So after this excursion I would like to come back to the problem of behavior and comment first on the motif of loneliness.

One may wonder whether it is physical, or spiritual or mental loneliness which seems to invite possession by evil. Personally, I would say both. In the stories I told you it is mainly physical loneliness, being alone out in the woods or mountains, though nowadays with the overpopulation one can be just as lonely in a tenth storey flat in a town as people were in the Amazonian forests. That is mental loneliness but also, in a way, physical loneliness. The Arabs in the Sahara desert say never approach a woman who lives alone close to the desert, for she certainly has a secret lover, a djinn, a desert spirit. There again is the motif of loneliness. On the other hand, in Christian and Buddhistic tradition loneliness is something sought after by people who strive for saintliness and higher spiritual and religious conscious development. If you take that into account you can say that loneliness invites the powers of the Beyond, either evil or good. The natural explanation would be that the amount of energy normally used in relating to one's surroundings is dammed back into oneself and activates the unconscious, loads up the unconscious part of the psyche, so that if for a long time one is alone, one's unconscious will come alive, and then you are caught for better or for worse; either the devil will get you or you will find greater inner realization. If you introvert in this way, as has been reported by people who strove for saintliness in the past, at first you will always be attacked by devils, because at first this energy strengthens what we would call the autonomous complexes in the unconscious. These become more intensified and before you have worked them out the fruit of loneliness will not be positive but it will mean fighting with 20,000 different devils.

I once tried that myself. Having read in Jung that the saints in the desert found that such isolation strengthened their conscious, I thought that I must try that out! It was my curiosity behavior, you see, the one thing I warned you against! I naturally tried it out in my youth, and so imprisoned myself in a hut in the mountains in the snow. I felt perfectly happy because I occupied myself the whole day with cooking, with what I was going to eat next, and that one pattern of behavior prevented me from getting caught by other devils. Being by nature introverted, if I went once a day to the village to get bread and milk and exchanged comments about the weather, that was quite sufficient to keep me in balance, so the effect was nil! But then I reinforced the cure and bought everything in tins so I would not have to go to the village. But I still went around skiing, so that I also stopped. Finally I forced myself, with only a pencil and paper to write down my dreams and possible fantasies, to sit the whole day and do nothing, to cook only very quickly cooked boring stuff — spaghetti or something like that — so that couldn't take all my energy, and the first experience I had was that time began to drag! It dragged like hell! I looked at my watch and it was ten o'clock. I sat and listened to the birds and the snow water dripping on the roof and thought I had sat an eternity but it was only ten-thirty and not yet time to cook the spaghetti, and so on, forever. It was interesting, because I had once had a woman who had been in an acute psychotic episode in Burghölzli and the first day she was in the asylum she had exactly the same experience, namely that time dragged, minutes were eternity. This got worse but I stuck it out, and then the unconscious became

151

alive because my mind got wandering on the idea that sometimes burglars got into such huts, especially escaped prisoners looking for weapons, a revolver, or civilian clothes, if they still had on their striped things. That fantasy got me completely, and not seeing that it was just the thing I was looking for, I was absolutely panic stricken. I took the axe for chopping the wood and put it beside my bed and lay awake trying to decide whether I would have the courage to bang such a man over the head if he came in, and I couldn't sleep. Then I had to go to the toilet which was outside in the snow in the wood, and in the night I put on my skiing trousers and went through the snow and suddenly something plopped behind me and I ran, and fell on my face, and got back panting. Then I realized it was just the snow which had fallen off the tree, but with my heart pumping and the axe beside my bed I still couldn't sleep.

Next morning I thought that now I'd had it and must go home, but then I had a second thought and said, "But that was what I was looking for!" Those were the devils I wanted to meet, so now I was going to make a fantasy with a burglar. I sat down and at once I saw the burglar coming in. So I did what we call in Jungian terms an active imagination and felt absolutely fine! After that I stayed another fortnight and put the axe back and did not even lock the door. I felt absolutely safe. But whenever such a thing came up I wrote it down and dealt with it in active imagination and then there was complete peace. I could have stayed weeks more without the slightest trouble, but when I met it without the means of coping with it by active imagination, I was on the right way to being really nicely possessed. I was even stupid enough, though I knew something of Jungian psychology, not to see that this burglar was the animus invading my territory. I was just absolutely terrified of a real criminal who would come in the night.

That experience taught me that loneliness piles up whatever you have in your unconscious, and if you don't know how to cope with it, it comes first in a projected form. In my case it was projected into the idea of a criminal, and if I had belonged to a layer of civilization which still believed in demons, then I would have thought the Kurupira was coming or that the "IT" from the mountains had thrown snow at me. I would have given that name to it, but because I am more modern I gave it the name of an escaped criminal. Yet the thing itself is absolutely the same. Most people are not capable of standing such situations for a long time; they need the companionship of other people to protect themselves against "IT."

In the book *Goldener Ring über Uri*, which I mentioned earlier, Renner explains very clearly that a man who lives alone in nature must constantly draw a ritual golden ring around himself, a mandala, either by the prayer call in the four directions of the horizon, by sending a prayer over the Alp in a circle, or by making the gesture of the circle. (We have also such gestures of swinging the Swiss flag up in the air in a circle.) If you don't know of such ritualistic protective practices you cannot live alone in nature. It will surely get you, for you need the ring, or at least a minimum thing, namely your own objects around you.

Our Alp cowherds believe that if a hut has been left unoccupied during the winter, and that happens to all our mountain huts, the "IT" takes possession of it again. Unconsciousness and nature invade it, and if you come back in the Spring you have first to exorcise this by certain religious rituals before you can take possession. You cannot simply move in. If you have ever moved into your holiday resort after the winter you will know exactly what that feels like; the lid of the pan falls on you, you bump into the spiders' webs, the bed is cold, and you have rheumatism the next morning when you wake up. You feel as if you were fighting with 20,000 devils until you have established yourself again in your living realm. So you need the protective ring of human beings, and also of your beloved objects.

Here I want to make a side attack on modern psychiatric treatment in hospitals. With the terrible excuse of wanting to prevent those who come to the hospital from committing suicide, in most asylums in Switzerland and in America all private possessions are taken away from the patients. They are not allowed to have around their beds either Mamma's photograph, or a beloved's letter, or their bag, or even a dirty handkerchief, all the little things with which one loves to surround oneself. I have heard again and again from patients that from the moment things were taken away they felt doomed, as if that were the end and then they were lost, nakedly delivered up to the powers of evil, and they gave up fighting with evil themselves. It was as if their last stronghold had been taken away. Why haven't psychiatrists discovered this yet? Naturally, you must take away a knife or a revolver and things with which they could really commit suicide, but leave them a handkerchief, something so tiny that they really can't hang themselves with it, just that little bit of the "golden ring," so that they may be surrounded by the things to which they have an emotional affective relationship, the things which belong to them.

Primitive man does not only relate to human beings, but also to objects. Such objects make a ring around one and protect one from complete exposure to the super-personal and terrifying forces of the unconscious. You know that schizophrenic patients complain that they are haunted by devils and evil forces, so why not let them at least keep their little ring of objects around them when they themselves have already cut off all human relationships by misbehavior.

There is another way in which loneliness attracts evil: if you live alone and away from a human community for a very long time then the tribe, the other people, project their shadow on to you and there is no correcting fact. For instance, after very long holidays in which I do not see my analysands, I often find that when I come back they have slowly spun a web of the most amazing negative ideas about me. That is why the French say: *les absents ont toujours tort* (the absent are always wrong). They think I do this or that, but when they see me again they say, "Why on earth did I believe that? Now that we are together again I cannot even imagine that I could think such things about you." The actual warm human contact dissipates those clouds of projection, but if one is away for a long time and the tie of affection and feeling loosens, people begin to project.

So people who live alone not only attract evil of their own nature and constellate it by their unconscious, they also attract projections. That is why lonely people are often thought odd, and if something disagreeable happens the villagers are apt to think they must be the cause. When one joins the community again one can argue or hit back, or explain one's behavior and so dissipate those black clouds. Or perhaps one does something unusual, and people get the most fantastic negative explanations, but if one goes to the inn and has a bottle of beer with those people, then they begin to tease you and an explanation can be given and everything is all right again. But when people can't understand, they project their own evil.

It is just these common basic human experiences which one has to keep in mind, because they are closely related to the problem of evil. One sees how loneliness can cut one off from the community. In former times and in primitive society that was much more so. The stranger was wrong, was

154

dangerous, brought with him the atmosphere of illness, murder, death and disturbance of human relationship, and therefore had to be approached with all sorts of precautions.

CHAPTER III

MEETING THE POWERS OF EVIL

In the last chapter I tried to describe attitudes or situations which, according to fairy tales, seem to attract evil: drunkenness, physical or psychological loneliness, being a stranger or isolating oneself too much. These are not necessary conditions, but they exist at the beginning of some of the fairy tales. Other initial situations are also worth attention. In the story of the Kurupira who ate all the hunters, the hunters had especially good luck and their camp was full of the apes they had killed. Next day they went hunting again, but at night the Kurupira and his wild animals came and ate them.

This seems to hint that by killing too many animals the hunters have annoyed the Kurupira, who is the Master of the Woods. Perhaps, though the story does not say so *expressis verbis*, what from a human standpoint is particularly good hunting luck has gone a bit too far, beyond the usual measure, transcending the natural limit, and so the hunters have possibly attracted evil. Either they became secretly inflated through their good luck, or, to put it more simply, they annoyed the Master of the Woods by taking too much away from him. This would not be surprising, for in most primitive societies there are certain rules for hunting. Too many animals may not be killed at a time. There are taboos. A certain number of animals must be spared if you do not want to disturb the natural balance of things and attract evil onto yourself, or the revenge of the spirit which protects the animals in general.

We are now becoming aware that man is capable of disturbing the biological economy of his surroundings, thereby attracting evil in reaction. We begin to wake up to the fact that we too have annoyed Kurupira, to such an extent that probably all our bones will soon be broken. By contaminating the waters we destroy the animals and the biological balance of nature. This seems to have its roots in the very earliest days.

When man began to use weapons he made use of an illegitimate trick. He no longer fought the animals on a level of equality and fairplay. From the beginning this must have given him a bad conscience, a feeling that he

156

must be wise and spare certain animals. For example, in old China the hunting rule was that the animals might be driven together by men to three corners of the horizon, but the fourth corner had to be an open space to give them a chance; God would inspire them to escape in the right direction if their time hadn't come. I read in the paper that we have just now issued a similar rule. Where men hunt in groups and there are beaters to drive the animals out of the bushes, one of the four directions of the horizon has to be left open so that some animals may escape; you may not make a ring and slaughter them all. Switzerland with its new hunting rules published in the papers about four weeks ago has returned to an old Chinese custom, probably without knowing it, for it is simply natural wisdom.

So you see the problem of evil in the realm of folklore which I am now discussing is unlike a differentiated or specific religious problem of evil. What we call evil on this level differs even from the theological idea, for it is in the realm of purely natural phenomena. This is tremendously important in psychology, for I think I am not optimistic if I say that in ninety percent of the cases where one has to cope with evil, one is confronted with this natural evil on a psychological level, and only very rarely with a more absolute and deep-rooted phenomenon of evil. Eighty or eighty-five percent of the phenomena are just the Kurupira, Mrs. Trude and such creatures, which still exist in our psychological nature.

It is for this reason that fairy tales are so important. We find in them rules of behavior on how to cope with these things. Very often it is not a sharp ethical issue but a question of finding a way of natural wisdom. This does not mean that these powers are not sometimes exceedingly dangerous.

I want to go into more specific illustrations of the manner in which human beings meet these powers. We have seen that not infringing taboos and keeping within the rules of the tribe seems to be one of the most usual ways of trying to avoid evil. But for more specific details I want to give you a Russian fairy tale called "The Beautiful Wassilissa." It is a more elaborate parallel of the Mrs. Trude story except that here the girl is not eaten, but finds a way out of trouble.

There was once in a faraway kingdom a merchant and his wife. They had only one daughter called the Beautiful Wassi-

157

lissa (the word Wassilissa means queen, but it is just an ordinary name). When the girl was eight years old the merchant's wife called her child and said she, her mother, had to die but she would leave Wassilissa her maternal blessing and a doll. The doll Wassilissa was to keep with her always and never show to anybody; if she was in trouble, she should ask it for advice. Having said this the merchant's wife died.

The merchant afterwards married a widow with two children of about Wassilissa's age. The stepmother slowly turned hostile to Wassilissa, but the doll always comforted her.

One day the merchant had to leave the country for a long time. During his absence the stepmother moved with her three daughters to another house standing near the primeval forest in which, in a clearing, was the house of the Baba-Yaga (the great Russian fairy tale witch). Nobody was ever allowed to approach her and whoever fell into her hands was eaten like a chicken. The situation suited the stepmother because she hoped that Wassilissa would one day cross the Baba-Yaga's path.

One evening the stepmother gave her three daughters candles. Ordering them to embroider, to knit, and to spin, she left them and went to bed. In time the candles burned down. One of the girls took her knitting needle to clear the wicks but purposely used it in such a manner that the light went out. Then she said she didn't mind because she could do her embroidery without light, and the other said she could knit without light, but you, the two girls said to Wassilissa, must go to the Baba-Yaga and get fire so that we can have light again, and they pushed her out of the room. The girl went to her room and asked her doll what to do. The doll said not to be afraid but to go where the others sent her, and to take the doll with her and it would help her.

Wassilissa walked all through the night. Then she met a rider dressed in white, sitting on a beautiful horse covered in white, and the moment he passed her, day broke. After a while she met a second rider dressed in red, riding a horse covered in red, and at that moment the sun rose.

Having walked through the night, Wassilissa then walked through the whole of the next day. In the evening she arrived at the clearing where the Baba-Yaga's house stood. Round the house was a fence made of human bones, with posts made of skulls. The bolts on the doors were made of the arms of skeletons and the locks were made of a skeleton's mouth from which the teeth stuck out. Wassilissa was terrified. She stood nearly fainting and as though nailed to the ground, when suddenly a black rider on a black horse galloped by and it became night. But the darkness did not last long, for soon the eyes in all the skulls on the hedge began to glow, and the whole clearing was light as day. Wassilissa stood shivering with fear, but soon she heard an uncanny humming noise, and the trees began to rustle and out of the wood came the Baba-Yaga. She sat in a mortar and rowed with a pestle, and with a broom she removed her traces. When she came to the door she sniffed the air and said, "Ugh! It smells of Russians! Who's there? "

Wassilissa went to meet her and bowed and said, "It's I, Grandmother, my stepsisters have sent me to you to fetch fire."

"Good," answered the Baba-Yaga, "I know them. Stay with me for a time and then you shall have the fire."

Then she spoke some magic words. The door opened and the Baba-Yaga entered the courtyard and the door shut behind them. She then ordered the girl about, telling her to bring her food and heat the stove. And she ate a lot, leaving a little cabbage soup and a bread crust for Wassilissa, practically nothing. Then she laid down to sleep, but she told Wassilissa that next morning when she went out, Wassilissa was to sweep out the yard and the hut, cook the midday meal, do the washing and then separate the mildewed from the good corn. All had to be finished by the time she came home. Otherwise she would eat her.

The girl asked her doll for advice and the doll told her not to be afraid, to eat her supper and say her prayers and lie down to sleep, "morning is wiser than evening."

Next morning when Wassilissa woke up and looked out of the window the eyes in the skulls were already closing. The white rider rode by and the day began. The Baba-Yaga went off and Wassilissa went over the whole house, admiring all its treasures. Then she wondered which piece of work she should begin on, but the work had all been done by the doll, who was just separating the last black from the white corn seeds.

When the Baba-Yaga came back in the evening she found everything done and was very angry that there was nothing with which to find fault. Then something very strange happened, for she cried out, "My faithful servants, grind the corn for me," and three pairs of skeleton hands appeared and took the corn away.

She gave Wassilissa her orders for the next day, saying she

159

should do as she had done the day before, but in addition she should clean the poppy seeds. The next evening when the Baba-Yaga came she called up the hands again to press oil out of the poppy seeds.

While the Baba-Yaga ate her supper Wassilissa stood silently by. The Baba-Yaga said, "What are you staring at without saying a word? Are you dumb? "

The girl answered, "If I may, I would like to ask you some questions."

"Ask then," said the Baba-Yaga, "but remember, not all questions are good. To know too much makes one old!"

Wassilissa said, "I'd only like to ask you about the things I've seen: On the way to you a rider dressed all in white passed me, sitting on a horse. Who was that? "

"That is my day, the bright one," answered the Baba-Yaga.

"And then another rider overtook me, dressed in red and sitting on a red horse. Who was he? "

"That is my sun, the red one."

"And then at the gate a black rider came."

"That was my night, the dark one."

And then Wassilissa thought of the three pairs of hands, but she didn't dare ask and kept silent.

And the Baba-Yaga said, "Why don't you ask me some more questions? "

And the girl answered that those were enough, adding, "You said yourself, Grandmother, that knowing too much made one old."

Then the Baba-Yaga replied (and this is important), "You did well to ask only about what you saw outside and not about what you saw inside the hut. I don't like it when the dirt is brought outside the hut. But now I want to ask *you* something: How did you manage to do all the work I gave you? "

"The blessing of my mother helped me," answered Wassilissa. (She didn't mention the doll.)

"Oh, that's it, is it? Then get away from here, blessed daughter, I don't need any blessing in my house!"

And the Baba-Yaga pushed Wassilissa out of the hut and chased her out of the gate. Then she took one of the skulls with flaming eyes from the hedge and put it on a pole and gave it to Wassilissa, saying, "This is the fire for your stepsisters, take it, and carry it with you."

Wassilissa hurried away from the Baba-Yaga and ran through

160

the dark forest, lit by the light of the skull which only went out
when dawn broke. On the evening of the next day she reached
home. When she approached the gate she thought of throwing
away the skull, but a hollow voice said, "Don't throw me away,
take me to your stepmother."

So Wassilissa obeyed and when she brought the fire into the
room the glowing eyes of the skull stared unceasingly at the
stepmother and her daughters, burning into their souls, and the
eyes followed them wherever they went to hide. Towards
morning they were burnt to ashes, and only Wassilissa remained
unhurt.

In the morning Wassilissa buried the skull in the earth, shut
up the house and went into town.

The second part of the story I will tell very briefly. Wassilissa went to
stay with a nice old woman who bought thread for her with which she was
to make linen. The linen she made was so beautiful that it was used to
make shirts for the King. Through that she became acquainted with him
and he married her. When her father, the merchant, returned, he was
very happy over her good fortune. He lived with her in the palace, and
the positive old woman with whom she had stayed, Wassilissa also brought
to the palace (so she has two parents again), and the doll she carried with
her to the end of her life.

As we are concentrating on the dark aspect of things and on evil, I am
skipping this happy ending.

You see here the similarity. With Mrs. Trude there was again a quaternity of figures, also a green, a black and a red man: the charcoal burner,
the butcher and the hunter. Here it is the day, the night and the sun who
are the three riders.

In the Russian version one can see clearly that the Baba-Yaga is the
great Mother Nature. She could not talk about "My day, My night" if she
were not the owner of the day, of the night, and of the sun, so she must be
a great Goddess and you could call her the Great Goddess of Nature. Obviously, with all those skulls around her hut she is also the Goddess of
Death, which is an aspect of nature. (One is reminded, for instance, of the
Germanic Goddess of the underworld, *Hel*, from which our word hell comes.)
She lives in a subterranean hall where the walls are built of worms and human
bones. So she is a Goddess of day and night, of life and death, and the great

principle of nature. Also she is a witch, which is why she has a broom, like our witches who ride on broomsticks. She goes around in a mortar with a pestle, which makes her resemble a great pagan corn Goddess such as Demeter in Greece, who is the Goddess of corn and also of the mystery of death. The dead in Greek antiquity were called *demetreioi*, those who had fallen into the possession of Demeter, like the corn falling into the earth. Death and resurrection was supposed to be a simile for what happens to man after death, so those skull hands which took the corn and the poppy seeds had to do with the mystery of death. I will go into this further later.

Here one also sees a great difference from the Mrs. Trude story. There, the girl penetrated Mrs. Trude's house out of sheer curiosity, infantile daring as I called it, and she got turned into a piece of wood and was burnt away by the great witch. But this girl would never have dared, inspired by infantile daring, to go into the realm of the great witch. Wassilissa was pushed there by the evil stepmother and her stepsisters. The girl in the Mrs. Trude tale had no magical protection, nor had she looked for any. With her infantile daring she did not even think of anything of the kind. Wassilissa, however, takes her mother's blessing and the magic doll with her.

One sees, therefore, that actually the great battle between life and death, good and evil, the girl and the great nature witch, becomes a secret magical contest as to whose magical powers are stronger, the girl's or the great witch's, and the two respect each other's power mutually. Wassilissa does not ask the last question about the witch's secret and the witch either does not notice, or pretends not to notice, the girl's great secret. So they can part *partie remise*. Keep this in mind, because I will concentrate on the magical contest later, as it is one of the most important problems.

At first the witch got very annoyed with Wassilissa because she didn't ask questions, so she expected and seemed to want questions. The words: "Why don't you ask me any questions? " having been shouted at the girl, Wassilissa asks three and swallows the last one. This fourth question referred to what she saw inside the witch's hut. The riders are connected with the witch but Wassilissa had seen them outside. So we must assume that those skeleton hands have to do with the inner-most secret of the witch, who said something very strange, namely: "It is good that you didn't ask about the inside things, because one should not carry the dirt out of the hut." This is like our proverb which says one shouldn't wash one's dirty linen in public, and she means it in this ordinary sense. This is an interesting point. The witch has dirty linen and obviously is slightly ashamed of it, because if she were completely unashamed of the evil she wouldn't care if Wassilissa brought it out. But, like an ordinary human being, she felt slightly awkward about her dark side and therefore was grateful that the girl tactfully did not poke into this dirty linen business.

This shows that the Baba-Yaga is a slightly split figure, not completely one with herself. There is a secret something of goodness in her, just enough to make her slightly ashamed of her dark side and to give her a feeling that it oughtn't to be carried out of the hut. She is not completely a nature demon; there is a tinge of humanity in her demonic character. She has become slightly human and so capable of ethical human reactions. Just here the girl must not poke, because if she had touched this blind spot in the Baba-Yaga the latter would have howled in rage and devoured her in fury. A similar thing can happen to an analyst who dares mention the shadow side of an analysand; he or she often gets eaten right away in an outburst of affect. Naturally, with a fellow human being you dare do such things sometimes, but with a Goddess, if you dared to put your finger on the dark side you would certainly disappear from the surface of the earth.

We can conclude from this story that the Baba-Yaga is not totally evil; she is ambiguous, she is light and dark, good and evil, though here the evil aspect is stressed.

This motif, that one should not poke into the dark side of the divinity, whether a male God or a female Goddess, is widespread in folklore stories. There is, for instance, an Austrian tale called "The Black Woman." A girl becomes the servant of a black witch in the woods. There is a forbidden chamber, as in the Bluebeard story, into which she may not go. She has to clean the house for many years. As always in these stories, she eventually opens the door of the secret forbidden chamber and finds in it the black witch who, through her cleaning, has already turned nearly white. The girl shuts up the room again but is then persecuted by the witch for having transgressed the taboo, and, strangely enough, in the original versions, the girl absolutely denies having seen anything. There is an infinite number of such stories. In the main story she sees the black witch turned nearly white;

163

in another story she sees a skeleton nodding all the time over a fire; in another she sees a goose, in another a petrified feminine figure surrounded by petrified dwarfs, and so on. Always the Goddess who sat in this forbidden chamber persecutes the girl, takes away her children and brings every kind of misery over her, pressing her, "Have you seen me in the chamber? " And the girl lies in a determined way, lies and lies, till finally the Goddess turns and says, "Because you have lied so consistently, because you have not given away my dark side, I will reward you" and then does so on a big scale.

So, contrary to our Christian morals, these stories say that there is a form of tactful lying about the evil or the dark side of these great divinities which is not immoral. On the contrary, to be capable of having seen into that abyss of evil and pretend not to have seen it is the highest achievement. This version shocked later Christian European story tellers so much that many of the modern versions transform it and the girl is persecuted because she lies. Finally she breaks down, tells the truth and then the Great Goddess rewards her. But this is an artificial version, changed by later writers who did not understand the old motif and were shocked that the child should be rewarded for consistently not telling the truth.

Question: The girl is thanked for not having revealed or given away the Goddess' dark side, but isn't it really the transformation she doesn't reveal? It isn't the witch's uttermost evil that she is being transformed and becoming white. Isn't that so?

Well, in the story the black woman is slowly turning white, but it is having seen the evil which is the problem, not having seen the transformation. For example, in one variation the witch says, "Child, have you seen me in my misery? " And the child says, "No, I didn't see anything." That is the same motif. The witch is ashamed of her darkness, of her misery, or of being stuck in the filth and misery of the mystery of evil and death, and does not want the child to mention it or bring it into the open.

Question: And then the removal of the seeds by the skeleton hands?

That would be the terrible secret in *this* story, where it is the untouchable secret. Because poppy seeds have a slightly soporific effect they have always, from antiquity, been ascribed to the Gods of the underworld. The poppy has to do with Hades and the mystery of sleep and death; and the corn, as I said before when mentioning Demeter, also has to do with the mystery of death and resurrection. So it is strange, in a way, that this should be such a shameful secret; it does not feel so evil, it feels more awe inspiring, the untouchable, terrifying secret of the Gods, which man should not penetrate, if not forced to do so.

It is obvious that what looks like lying is rather a gesture of reverence, of respect towards the otherness of this divinity. We can compare with it situations which occur sometimes between two human beings. In the last paper he wrote, Dr. Jung tells of the case of a man who, if I remember rightly, came to him with severe compulsions. He came always for short periods of analysis, because he came from a foreign country and could only stay for about three or four weeks each time. This man made a very consistent pseudo-analysis. Dr. Jung saw in the first therapeutic hour that he was hiding some kind of secret and had all the symptoms of a bad conscience. For some strange reason, Dr. Jung had a kind of feeling inhibition from telling him right out about it, so the man did a swindle analysis for ten years and Dr. Jung always felt very awkward because they talked about dreams and this and that, yet it was all a swindle. But Dr. Jung did not poke into the affair because he noticed that the man's symptoms slowly cleared up and he got better each time he came, which normally doesn't happen if you make a swindle analysis. Finally, after many years, the patient said, "Now Dr. Jung I want to tell you how grateful I am to you for not ever having asked me before, for I just couldn't have told you, and it would have ruined the analysis." Then he confessed some rather awkward sin he had committed which he couldn't face. He had to have built up a relationship to Dr. Jung and re-built his own self-esteem and energy before he himself could face what he had done and share it with the analyst. So Dr. Jung, who had only followed a kind of irrational feeling in not poking into the secret of this man, was rewarded by seeing after the event that his feeling had been right. It is important for all people who may be unwisely tempted to use confession drugs to know about this.

Remark: I see here an exact parallel to Apuleius' story, Amor and Psyche, *where there are two evil sisters who push Psyche and she looks into the big secret, but the magic protection is there. Then she brings up from the*

165

underworld the box in which there is the ointment for Aphrodite's beauty, and immediately falls asleep herself. I think it is an amazing parallel. Perhaps you will correct me if I am wrong?

No, you are absolutely right. It is a parallel, though there are certainly other nuances. But the parallel is that she should not look into the secret. After doing so she collapses into the eternal, death-like sleep. That is an exact parallel. The stepsisters pushing her into it is also a parallel. The underworld Gods are usually the Gods of the great mystery. There is the great secret in all religious systems, and always this parallel of not opening the forbidden chamber, of not looking, with sometimes the exception of having to do so.

I have stressed the point that here the good outcome is brought about by *not* looking into the secret, even by consistently lying about it. But I could tell you other stories where it is just the opposite, where the secret had to be disclosed. That's why I told you at the beginning that it is always a paradox, it is always a Yes and a No.

Question: Has that got to do with the time when the story originated?

No, not as far as I have seen.

Question: Because in medieval times people were not aware of the dark side of God as we are now becoming aware?

As far as I can see this is not historically conditioned. On a most primitive level both rules already exist: the opening of the door as the right thing, or something a chosen hero may do, and its opposite. In certain periods in history it might be that the one has more often to be done than the other, but as far as I can see it is an archetypal motif from the beginning, which does not have to do with specific evolution. It is an archetypal pattern that one must, or must not penetrate that secret, and it means walking on the razor's edge, for it may cost you your head if you do the wrong thing. An analyst who stands a swindling analysis for ten years does absolute harm to himself and the patient! He *should* say, "Now come on, don't beat about the bush! What's the matter with you, you are telling me rubbish!" and so on, but to take his money and pretend not to notice anything for many years is plainly immoral, from the therapeutic standpoint. But in the case which Dr. Jung tells it was just the other way round. He would have destroyed the rapport if he had asked one minute sooner! So the terrible conflict is to find out which situation is it now? Is it the one where I have to poke into the forbidden chamber, or must I pretend not to have noticed, even if I have done so?

Question: It seems to me that on both sides: the human and the inhuman, the human and the God, there has to be a balance, but in the case of the infantile child and of the man who swung too far and dropped into the abyss, it was unconscious evil. But the God musn't show all his evil either! In the case of those two humans one wonders why such an imperfect human was produced! Why did they have to be nothing but that and why did they have to be completely swallowed up? It wasn't their fault?

No.

Question: There it is as though the other side had made an "overstep" onto the side of evil?

Yes. Well, I like your idea that it is a question of balance. We might even go one step further and say it is a question of the possibility of relationship, or confidence. Between such a great God and an eight-year-old girl there couldn't be a relationship, really. There couldn't be mutual confidence. The two positions are too far apart – the great nature Goddess and a little harmless girl – so that is probably why there the secret has to be kept; while in a state where the human being has become more conscious, the Godhead can also show more of its secret. I don't know, that is the great puzzle.

Question: Yes, why were they produced?

Why are we such incomplete creatures? We didn't make ourselves as incomplete and deficient as we are. But it seems that the Divinity of Nature, this Goddess of Nature has itself the same problem. That would explain why we are like that, for Nature itself is like that.

In another Russian story the Baba-Yaga shows more her positive side and I want to give this story as an amplification, first because it illustrates how a man might cope with her differently from an eight-year-old girl, and secondly because it shows her relatively positive side.

167

There is a Russian story, (No. 41 *Die Jungfrau Zar*) called "The Virgin Czar" where the hero rides to the end of the world, to the kingdom under the sun, to find the beautiful Maria with the golden plait and bring her home. On his way he comes three times upon the hut of a Baba-Yaga. It is a rotating hut, standing on chickens' feet, and by using a magic verse he makes it stop and then enters. In it he finds a great Baba-Yaga poking the fire with her nose, combing silk strands with her fingers and watching the geese on the field with her eyes. When the hero, Ivan, enters, she says, "Have you come voluntarily or involuntarily, my little child? " Ivan bangs with his fist on the table and says, "You old witch, you must not ask a hero such questions! I want something to eat and drink and if you don't serve me a good meal, I shall box your ears, so that (and then comes an obscenity which I am not translating)...." And the Baba-Yaga turns very nice and serves him a wonderful dinner, makes a bed for him and the next morning shows him the next step. This happens three times so that she becomes an absolutely protective and helpful Goddess who even shows him the way.

That is the difference between a man and a girl's way of treating the Baba-Yaga. Ivan is a grown-up man, while the girl is an absolutely helpless young creature. But it also shows here that the Baba-Yaga is not evil at all, she is just plain nature. If you know how to cope with her, she is all right. It's up to you which side of her you experience, and here comes the first intimation in these stories that somewhere the problem of evil has to do with man, that evil is not right out in nature, a just-so story, as I represented it to you at the beginning. Here we begin to touch the problem on a higher level, where it has begun to dawn on man that evil is not only a nature phenomenon, but is dependent on man's attitude and behavior.

The Baba-Yaga addresses Ivan as "little child!" He is a grown-up young man and so you see what the great mother does. She tries to reduce him to infantile helplessness. Though it sounds very nice, "Did you come here voluntarily, or unvoluntarily, little child? " it is a real hit below the belt. She wants to depotentiate him and treat him like a small boy and then she would have nicely eaten him for supper. But he is up to her and does not take this wicked stab. He answers back and then she becomes amiable.

168

In both these Russian stories, the Beautiful Wassilissa and the Virgin Czar story, there is great subtlety. It is in a tiny conversation, just a few sentences of the story, that the whole problem of good and evil is decided. It means walking on the razor's edge to be able to say the right thing, or have the right reaction at the crucial moment, for that turns the whole problem.

I want to dwell shortly on one more small motif in the story, the fiery skull which Wassilissa takes home burns the stepmother and the stepsisters to death. These fiery eyes which persecute them wherever they go have been amplified in mythology and generally are associated with a bad conscience. There are Jewish traditions in the Midrashims where after the murder of Abel the eye of God followed Cain all over the world and he couldn't escape it. There is also a beautiful poem by Victor Hugo in which Cain, after the murder of Abel, runs away into the woods, and all over the place, and hides, and everywhere *God's eye* follows him; finally he digs a grave and buries himself alive, drawing the tombstone over himself, but in the dark — a typically pathetic Victor Hugo touch — *"et l'oeil de Dieu le regardait toujours!"* There you see the same motif of the eye pursuing the evil deed absolutely and inescapably. In that way the eye represents the original phenomenon of a bad conscience with its terrifying effect.

As I mentioned before, Dr. Jung in his article on "The Conscience" pointed out that the original phenomenon of conscience is an immediate experience of the voice of God within oneself, or a manifestation of the Self within the psyche, if you want to put it into psychological language. Here there is this immediate phenomenon; the stepmother and the stepsisters are destroyed, not by the girl, but by the phenomenon of evil, the bad conscience, their own evil, so to speak, in an immediate form.

There is another item which one might miss if one didn't watch the text closely, and that is that after the skull with the fiery eyes has destroyed the stepmother and stepsisters, Wassilissa buries it and leaves the place. She doesn't stay with it, or keep it to burn up other enemies later on. She could have said, "Oh well, this is very useful! I'll put it in my bedroom drawer and whenever somebody annoys me I can take it out and use it against them!" But she gives it up, she doesn't keep its power. A magical power of revenge has been placed in her hands by the witch, a revenge which takes place though she hadn't intended to use it that way, it just happened so. She didn't know it would burn her sisters and stepmother, but afterwards she buries it and leaves the whole problem. She detaches from it completely.

Here we return to another rule of wisdom which we find in fairy tales. Everything of evil tends to produce a chain reaction, whether it be suicide, or revenge, or paying back evil; the emotional chain reaction tends to go on in some form and therefore it is wiser to interrupt it. When the right moment comes, one has to stop being caught up in the chain reaction and bury it, leave it alone, detach one's own integral personality from it and give up the power. It would have been very human to say, "Ah-ha, that serves them right" but then Wassilissa herself would have been caught up in the evil thing she had used, the evil medicine, to use African language. But we hear nothing of any triumph. She buries the skull and leaves at once. This is very difficult to do, because if one has once learnt not to let evil catch one, one can often experience that it hits or lashes back onto the people who produced it. Not to triumph or think, "Ah, that's the way to do it, just turn it back onto the other," but to detach and step out of it at the right moment, is of paramount importance. It is a rule as imperative to follow today as it was in the stone age.

I would like to amplify on those hands which take away the corn and the poppy seeds. The terrifying secret of the hidden side is frequently associated with death. In this primitive form the skeleton represents death. I told you another story where the girl opens the forbidden door of the room in which there is a nodding skeleton. Primitives associate death with evil and there are Indian tribes in North and South America who will never touch a corpse. A dying man is put in a separate tepee, or hut, and as soon as he is dead the hut is shut, or walled up, or burnt, and people keep away from it. The phenomenon of death and corpses releases tremendous and genuine primitive fear. One does not know whether it is the fear of evil or of death, it is the same thing.

In Egyptian mythology and in some African tales death is personified as the enemy which kills at the end of life. We still have this in the word agony (Greek *agon*) which means battle. Nowadays this is rationalized in the idea that the dying person fights for life, for breath, but originally the battle was with the invisible enemy, death. Rostand reproduces the same conception in his play "Cyrano de Bergerac" in which the last enemy Cyrano has to fight is death.

Till nature invented man, practically no warm-blooded creature died of old age. In nature, when the physical forces fade to a certain degree, one is eaten, or one dies of hunger and cold, or of thirst, if in the desert. So in spite of present day civilization, our pattern of behavior, our instinctual adjustment to death still functions in the age-old way, representing death as that last thing which cuts your throat, which bites one to death as it did in the past.

In his book on the life of the Kalahari Bushmen Laurens van der Post describes how the old people run along in the desert with their tribe as long as their strength permits. When they can no longer keep up, the tribe gives them food and water for three or four days, says Goodbye and leaves them, and they quietly settle down to wait for death. Naturally, eighty-five percent of the time they are eaten by the wild animals of the country. That is death under natural conditions. Death prolonged by chemicals as we have to undergo it now in hospitals did not exist and we are not yet adapted to it.

If you think back to such natural original conditions, you realize how closely being overcome by evil, by the enemy, being eaten, and death are connected. It is as if one's life were a radiant light which keeps the lions and tigers, and even one's human fellow beings, at bay, but when that light dims and vitality fades, then all that darkness breaks in and gets one, so to speak. So the last battle is always defeat by the dark side — that is, on the physical level. That probably accounts for this great closeness of the symbolism of death and evil, and is why we in German still combine *Tod und Teufel* (death and the devil). A German proverb, for instance, says "he fears neither death nor the devil," taking the two things as a kind of twin couple.

But it seems to me that this biological angle is only the substructure of something which goes even further. In my experience, though nobody can judge what is really evil or good and I wouldn't dare to say, what impresses one as really evil in human beings, if one looks at it naively, is a kind of psychological death wish.

I want to tell you of a case because I think it illustrates a very important factor. Miss Barbara Hannah and I each had a difficult case with which we

171

couldn't cope. We each had a woman analysand very much obsessed by the negative animus and so, in those past times when Dr. Jung was still our control analyst, we asked for help. By chance, he saw those two ladies, one after the other, on the same afternoon. He was very nice to both of them, as he always was in such one hour interviews, and accepted them completely. In my case the woman was quarrelling with the male analyst, the medical supervisor of the case, and she told Dr. Jung all about that. To cut a long story short, Miss Hannah's case went home and drew a beautiful picture as a kind of reaction to what she had got from Dr. Jung. My analysand went home, rang up the medical doctor analyst and told him everything Dr. Jung had said against him, plus a bit more, making mischief with it.

Dr. Jung said that this was very important, because if one gave psychic energy to anyone one should always see what they did with it. If there was a slight, or momentary recovery, even if that collapsed again, one could go on giving charity, or giving concern, giving energy to the case; while if it had a contrary effect then one would know that one was feeding the demon of that person and that the person didn't get what one gave. He did not condemn my case, but it was as if her evil animus was sitting in front of her mouth and whenever one gave her a good bit, he got it. In effect the demon got fatter and she got thinner.

In such a case, if one goes on treating the person with Christian charity, love and concern, one is acting destructively, and that is a mistake which many naive young psychiatric doctors make. In their Christian tradition, but also in the tradition of physical medicine (Hippocratic oath!), it is absolutely imperative that one is always charitable; such people don't notice that they are feeding the devil and making the patients worse instead of better. Therefore if one sees that the devil snaps up everything one gives, one can do only one thing — turn off the tap and give nothing.

Dr. Jung told me — it was my very first case and I was terrified to do it, I even disobeyed for a week before I could make up my mind — to kick that lady out of analysis, telling her what a cheating, lying devil she was. But one is kind of lovingly attached to one's first case, so for a week I hesitated, and then I did it. The plain result was that from then on she was much better. After many years of *no* treatment she was practically all right! The kick in the pants did it, and after eight years I even got a letter from her thanking me.

172

In this case it was not only that her demon was eating everything she was given so that one couldn't get anything into her, neither human feeling nor psychological food. It was much worse, for one saw how the animus was working everywhere against life. If she got life energy from Dr. Jung, she tried to hurt the other medical doctor by making mischief out of what Dr. Jung had supposedly said against him. She was working for destruction, for what I would call a psychological death atmosphere.

Such a thing can begin on the simple level of the spoilsport. When people are having fun, somebody turns up with a sour face and tries to put a wet blanket on it; if one person has a nice present, the other makes a jealous remark, spoiling it. These are minor manifestations of something which tries to destroy the flame of life. Whenever psychic life, pleasure — in the highest sense of the word — being alive, that burning fire or spiritual elation comes up, there are always people who try to cut it with envy or criticism, and that is an aspect of real evil. If I notice this kind of demonic desire to destroy all psychological life, then I prick up my ears.

So, in a way, evil *is* a skeleton. It is that spirit of "no life and no love" which has always been associated with the essence of evil. It is destructiveness for its own sake, which everybody has in himself to some extent. But some people are completely possessed by it, as was this woman. This kind of death-devil is best simply starved to death. One hands back what the person is, what he or she does, one gives no life. One stretches out a skeleton hand to shake the skeleton hand, one gives no blood, nor warmth, nor life, and that makes the devil turn back to where he came from.

Before we go on I want to point out again that in dealing with evil in fairy tales and folklore material the ethical conflict is treated with a kind of natural wisdom rather than with religious awareness of the problem of good and evil. This is very different from the Judeo-Christian tradition which has worked for 2,000 years sharpening our conscience to a much more acute awareness of evil and trying to establish absolute rules of behavior. This, it seems to me, is quite all right when used as an instrument for the acquisition of higher consciousness and a more subtle conscience about the problem of good and evil. But if we apply it to other people, it produces the effect I tried to describe before; the evil gets more and more hooked into others, causing chain reactions of vengeance and punishment, heaping coals of fire on their heads and drilling into them that they ought to have a

173

bad conscience until they turn really wicked out of that repressed bad conscience. All those abominable effects have made us into the most restless and disagreeable crowd of people on the planet. In my opinion this is directly linked with higher morals which we use in a wrong way, namely on other people instead of purely on ourselves.

Nature wisdom has this disadvantage: if one uses it too much on oneself it creates a certain relativistic ethical attitude of calling white a bit black and black a bit gray, till finally everything is a kind of soup in which everything gets both lighter and more shadowy, and there is no moral problem! This naturally is not right and we cannot return to unconscious unawareness of sharp differences of behavior. But, as Dr. Jung wrote in *Aion*, before Christianity, evil was not quite as evil. The rise of Christianity added a kind of spirit of evil to the principle of evil which it did not have before. The sharpening or differentiation of ethical reactions into too clear-cut black and white lines is not favorable to life. So, after having dealt with fairy tales for many years, I think that it is probably better to treat evil outside oneself according to the nature wisdom rules of fairy tales, and to apply the sharpened conscience only to oneself.

I want now to tell you two stories which will lead us into the paradox of charity. Should one be charitable with evil or not? This is a modern question in the form of the problem of the death punishment which some countries still impose, or want to abolish. The modern version has its political and religious backgrounds, which we will not discuss, but we shall look at the problem from this simple folklore level. But first do you want to discuss the problem I am now leaving?

Question: I just want to ask whether dealing with oneself and not applying moral precepts to others connects at all the the Baba-Yaga's remark about the inside and the outside?

Yes, round the corner, twice round the corner it is connected, I would say, but not in a simple straight line. With the Baba-Yaga it is quite clear that with such unequal partners there could be no balance of power. It was not even wise for Wassilissa to carry outside the things from the Baba-Yaga's hut, poking about there and looking at the Baba-Yaga's shadow instead of at her own. Traditionally, that would be skipping the enormous difference between a deity and a human being, but on top of that there is a lack of religious respect for the Divine figure. The same thing occurs in "Answer to Job." Job insists on being right. God might have thought that Job thought he was wrong, and God does have that reaction and attacks Job about it, but Job does not say, "Ah yes, but I think you have fallen into your shadow!" That would be treating God as if he were sitting on a school bench with him. Job answers, "I will lay mine hand upon my mouth"; he makes a gesture of reverence. It is not man's task to rub God's nose into his shadow, so to speak. That would mean such an inflation and such absolute unawareness of psychic realities as they are that it would deserve immediate decapitation. Then Job says, "I know that I have an advocate * in Heaven," – I know that he who stands up for me is in Heaven, meaning God himself. (Ich aber weiss: mein Anwalt lebt, und ein Vertreter ersteht (mir) über dem Staube.) That would be equal to saying reverently, "This is between God and Himself." And then God turns, because Job does not throw it back at him or poke into it.

That is a very complicated and specific situation, but if we take the situation of two human beings, then, in a way, if you do *not* point out his darkness to the other you do not take away his chance of finding it himself. If you say that he, or she, has done this shadow thing, then you put yourself above the other. But if you say nothing, the other can go home and find out himself. If the feeling relationship is not well established and there is uncertainty and the other is afraid that you are too powerful for him, then very often it is better to leave it, because then the other has the honor of finding out and that stabilizes his prestige. So sometimes not to point out the shadow means respecting the integrity of the other person's personality. You respect that person as an ethical being, able to find it out for himself. As soon as you have a very good relationship you do not need such complications any more. Then you can say, "Ah, now there you were in the animus" and there is no prestige problem between you. Among friends you can say, "Oh come on, don't be such a damn fool" and the other doesn't experience that as a loss of prestige, for each respects the other.

So I would say it depends very much on the relationship. As long as the partner is in any way uncertain or in danger of losing his self-esteem,

* " 'Vindicator' is RSV alternative reading for 'Redeemer,' and comes very close to the Z.B. 'Anwalt' – 'advocate'." (Translator's Note on p. 369 of CW XI, "Answer to Job," *Psychology and Religion*.)

MEETING THE POWERS OF EVIL

it is better to leave it alone.

Remark: I think Job goes a little bit further because after the Lord has given him the list of his power: "Canst thou bind the unicorn..." etc., Job says, "I know you can do all that. Once I have spoken, but I will not answer, yea twice, but I will proceed no further." I think he sticks his neck out a little bit more.

I am not quite sure that you couldn't interpret it more simply and say, "Yes, I know you have all that power, and just because of that, because you are so much greater than I, it would be inadequate for a louse to tell the Universe that it is all wrong." As I understand it, it is not as happens often in ordinary life where we say, "Yes, Yes, I know," and between the lines it is clear by our expression that we think the other is wrong but don't say so.

Remark: That is what I think.

I have always understood it differently. I think Job was just respectful enough, he really took it that he was a louse who could not reproach God. That was a turn to humility, to really not feeling entitled to reproach God. But of course that is a different shade of understanding, it can be taken this way or the other. I couldn't prove my point.

Question: I want to refer to the conversation between Wassilissa and the Baba-Yaga when at the end the witch gave her the fiery skull. Was it because Wassilissa was tactful, or was it because the Baba-Yaga respected her mother's blessing?

No! She hated her mother's blessing! I will read you the extract. The Baba-Yaga says: "Now I am going to ask *you* a question! How did you manage to do all the work I gave you?" We know that the magic doll did it, but Wassilissa keeps her secret as well as the witch did hers and says, "My mother's blessing helped me." She doesn't tell the whole story, only half of it. She got her mother's blessing, plus the doll, and she mentions only the blessing.

Question: But she gives her a blessing too, doesn't she?

She gave her the skull. She threw Wassilissa out of the room and out of the gate and then took from the fence the skull with the flaming eyes, put it on a pole and give it to Wassilissa, saying, "This is the fire for your step-sisters, take it and carry it home." Wassilissa came originally to fetch fire, or the sisters ordered her to get it, so the witch gives the girl exactly what the stepsisters wanted. One could say that she is the function for trans-mitting evil to the evil sisters, but it doesn't look like revenge. They get what they wanted!

Remark: They wouldn't welcome the light, would they? Originally they wouldn't have it! So they got a different kind of light in the end, the kind of light they didn't like.

Yes, they got another light, the light they didn't like at all. If we put that into psychological language, they refused to become conscious and unrealized consciousness becomes a burning fire, coals of fire on their heads!

That is why, according to Dr. Jung, not becoming conscious when one has the possibility of doing so is the worst sin. If there is no germ of pos-sible consciousness within, if God made you unconscious and you just stay that way, then it doesn't matter; but if one does not live up to an inner possibility, then this inner possibility becomes destructive. That's why Dr. Jung also says that in a similar way one of the most wicked des-tructive forces, psychologically speaking, is unused creative power. That is another aspect. If somebody has a creative gift and out of laziness, or for some other reason, doesn't use it, that psychic energy turns into sheer poison. That's why we often diagnose neuroses and psychotic diseases as not-lived higher possibilities.

A neurosis is often a plus, not a minus, but an unlived plus, a higher possibility of becoming more conscious, or becoming more creative, funked for some lousy excuse. The refusal of a higher development or a higher consciousness is, in our experience, one of the most destructive things there is. Among other things, it makes people automatically want to pull back everybody else who tries. Someone who has unlived creativeness tries to destroy other people's creativity and somebody who has an unlived possi-bility of consciousness always tries to blur or make uncertain anybody else's efforts towards consciousness. That's why Dr. Jung says that if a patient outgrows his analyst, which happens frequently, he has to leave

177

the analyst because the latter will probably try to pull the patient back onto the old level.

The desire to prevent other people from becoming conscious because one does not want to wake up oneself is real destructiveness. I saw this in the mother of a friend of mine. She ate up my friend and her brother absolutely naively, she was a devouring mother who had never heard of psychology. She was a big, fat, friendly, genial extravert who spoiled her children to death, always poking into their affairs and never leaving them alone. She arranged everything for them till they were absolutely dead. They couldn't move a finger without her benevolent interference. She destroyed both of them without the slightest bad conscience. She was blissfully happy. The only thing which worried her was that her daughter didn't get married and her son was constantly ill and visibly neurotic, but she thought that was just a strange fate. She had done everything she could for her children but they had this horrible fate, which made both her children unhappy. I wondered why she hadn't a bad conscience and asked Dr. Jung about it. He said that that could happen, but let her once have a pamphlet on psychology and read about mothers having to do with such developments in their children and after that she wouldn't be able to do it happily any longer. That happened! I didn't play that trick, because I don't interfere with other people's lives, but another benevolent person interfered and got that mother to read some psychology. After that she became more destructive, because she wouldn't give up eating her children, but from then on she did it with a bad conscience as well.

So you see, having the possibility of becoming conscious and not taking it is about the worst thing possible. You are quite right about this business with the light. The stepsisters did not want the right light, but put it out. They wanted the devilish light and got it quite rightly! There are subtleties in fairy tales which one doesn't expect.

CHAPTER IV

HOT AND COLD EVIL

We discussed the Russian fairy tale in which the girl asked three questions and, though the Baba-Yaga tempted her to ask more, she avoided asking the fourth question which alluded to the dark secret of the witch. This contrasts with other fairy tales where entrance into the forbidden chamber, or asking the forbidden question, finally leads to a higher development of consciousness. Here the actual moral of the story is to let sleeping dogs lie; not to penetrate into the mystery of iniquity unless there is an urgent reason for doing so.

This seems to be related to another set of stories with the motif of the "getting angry" contest, which usually is found in Nordic and German fairy tales. I have not come across this motif in many other countries, but I think it describes a feature which might be of general importance, so I will tell you an actual version of this type called "Getting Angry."

There was once a peasant and his wife who were very rich and very stingy. They had not even a child — they were too stingy for that! As this stingy peasant grudged paying a servant his wages, he went to a poor brother and said he should let one of his three sons come and work at the farm. The arrangement should be that whichever got angry first would have to pay the bill, irrespective of whether master or servant. If the master got angry first, the other would get the farm and could even cut off the master's ears and have all his money; if the servant got angry first his ears would be cut off and he wouldn't get any wages. "This is only," the peasant said, "because I want to live in peace and friendship and not have any quarrel with you," but in his heart he knew it was a trick not to pay any wages.

The eldest son, Hans, went first. He got practically nothing to eat and had great difficulty in not getting annoyed. When the year was up the peasant thought he would find a way to cheat him out of his wages. He told the boy to drive the cows out to the meadow and that his wife would bring him his dinner. Hans did so but the dinner never came. The peasant

thought that way Hans would come to the house in a rage.
But when dinner time went by, and the boy was very hungry,
he called to a butcher, sold him the cows and stuck their
tails in a nearby moor. Then he fetched the farmer and said,
"Come quickly, the cows have sunk in the mud." The man
came and pulled up a tail and fell backwards! He did the
same with the other tails, but he made no comment, for
when he saw that Hans had sold the cows, he was more
friendly than ever to him, knowing that he would lose his
farm too if he got angry.

The two then went home together and the farmer's wife
gave her husband his supper, but gave nothing to Hans, who
by that time was so hungry that he couldn't contain himself.
He raged at the farmer, who cut off his ears.

So Hans went home with the money he had from selling
the cows, but without any wages. The next day the second
brother went. When his year was nearly up the farmer, wanting to cheat him too, told the boy to take the horse and cart
into the forest to fetch wood and that he himself would
bring him his dinner. But the same thing happened; the dinner was not brought, and the boy sold the horse and cart to
a passer-by, telling his uncle that a lion had eaten them up.
The farmer pretended to believe it, but when it came to
supper time and the farmer's wife gave the boy nothing to
eat, he was starving and tried to take the bowl from the
farmer, who cut off his ears.

The next day the third brother came, a very simple-
minded fellow. His brothers were sorry that he should
starve, so they brought him food every day wherever he was.
The rich farmer was astonished that, in spite of the miserable
food he gave him, the boy was always friendly, and he became suspicious. So he told his wife to dress herself up as a
cuckoo and go into the wood and call out "Cuckoo" three
times, and the boy would think that his year was up. And
to the boy he said, "When the cuckoo has called three times
you will know that your year is up, because you came with
the cuckoo." The boy was delighted for he did not have it
in mind to play tricks like his brothers, but simply wanted
to take home his wages. He begged the farmer to lend him
his gun, so that, out of pure happiness, he could let off a
shot. The mean farmer was quite ready to do this because
he knew that in the gun there was an old cartridge which

180

would probably explode.

So one day the stingy farmer's wife rolled herself first in some syrup and then in feathers, and when the boy went into the wood to work she climbed a tree and called, "Cuckoo!" But she had hardly called once, before the boy seized the gun and shot at the supposed bird, killing the woman by mistake. The peasant, who had hidden nearby, came out and raged and stormed at the boy, who said, "Uncle, are you angry? " The farmer answered that in such a situation even the devil would be angry, so the boy got the house and farm and was even allowed to cut off the farmer's ears.

There are other variations of this story where the participants tease each other almost to madness. Naturally, it is generally the evil-doer who invented the trick who loses in the end. This may seem to be a naive and primitive story, but we should remember that the people of that time had not yet learned to control their emotions. To do so would mean a tremendous cultural achievement. As a matter of fact we need not boast about having reached that level ourselves. The one who can control his emotions is the more conscious personality of the two, but we must look a bit deeper, for in other stories there is, so to speak, a "cold" kind of evil and a "hot" kind of evil. The hot evil is carried, no matter whether by demons or by ' human beings, by an unquenched emotional affect underneath, like a suffocated fire burning and smouldering all the time, and this kind of repressed affect is highly infectious. It can be seen in cases of explosions or destructiveness in families or nations, or in other social situations.

The infectiousness of affect, or emotion, is a great danger and is responsible for a tremendous amount of evil. If, for instance, you tried to discuss the race problem with an American before the last election, you could go far before you met somebody who could treat it with an absolutely objective attitude. Most people got emotional. As soon as somebody gets emotional, it does not matter which side that person takes, the fire has taken hold and the situation is dangerous. That is a recent example, but there are such examples everywhere. Emotion gets the person from underneath. The affect gets him and objectiveness and the human attitude goes. The best way of knowing within oneself whether one has been caught is to see if one has kept one's sense of humor; if that has disappeared one can be sure that an emotional fire has caught one somewhere and then one is in danger of falling for the principle of evil.

The capacity for overcoming anger or affect is not just a primitive affair, for it is still a decisive factor in us. Many people in our society can control their anger outwardly, can keep their persona and cover up their emotions, but inwardly the thing still grinds at them, influencing their inward thought. That is only apparently overcoming affect. Most people can take this first step, but few can manage the second and can detach completely from a strong emotion. Emotion is so dangerous because of its tremendous infectiousness. If one loses one's sense of humor and gets into a snarling mood it is difficult for others to stay out of it. This seemingly funny little peasant contest of getting angry is a deep story and sheds light on a very essential aspect of the problem of evil.

We shall see that this seems to be even more important in the contest with the Devil himself. Later I will tell you a story where the hero has to fight with the Devil; the question is whether he can make him angry. If he can, the Devil has lost the game. So even with supernatural figures the same game has to be played, and the one who stays human wins against the one who is carried away by his unconscious nature.

Question: You spoke of this as being mainly applicable to Northern and Germanic countries. Isn't this a Wotan manifestation?

Oh yes. Wotan is a God of emotionality and uncontrolled rage, either bad or holy rage, or any kind of emotionality, so it is a specific and acute problem among the Germanic races which have this kind of aggressiveness. But other people might think about it as well, because non-Germanic people are also sometimes in the same kind of plight.

Though it seems to have no connection, the common denominator of this story and the last one is that one has to keep away and detach from darkness, retire from it. Our servant keeps away and avoids getting contaminated by the uncle's trick. The two elder brothers switch on to playing tricks on their uncle. They do not fight with their emotions, they see that they have to keep the weapon of hatred and emotion in their pockets but they still try to fight by playing tricks. One sells the cows and cuts off their tails, the other sells the horse and cart, so they do something actively evil on the intellectual level and only avoid the emotion. With that they have entered the fight, though with weapons different than those

182

decided upon. That, the story tells us, doesn't work either, for in the end they fall into affect all the same.

The youngest does not go in for any evil doing. Even the shot is a *Freudenschuss*, a shot of happiness, to express his pleasure and say, "Hurrah, Spring is here and now I can go home!" In a naive kind of way he keeps even, not only with his emotional personality, but also with his mind, as far as he has one — he does not seem to have much. He keeps uncontaminated by dark forces and because of this things work out by themselves.

The interesting thing is the symbolism of the rifle with which he shoots his uncle's wife. In shooting, explosives are used. Here there is a transformation of explosive rage. He uses in symbolic form the explosiveness of the old uncle, turning it against him in the form of his wife. As a finale the uncle then explodes actually, not only symbolically. In a symbolic gesture, a magic gesture, the boy uses the uncle's explosiveness against him without knowing what he is doing. He doesn't borrow the rifle with the intention of shooting his uncle's wife, it just happens that way.

When one is able to work out a problem on a symbolic level and with a pure intention, things often seem to occur in exactly this way. An example is the use of Dr. Jung's technique of active imagination for the purpose of overcoming overwhelming emotional affect. This technique is applicable in many situations, but one of the moments where active imagination is indicated is when people are overwhelmed by an emotion. It needn't be anger, it can as well be when in love in a possessed way, or not knowing how to keep one's head, or in any kind of emotion where the subject feels overwhelmed, too much subdued, helplessly unfree. We generally advise people in such a situation to personify and talk to their affects, to let the affect come up in some form and to try to deal with it as if it were an actual being. It is the only way, if you have suppressed an overwhelming emotion outwardly for personal reasons but cannot overcome it inwardly. People say, "Yes, I do behave, I don't let out my anger, I swallow it, but I can't get rid of it all the same, it bothers me day and night, I don't know what to do and I can't help thinking of it all the time." The only thing to do is to personify this impulse and try to have it out with it in active imagination.

This is, as it were, transforming the whole battle, taking it away from the naive onto a symbolic level. That is what unknowingly this young man did when he took his uncle's rifle. He took the whole problem onto a symbolic level, reacting or playing with it on that level and it had the strange, magical repercussion that the shot went back onto the uncle.

I am making a dangerous statement here, because if one has once experienced this phenomenon, the next time one does it, one has a sneaking feeling of being involved in black magic. The first time you are like this simple young man; you try honestly to overcome your own affect in active imagination, things turn out well for you, and the other person who has annoyed you gets it back through a synchronistic event. So you think that's marvellous, but the next time you fall into black magic and say, "Now I am going to overcome my affect and I hope the other will get it through that!" Then you are in it again! It becomes more and more difficult to keep one's purity of intention. That is why it is stressed that this young man had absolutely no evil intention in what he did; he had kept his original pure naiveté. If you do active imagination you must try to get yourself first into this attitude of doing it honestly and only for your own sake, to keep yourself out of evil, without looking at what is happening synchronistically outside. Otherwise it is simply the old mischief of black magic.

Question: What is the symbolism of the brother being simple-minded? Why did he have to be simple-minded in order to combat the situation?

That is what I tried to explain. Because of his simple-mindedness he had purity of intention. He didn't speculate, intellectually deciding that he would do this or that, as the others did who played a trick in order to have no affect but to annoy the other.

Question: By simple-minded do you rather mean single-minded?

No. This is rather the famous fairy tale motif of the Dummling, the simpleton, who appears in an infinite number of fairy tales. For instance, a king has three sons and the youngest is a fool whom everybody laughs at; but it is always this fool who becomes the hero in the story. Or there is a peasant who has three sons; two are all right, but the youngest only sits by the stove and scratches himself all day and finally he is the one who becomes the hero, marries the princess and becomes Czar.

184

So the simpleton is a general figure, not only in fairy tales, but a general mythological motif. He symbolizes the basic genuineness and integrity of the personality. If people have not in their innermost essence a genuineness, or a certain integrity, they are lost when meeting the problem of evil. They get caught. This integrity is more important than intelligence or self-control, or anything else. It is this genuineness of the servant which saves the situation.

Question: But it is the uncle who gives the nephew the gun, isn't it? The boy doesn't take it?

Yes, but the boy asks for it, saying that if the cuckoo calls and he is free and can go home, then he would like to have a *Freudenschuss*. The uncle gives him the gun because he thinks there is an old cartridge in it which might explode. An old cartridge in a rifle at that time would mean trouble. Nowadays weapons are better.

Question: So the old uncle is really at the bottom of the plot?

Yes. The simpleton wants the gun for naive, simple reasons, for fun. The uncle sneaks an evil plot into it and gets it turned back on himself.

Question: You spoke before of black magic. Doesn't the girl Wassilissa belong there? She had the black magic in her hands but she buried the skull to regain purity for future events.

Yes, that would correspond to the burying. She could just as well have said, "Ah, now I have something I can take about with me and if there is anybody I don't like, I'll turn the fiery skull onto him." But she gave up that power which had been given her by the Goddess.

Remark: In our present society, we would call that stupid!

In our present society — yes! To bury laser rays voluntarily would be stupid, we would say. But fairy tales decide differently, or the collective unconscious thinks differently in this respect.

Are you satisfied with the answer about the simpleton?

Question: I suppose the idea is to emphasize the guilelessness of his personality? Simple-minded seems stupid.

185

Yes, but you see evil people would call guilelessness stupidity! If you keep your integrity, from a certain social angle you look stupid and people accuse you of being stupid. In politics, if you are naive, that is the end of you! To be honest, and guileless and naive is idiocy!

Question: The story starts off with the idea that the uncle and his wife live for wrong reasons. They were the stupid ones at the beginning, weren't they?

Yes, exactly. In the beginning it is clear that they are the stupid ones because they are sterile. They are so ungenerous and sterile that they are already completely off the track, so it is they who are really stupid. But naturally, they think (I haven't given you the details of the conversation) that they are the clever ones. They think that with their trick they will get service for nothing, they can cut off the servants' ears and not pay them. They feel marvellously right, but with the youngest son the story turns. The youngest son is so innocent. He has a kind of innocent stupidity which begins to bewilder them. It is so candid that it makes them nervous. They feel this young man has a value which they do not understand; he lives without great ego demands and enjoys life. Even small pleasures mean a lot to him. So the uncle and his wife feel they are not up to this one. They have no empathy with his innocence, which makes them nervous. They want to get rid of him and they lose the battle because, being nervous, they are slightly frightened and do everything wrong. They begin to play tricks and lose the game.

Thus underneath this funny, simple story there is something exceedingly subtle. One might say that this kind of simple-minded, candid integrity is a great mystery and is already the secret of an individuated personality. The gift of guileless integrity is a divine spark in the human being. In analysis, I would say that it is the decisive factor as to whether an analysis goes right or wrong.

Question: It is the natural instinct?

It is very close to the natural instinct, yes. We shall come to that in a later story.

Question: I was wondering whether this whole question might not under-

186

lie the problem of the better integration of Jungian psychology? There is difficulty in maintaining, integrating and developing Jungian psychology in the United States without being caught up in a power attitude and emotional affect. Do we perhaps become more involved in affect in relating to Jungian psychology than interested in the inner integrity?

I think that difficulty is everywhere, not only in the United States. In my experience this candid attitude is exactly what Dr. Jung had and which you feel so much when you read his memoirs. Some of the reviewers of the book shook their heads, saying that the man was a big simpleton! How naive could he be, to publish such things? They have lost the feeling for this subtlety. Dr. Jung was not naive at all! But he had this innermost integrity. A person who approached him with honest integrity always got an answer of honest integrity, though Dr. Jung was wise enough to use integrity when he thought it appropriate and to hide this side of his personality when he was up against darkness.

I think this integrity of the nucleus of the personality is what we would call an aspect of the Self and it is the essence of Jungian psychology. You are quite right, we must not leave that on any account. As soon as we begin to make Jungian psychology more widespread by using tricks in fighting other schools, for instance, we have already lost our integrity. We are not behaving in accordance with the standards of Jungian psychology. That is difficult. People will always say, "Yes, but listen, if you don't do something against it, then they'll take all the power — we *must* do something." That is always the argument and if you walk into *that* trap you are lost! *Do* something! The others do something and therefore we must! We don't *want* to, but we *have* to!

Question: Doesn't this contradict what you said the other day, that sometimes you have to take action? You spoke of the time when you threw out your analysand.

Yes, exactly, it is a complete contradiction, but I did say at the beginning of my lecture that with all these questions I shall move in complete contradictions!

Remark: This sounds highly theological!

It is becoming "highly theological" because it is, as we say, a paradox!

187

The task is to decide each time with your own conscience which is meant *this* time. And for that one has one's own dreams. But general rules can only state a paradox, though in the actual individual situation there is no paradox. There is just *one* line: now I must act against all the rules of analysis; the next moment, I must not get contaminated. In the real situation it is something unique which has to be decided from one minute to another. If you take this attitude, life becomes a constant ethical adventure. That is why we are annoying to people who try to learn from us. We have no rules of behavior. We have no therapeutic rules, absolutely none.

Remark: The ears come in here. If people block their ears they can't hear!

Yes, they can't hear the grass grow! They can't hear the subtlety any more. One has to keep one's ears open and listen all the time to know that the innermost order of the Self at this minute is to do this, and the next moment not. But when moving in general commentaries I shall always contradict myself. With honest conviction!

Question: You were going to give a definition of "hot" evil and of "cold" evil.

We are soon coming to "cold" evil. We have had "hot" evil, but first I want to introduce another aspect, because "cold" evil will lead us to the next motif of magical contests, magic competition. I want to take that later because it is more complicated. Now I want to stay with more simple rules. Our next step will be the problem of charity. Should one be charitable towards evil or not? Should one, as it is said in the Bible, turn the other cheek, or should one hit back with all one's strength? Which is right? I am going to tell you two stories which seem to run parallel but are completely contradictory, so you can catch me once more!

This one is from the same volume: *German Fairy Tales Since Grimm*. It is written in the Southern dialect and is called, "Vun'n Mannl Sponnelang" ("About a Man a Span Long").

> There was once a poor girl who had lost father and mother
> and had no home. She did not know where to live so she set
> out to find a place as a servant. While walking in the woods
> she lost her way. Night came on and to her great joy, just

when darkness fell, she saw a tiny little house in the woods and she thought she might go there to find shelter. The whole house was in an awful mess and disorder so she started to tidy things up, washing the pans and putting up the towels, etc. Suddenly the door opened and a tiny little man came in, a dwarf with an immense beard. He looked round and cleared his throat and when he saw the girl sitting in the corner he said:

> I am the little man who is a span long,
> I have a beard three ells long!
> Girl, what do you want?

The girl asked if she could stay the night and the man answered her again in verse and told her to make his bed. She did that and then he told her to get a bath ready for him. She did that, too, and gave him a good bath and he became quite nice looking. She cut off some of his beard, and the little man thanked her very much, saying she had redeemed him and he would reward her. He gave her his beard and disappeared.

The next day the girl took the beard with her and started spinning with it. While she was spinning, it turned into pure gold. Naturally everybody wanted to have this golden yarn. So she became very rich and married and if she hasn't died she is still alive.

I shall not discuss this story by itself but together with its contrasting parallel, the Grimm fairy tale of "Snow White and Rose Red."

> There was a poor widow who lived alone in a hut. In the garden in front of the hut there were two rosetrees, one with pure white and the other with red roses. She had two girls who looked exactly like the rosetrees, and she called them Snow White and Rose Red. They were very pious and worked hard, as did their mother. Snow White was quieter and more gentle than Rose Red and Rose Red was more lively, but the two girls were so fond of each other that they always went out hand in hand. They often went to the woods and collected berries but were never harmed by any of the animals. Even the stag did not run from them, and the birds stayed on the branches and sang for them. Sometimes when night overtook them they slept on the moss until morning; their mother knew this and was not afraid for them. One morning when they woke up in the woods they saw a

beautiful child dressed in a white shining dress sitting beside them. It got up and looked at them in a friendly way and then disappeared. Their mother said that it must have been the angel who watched over good children.

One winter evening when they had finished their work and their mother was reading fairy tales to them, there was a knock at the door. Rose Red went to answer because they thought it might be a traveler who was looking for shelter, but instead the black head of a bear poked in. The children were frightened but their mother said to let him come in and warm himself by the fire. The children brushed the snow off his coat and they soon dared to put their feet on his back and shake him to and fro, or to hit him. The bear was good-natured, but when it got too bad he would say, "Don't kill me, children!" and added, "Snow White and Rose Red, don't kill your suitor!"

They kept him at the hut, and it became the custom all through the winter for the bear to go off in the daytime and come back at night. When the Spring came he said Goodbye to them, explaining that he could not come any more because now was his troublesome time when he had to protect his treasures from an evil dwarf who tried to steal them. He said that in the winter when the ground was frozen the dwarfs had to stay underground and could not do any mischief, but as soon as the sun had thawed the ground, then the dwarfs came up to hunt and steal, and he had to protect his treasures.

One day in the Spring the girls went out into the forest. Suddenly they saw a tiny creature hopping about in a funny way. When they came up to it they found a dwarf whose beard was caught in a cleft in the wood. He had tried to cut the wood and his beard had gotten into the cleft which had closed again. Now he was jumping about like a little dog and didn't know what to do. He stared at the girls furiously with his red, fiery eyes and he asked them what they were standing there for. Couldn't they do something to free him? The children did their best but could not find any way of freeing his beard. Rose Red said she would run and get help but he only called her a sheep's head, so Snow White fetched some scissors and cut off the end of his beard. Instead of being grateful, the dwarf was angry and scolded them for having cut off his beautiful beard.

A little later the two girls found the same dwarf, who, while trying to catch a fish, got his beard caught up in the fishing

line. At the same time a big fish bit. The dwarf was not strong
enough to pull against it and was in danger of being pulled in
himself. The girls hung onto him and tried to get the beard free
but couldn't, for beard and line were all tangled up together.
There was nothing to be done but to cut off the beard. But the
dwarf got quite wild and said that now they had cut away the
best part. (I forgot — I should have said at the beginning that
in their home they had a little white lamb and a white dove.
That belongs to the atmosphere!)

A third time, when they were again walking in the woods,
they heard cries for help. They saw a big eagle who had caught
the dwarf and was just about to fly off with him. The children
hung onto the dwarf, finally succeeding in getting him away
from the eagle. But he scolded them furiously for not being
more careful, saying that they had torn his coat to rags and
now it was full of holes, stupid creatures that you are!

Then, as they were going home, they surprised the dwarf.
He had not expected anybody to be about so late and had
found a clean place on which to shake out his sack full of precious stones, and the evening sun shone on the glittering stones
in all different colors. The children stood there looking at
them. And the dwarf shrieked at them, his gray face becoming quite scarlet with rage. But just as he was going away
the bear came out of the wood, growling. The dwarf jumped
up but couldn't get to his hiding place. He begged the bear
to spare his life and said he would give him all his treasures.
"You won't notice me between your teeth," he said, "but
take those two Godless girls, they will be a tender morsel
for you!" The bear paid no attention to what he said but
gave him a whack with his paw and the dwarf never moved
again.

The girls had run away, but the bear called after them,
"Snow White and Rose Red don't be afraid, wait, I want to
go with you." They recognized his voice and turned round,
and as the bear reached them his bearskin fell off and there
stood a beautiful man dressed all in gold, who said, "I am a
king's son and have been cursed by this impious dwarf who
stole all my treasures. I was to run wild in the woods as a
bear until I was redeemed by the dwarf's death. Now he has
received his well-deserved punishment."

So Snow White married the bear and Rose Red married his
brother (who apparently turned up out of the blue) and be-

191

tween them they divided the treasures which the dwarf had collected in his cave. The old mother lived many years happily with
the children and they took the two rosetrees with them. They
stood in front of the window and bore the most beautiful red
and white flowers each year.

This is a silly, sentimental fairy tale, but it is a nice contradiction for
the other story. In the one there is the girl who with simple-minded integrity tidies up the dwarf's house and is charitable to him. The golden beard
is the treasure she is rewarded with for having bathed the dwarf and cleaned his
home. In the other story it is just the opposite: the girls are always charitable to the dwarf and thereby prolong the life of the evil-doer who should
have been eliminated long ago. They also prevented their suitors, the bear
and his brother, from coming and marrying them, so they prevented the
possibility of their own marriage by being wrongly and sentimentally charitable to this dwarf.

So we are again up against a paradox! But if you look at the whole atmosphere and the description around the motif, there are indications to
show which is which.

In "Snow White and Rose Red," the women live together with no man
around, only a little white lamb and a white dove. There is an infantile,
sentimental paradisiacal atmosphere, an innocence which is not the integrity of the simpleton but a kind of unreal paradise, a kindergarten, a de-
lusional world with protecting angels and what not.

This story makes fun of a certain Christian, kindergarten attitude which
is still widespread among people who mix up the kindergarten motif of
having a certain candid integrity of the personality. Dr. Jung always stressed
that Christ did not say, "If you remain children you will find the Kingdom
of Heaven" but, "Except ye *become* as little children." Becoming children
again means not to stay in the kindergarten, but to outgrow it and become
adult, aware of the problem of evil in the world; to re-acquire one's inner
integrity or find the way back to this nucleus or innermost integrity, but
not to stay like a big baby in the woods and think that this is it. Sometimes the difference is very subtle. It is sometimes even mixed up in people.
There are some who have an incredible naiveté. One wonders whether it
means a higher integrity or is just a hopeless kindergarten attitude, a baby
in the woods walking about with damn-fool sentimentality. In the fairy

tales it is clearly differentiated, but in reality the two are sometimes one millimeter apart. It can be very difficult to know which is which within a person, and also within oneself. But in this story the lamb and the dove clearly point to a kind of Christian infantilism of the worst kind.

Remark: But they were kind to the bear!

Yes, that was all right.

Remark: But it wasn't all right to be kind to the dwarf?

I think that's the essence of the story. It's all right to be kind, but only with the right people or with the right object. This kind of Christian innocence and kindness and charity is quite all right if you know where to apply it. If it is combined with the capacity for discernment and understanding, then there is nothing wrong about it, but it must be coupled with a certain amount of wisdom.

Remark: Probably what they should have done was to stop helping him after the first time when they saw that the dwarf was angry and impossible.

Yes. People who have a more instinctual reaction would say, "The next time he is in trouble I'll leave him alone." They would pass by and say, "Goodbye, I am not going to cut off your beard and be shouted at again!" But these two didn't learn. They were obstinate, keeping to what Mama said.

Question: What can one say about the dwarf? He has not a common character throughout fairy tales, has he? He is not always the same. Is the dwarf in the first story...

A different one from the dwarf in the second story? Yes, well, No — Yes and No!

Question: In a fairy tale the dwarf does not necessarily stand for good or evil, does he?

Well, dwarfs are nature spirits, impulses of pure nature. They are partly good and partly evil in comparative mythology. Here is an evil dwarf and in "Rumpelstilskin," for instance, there is an evil dwarf, an evil-doer. Generally I would say that eighty percent of the dwarfs are good. They do your work in the night and give you treasures. I'd say that they are eighty-five percent good and sometimes really witty. So the figure of the dwarf in itself doesn't say anything, it's neutral. The girls couldn't have concluded from the fact that it was a dwarf whether it was a good or bad creature. It's not that simple. But as you said, they should have tested him and drawn their conclusions from that.

Remark: But the mother had the right idea when she let the bear in!

Yes, the mother knew that the bear wouldn't behave badly and that he should be let in charitably, but she was not mixed up with the dwarf. We don't know what she would have said there. She is too vague a figure for us to know whether she would have said, "No children, leave that dwarf alone," or if she would have had a rigid principle.

There is another interesting scene in the beginning. For a long time they were protected by a guardian angel. There is a widespread folk belief that children are specially protected by a guardian angel. If a child upsets a pan of hot water, or does any of the silly things which children do, and escapes, then people say, "Oh well, it has a guardian angel!" In Bavaria it is said of people who are always lucky that they have a guardian angel like a prize boxer! In life this is true. One has only to see what children do: they take scissors and poke at their own eyes, they walk down the stairs with an open knife, they seize the hot water pan. It's a miracle how comparatively few get killed, so you could say that children have a guardian angel. But in general that guardian angel motif has to do with the unconscious of the parents! If the marriage of the parents and the atmosphere at home is harmonious, and the unconscious atmosphere is full of life, then the instinctual vitality of the child somehow lets it escape. If the marriage of the parents is disharmonious, if the atmosphere at home is bad, then father and mother can cluck and fuss from morning to night and pay a governess to watch the child, and in spite of that it will manage to fall out of the window and kill itself.

That is what we observe with our disagreeable faculty of being able to see behind the scenes; it is more important for children to have a harmonious life at home than to have someone to take them across the road every time and watch them all day long. In a child there is a tremendous natural urge towards life and a great connectedness with the life instinct. If the

194

basis is healthy, that life instinct will save the child. On the other hand, if the atmosphere is unhealthy and morbid, then the child will be undermined. Having the usual childhood accidents all children have, it will have them in a bad way.

Question: In the story, I wonder if they would have found the treasure if they had left the dwarf in that fishing line when they came across him the second time?

Yes, you are right, they might have not seen him spreading his treasures. Perhaps one has to make those mistakes in order to get deeper into trouble and through that, out of it. There are fairy tales in which such mistakes are made where it is clear that but for the mistake there would not have been the good outcome. But here you could imagine that if he had been left alone after a while they might have seen him spreading his treasures. So here at least *expressis verbis* that is not said. In other stories it is sometimes like that, so I am not sure here. But I think they are just silly sentimentalists.

Question: Something you said earlier mystifies me. You spoke of hiding your integrity when up against darkness and I don't follow what you mean.

I will try to give you an example. I said that if one is up against evil people one should hide one's inner integrity, or that innocent nucleus of the personality, and not display it like a fool. I could go back to something I said last time. I told you of the case where Dr. Jung said that one should give a certain amount of concern and libido and participation only to the patient who does not make an evil use of it; otherwise one feeds the evil instead of the good side of the person. He induced me to kick out the person who always, when I did anything charitable for her, got worse. He had the idea that this would be therapeutically good for her, but he did not tell me that. Afterwards, when I told him that she had been cured by being kicked out of the analysis, he grinned and said, "That's what I expected would happen. I hoped so, but I didn't say so!" He had kept it completely to himself. He had not even shown it to me, even less to the patient.

That woman was completely possessed by the animus. If she had guessed that she had been kicked out in order to be helped, she would have started arguing, "You kick me out in order to help me, but I know that won't help me. I know that that is how you will kill, not help me!" Or she would have made a theatrical display of getting worse to prove that having been kicked out did not help her. So the intention of helping that person had to be completely hidden, it had to hit her animus with a blow – and Adieu! She had to experience it like that, even to the extent of being treated just as the bear did to the dwarf. There was no charity and no argument!

I think it would be worth while to go a bit deeper into this motif of hiding one's integrity. Dr. Danelius mentioned that to remain a civilian when on military service can sometimes get you into that kind of situation. I would say that to remain the one who has a different personal idea of things within a strongly collective organization is always close to that problem, because collectivity, according to our ideas, is always ethically on a lower level than an individual can be. That's why Dr. Jung always quoted the Roman proverb: *"Senator bonus vir, Senatus bestia!"* (One Senator is a good man, but the Senate is a beast.) One could say that whenever one is in a group one has to hide one's best nucleus, or very rarely let it come out. One has to draw a veil over a part of one's personality because of the automatic lowering of the ethical level.

This is again one of those paradoxes, for sometimes, but very rarely, it is just the other way round. In ninety-five percent of the situations one must hide one's inner nucleus of integrity when in a group, but I might mention the exception so that whenever you meet it you may know what it would be.

I remember once a small party at Dr. Jung's house where something occurred which you might have experienced sometime. There was a kind of perfect collective harmony, not a lowering or falling down into a *participation mystique,* but something which gave one the feeling of a magic presence. The old Romans or Greeks would have said that the God, Hermes or Dionysus, was there, and the early Christians would have said that the Holy Ghost was present then. There is sometimes a kind of super-personal harmony which makes everything which happens numinous. One goes home feeling that was an unforgettable evening. This happens very rarely and I was so impressed on that occasion that I talked to Dr. Jung about it. He said, "Yes, normally, it is when one is alone that one meets the Self, but there is an exception sometimes when the Self can manifest as a collective factor, generally only in a small group of friends, and then it is a specially numinous experience. It is even experienced as something more numinous than when you experience it alone."

This underlies symbolism such as the Round Table of the Knights of King Arthur, the small group of people united in the spirit, so to speak. It points to a group experience of the Self, which is a higher form of the old archetypal pattern of the totemic meal of the primitive, where all participate in integrating the one God. It also underlies the idea of the Eucharistic meal. Whenever you are in a group you have to hide your innermost integrity or the kernel of your ethical personality with the exception of such an event which might happen once or twice in a lifetime, where one feels one is "in oneness" with the surrounding people. This is easily confused with a drunken *participation mystique,* which has nothing to do with it, but is just slipping down onto the lower level — also an agreeable experience, but not the same thing. That generally leaves you with a hang-over the next morning, while the other has an opposite effect.

Hiding one's inner integrity can be a self-protective gesture. Nothing irritates evil emotions in a gathering more than if one plays the superior saint or something like that. So if you feel different you have to hide it completely, not to give motivation to others to say, "What, d'you want to be better than we are? " There is also a deeper reason. You might say this inner ethical integrity comes not from the ego, but from the Self. It is a genuine reaction which comes from the depth of the personality. Therefore it can never be consciously planned or applied, because that would mean being in the ego. The deepest penetration I know into that problem is to be found in Zen Buddhism, where the Zen Master often displays absolutely irrational genuine reactions towards the pupil. One feels that it is not planned. There is no kind of pedagogic plan and intention. The genuineness of their personality simply acts at the moment upon the pupil and awakens him through this manifestation. Planning or thinking ahead would weaken this effect or prevent it. If we translate that into our language it means that one has to dim one's conscious light and not concentrate with the ego too much so that this more genuine situation can come through.

When Dr. Jung was old he didn't give many analytical hours, and when

197

his pupils or other people saw him they naturally did not talk about their own problems and dreams. It happened to me often that I had some problem I was battling with by myself, which I didn't mention, and in the first five minutes Dr. Jung would start to talk about just that problem, giving all the answers or hints I needed! Afterwards I often asked him how it happened that he started to talk of that particular thing. Generally he said he had no idea, but when he sat down it had come into his mind. It was just the thing I needed!

I remember one such incident. I madly wanted something in my own life, but was too shy to stretch out my hand and get it. I visited Dr. Jung just when he was feeding the ducks and there was a little shy duck which came close and wanted some bread but was always frightened of the other ducks so went away again. Dr. Jung saw this poor thing and threw a piece of bread at it, but it swam away nervously, and then went back, but it was too late. That happened two or three times and then Dr. Jung turned round and said, "Oh well, silly damn fool, then you can just starve if you haven't the courage to take it!" That was my answer! I at once related it to my situation. Afterwards I asked Dr. Jung if he had said that on purpose. He said he had only thought of the duck; he had no idea that it coincided with my inner question:

That happened constantly. Easterners would call that being in Tao. If you are in Tao, that is, if you are in harmony with the deeper layers of your personality, with your totality in the Self, then it acts through you in this way. But for that you mustn't have ego intention. If you *intend* to do the right thing, want to help other people and so on, then with your ego you block this effect. You put yourself between the natural possibility. That's why Dr. Jung went so far as to say that an analyst who has the wish and intention of curing his patients is no good. Even that one mustn't have, for to want to cure one's patients is a power attitude: "I want to be the analyst who cures that case!"

In another connection, but a similar thing, Jung often doubted whether women could be good analysts because with their maternal, clucking feeling, they tended to prevent the patient from getting into his inner hell. It is only when the patient can get into his innermost hell with no outer help that he can have a numinous experience; only then does something come from within which helps him. But if you cluck and prevent the thing all the

198

time with motherly charity, you also prevent the other from coming into
his innermost positive experience and that — to get back to our fairy story
— is that Snow White and Rose Red false charity: to be always charitable,
to prevent evil, to do the right thing, to do the good thing and thereby prevent the deeper course of nature.

I am sure that if the bear had consulted the girls as to whether he should
kill the dwarf they would have said, "Oh no, the poor dwarf, don't kill him
now! Give him another chance!" Thank God he didn't consult them but
silently whacked him down. After the event there was nothing to be said!
That was also, so to speak, an action of the Self. Pure nature took its
course in the right way, with no human intervention; there was no planning
but just the thing which happened. That leads one close to a dangerous
borderline, because as soon as ego reflection acquires such a style it goes
wrong. That's why one has to notice such a thing and then turn away and
not reflect. Reflection is destructive here because it is an ethical problem;
that means it is a feeling experience where the intellect has no say. That
I lecture on this problem is another paradox or contradiction, because one
cannot really lecture on it. With the mind one cannot comment on it, or
can do so only if feeling remains in its own realm.

*Remark: I would like to say that the dwarf who gets entangled represents
to me an aspect of the animus that many of us know.*

Yes, certainly!

*Remark: One gets really snarled up and cannot possibly get out, one be-
comes more and more exasperated and bad tempered, and then also I
think we are aware of keeping him going!*

Yes, women have that kind of charity to their own inner bad animus.
It is a weakness of the ego personality which cannot say, "Now this is all
nonsense, I am not going to listen to all that nonsense in myself." Instead
of that one thinks, "Well, perhaps it is very important, perhaps I should
write it down and tell my analyst about it next time" and then one gets
entangled more and more. That's why, when you analyze such people and
they come in that kind of mood, you don't know what to do, because if
you go near them the line and the hook and the beard entangle you too!

199

Remark: But it isn't only confined to women!

Well, in men it's slightly different. In women there is this argumentative nuance — "Yes, but...." No matter what you say to them, there comes, "Yes, but didn't you say last time...? " So you get entangled in the line.

Remark: Haven't you seen that in men too?

Well, men also say, "Yes, but....", but it's more like a depressive mood which secondarily gets their mind into expressing itself that way.

I remember an analysand who came to me, saying, "Ah well, now life is over for me, I'm getting old and I'm not going to do anything any more, and I'm getting tired. I don't like my job, but I'm too old and tired to change it, and...." You know — deep melancholy!

"Did you have any dreams? "

"No, I had no dreams, except just a little fragment, but I know that's very negative."

The little fragment was that a voice ordered him to go into the woods and light a fire there. But then he didn't take any matches with him. He went home and got matches, but when he was back at the fire he discovered that he had a matchbox with only one match in it. Then he lit the fire and it began to smoulder and he wondered whether he should blow it or not and he gave a little puff — and it went out! And the voice said, "That's what the spirit does!"

This is a catastrophic dream. He didn't react normally by getting a terrible fright and saying, "Gosh, this is awful! I'm in real danger that the spirit may die. I must go home and next time take a matchbox and a lot of newspaper and make a decent fire!" For after all, making a fire in the woods — it wasn't even raining — even for a tired old man isn't such an impossible task! He just said, "Well, you see the unconscious says this too, this is the end, it says there is no more spirituality in me, so why should I try? "

I can't tell you all I said! I cursed and got absolutely wild, and he watched me in a sad, detached sort of mood, and then he said, "You see, *I* must be objective! *I* must allow for the other interpretation!" Then he walked out.

So it's the same thing — the wrong kind of argument — but it's based on a mood. I saw it in his babyish, sulky mouth when he came in. The argument is similar to that of the animus, but the underlying thing is the mood, the depressive anima mood which inspired him to say that he had to be objective — the male objective logos! It is only to justify a whining anima mood, but that's the form it takes in men.

Question: But the nature of the dwarf and his impatience...?

Yes, that impatience is typically animus.

Remark: But I have also seen it once or twice in men, and that must be from the animus of the mother.

Perhaps that plays a role sometimes, but impatience in men is generally a shadow reaction. One sees it in them often when they are intuitive. They just can't wait for things to come along. But getting entangled with the figure is general in men and women, anima and animus; getting into a regular tangle and not being able to snap out of it. One has to switch the situation somehow, either do it oneself, if one can, or the other person must do it for one.

On a minor scale it is the same thing when an analysand slips down into a psychotic episode. Then, as Dr. Jung says in his paper on the transcendent function, one can still sometimes break the catastrophe by making a switch in the outer situation, making the person suddenly change his job, or throwing him or her out of the analysis, or making a change in the therapist, or something like that, a powerful switch of the whole situation, so that they can snap out of it. It's like a stone beginning to roll down a mountain. If you don't interrupt the movement it becomes worse and worse, like an avalanche when a little snow starts rolling. If you can stop that then you can prevent a destructive emotion. The same thing applies with non-psychotic people, or those who get too much possessed by animus and anima.

I know a family where there were several brothers and one sister who, like all women, indulged in getting into the animus. The brothers knew nothing about psychology but they recognized this thing with their feeling, so whenever their sister got into the animus they would say, "Oh come, snap out of it!" It became a family habit to tell her to snap out of it. Without Jungian psychology they had realized that when females begin to argue in a certain way one must turn the wheel of the car right round and drive in another direction. Arguing, or entering into it is hopeless for the others as well as for the woman, for she *has* to argue on. The only thing to do is to cut or interrupt, which requires a certain ego strength and instinctiveness.

Now back to the problem of charity, but on a deeper level: I want to tell you a Nordic fairy tale, a Scandinavian story entitled "The Giant Who Didn't Have His Heart With Him." (*Nordische Volksmärchen*, II. Teil, Norwegen, p. 119.) This is our first example of "cold" evil.

There was once a king who had seven sons. He loved them so much that he never wanted to part with them all at the same time. So when they were grown up he sent six of them out to find wives for themselves, but he kept the youngest with him. He told the six others that they should bring a bride for the youngest. He gave his six sons the most beautiful clothes and each got a very valuable horse and a lot of money before they went out. They went to many courts and looked at many princesses and finally they came to a king who had six daughters. They had never seen six such beautiful princesses. So each took one and completely forgot that they were to bring a seventh bride for their brother, because they were so in love with their own brides.

When they had gone a good piece of the way home they came to a rock where giants lived. One of the giants came out and, by just looking at them, transformed them all into stone, princes and princesses both. At home the king waited and waited for his six sons but they never appeared. He became very sad and thought he would never be happy again. "If I didn't have you," he said to the youngest, "I would commit suicide, for I am so sad at having lost your brothers!" "Oh," said the youngest son, "I had thought of asking permission to go out and find them!" "No, on no account, I don't want to lose you, too," said the king. But the boy begged for so long that the king had to finally give in and let him go. He only had a sick old horse and no money, so the youngest boy had to take that. The boy didn't mind, but jumped on the horse and said goodbye to his father, saying he would certainly return and bring the six other brothers with him.

After a time he met a raven who couldn't move. He could only flap his wings, he was so starved. He asked for food and the king's son said he hadn't much food himself, but could certainly give the raven some and he gave him some of his provision.

202

A little later he came to the bed of a stream. Lying on the dry mud was a big salmon who couldn't manage to get back into the water. The son pushed the fish back into the water. Both raven and salmon promised to help him in return and to both he said that he didn't suppose the help could amount to very much. Then, after a long, long ride, he came to a wolf who lay in the middle of the road and begged to be allowed to eat the horse, for he was dreadfully hungry, not having eaten anything for two years. The prince answered that he was very sorry, but that first he had met a raven to whom he had to give food, and then a salmon, which he had to help back into the water, and now, he said, you want to eat my horse! But the wolf insisted and promised to help him later, saying the king's son could ride on him. The prince said he didn't think the wolf could help him very much, but he could have the horse.

After the wolf ate the horse the prince put the harness onto the wolf and he had become so strong that he could carry the prince with great speed.

The wolf said he would show him the giant's court. He took him there and showed him his six brothers and their princesses all turned into stone, and the door by which the prince must enter. But the prince said he wouldn't dare do that, the giant would kill him. "Oh no," said the wolf, "when you go in you will find a beautiful princess. She will tell you what to do to conquer the giant, just do what she says." So the prince went in, though he was afraid. Just then the giant was out, but in one of the rooms a princess sat, and she said, "God help you, how did you get in here? The giant will kill you, and nobody can kill him because his heart is not with him." "Yes," said the prince, "but now that I am here I will try to save my brothers." "All right," said the princess, "we will see what we can do. Now you must hide under the bed and listen carefully to what the giant says, but you must keep very still."

So the prince slipped under the bed and was scarcely there before the giant came back. He said, "Oh, it smells of Christians here!" "Yes," said the princess, "a raven flew by and dropped a human bone down the chimney and that's what the smell comes from." When the evening came and they went to bed the princess said that there was something she had wanted to ask him for a long time but hadn't the courage. "What's that?" "I would like to know where your heart is?" "Oh you don't need to bother about that yet, but it's lying

203

under the threshold of the door." "Oh," thought the prince under the bed, "so that's where it is!"

Next morning the giant went out early and the two rushed to look for the heart. But no matter how much they dug there was no heart. "This time he has cheated us," said the princess, "but let's wait." And she picked a lot of the most beautiful flowers she could find and strewed them over the threshold. When the giant returned there was the same thing again, for he said it smelled of human flesh and the princess made the same excuse about the bird. But after a time he asked who had strewn the flowers over the threshold. "Oh," said the princess, "I am so fond of you that I had to do it, because your heart was lying there." "Oh is that it," said the giant, "but it isn't there!"

When they went to bed she again asked him where his heart was. She loved him so much, she said, she must know. "Oh," he said, "it's in the cupboard there at the wall."

So the two went through the same thing again. But the heart wasn't there, and again they put flowers and wreaths there. A third time the giant said it smelled of humans and the princess made the same excuse about the bird and told why she decorated the cupboard. And the giant asked her if she was really stupid enough to believe that his heart was there; it was somewhere she could never get to. It was far away in an island on which there was a church which had a well in it on which a duck swam, inside which there was an egg, in which was his heart.

Next morning the giant went out early and the prince went to the wolf, having said goodbye to the princess. He told the wolf that he had to go for the heart. The wolf took him on his back and when they reached the sea the wolf swam across with the prince on his back. And they reached the island and the church. But the key was hanging up so high on the tower that they couldn't reach it. They called for the raven who got the key, and they went into the church where there was the well on which the duck was swimming, as the giant had said. They enticed the duck out and caught hold of it, but in the moment when the prince took it out of the water it dropped an egg in the well. Then the prince didn't know what to do. But the wolf said to call for the salmon, and the salmon fetched the egg from the bottom of the well. "Now," said the wolf, "you must squeeze the egg a little."

And when he did that the giant cried out. "Press again," said the wolf, and when the prince did it the giant groaned much louder and begged for his life, saying he would do whatever the prince wanted if he would only not press his heart in two. "Tell him," said the wolf, "that if he will transform the six brothers and their princesses whom he had turned into stone, back again, you will spare his life." So the troll (evidently the same thing as the giant) changed the six brothers and their brides back into human beings. "And now," said the wolf, "squash the egg!" And the prince squashed the egg into pieces and the giant burst.

So, having killed the giant, the seven brothers ride home with their brides. The king is delighted and says that the most beautiful bride is that of the youngest son and she must sit with him at the top of the table. For days they had a great feast, and if they haven't finished, they are still at it.

CHAPTER V

THE SEARCH FOR THE SECRET HEART

It is always useful with a fairy tale to count the figures involved. In the beginning of our story there are the king and his seven sons; eight men and no woman at this court. The queen is not mentioned all through the story, so we must assume that she is not alive.

I do not want to go into details, but generally, in Jungian terms, eight as a double of four points to the inner totality, to psychic completeness. So we can say that in the beginning there is a symbol of totality but in it the feminine counterpart, or element, is lacking. In practical language, this would mean that these eight people symbolize an outlook on life, possibly a dominant religious attitude, in which the symbol of totality is realized, as it might be for the period of this fairy tale, but only in its masculine features, its Logos aspect. The Eros, the feminine, the anima aspect, is lacking; it is a symbol of totality which is too high and only in the area of the mind and of masculine activity, a symbol of the Self which would correspond to the psychic pattern of the Self in men but not in women. There is a great deficiency somewhere.

Since the giant is the enemy, and since at the end of the story a church is mentioned, we must assume that this fairy tale is not older than the Christianization of Norway, meaning the second millenium of the Christian Era. Before then the Scandinavian countries had a rather masculine religion, predominantly of a patriarchal social order, but when they became Christianized they took over a purely patriarchal, spiritual religious outlook. The feminine element remained in a primitive undeveloped state.

Six sons go out on the quest to find the feminine element missing at the king's court and to bring home a bride. The king does not let the youngest go, but persuades him to stay at home. But the six sons, after finding their brides, come to a steep rock where there are giants, one of whom comes out and turns them to stone.

We must here go into the symbolism of the giant. Primarily he represents the remaining pagan element which has been repressed and had therefore receded into the rocks. Giants in Germanic mythology are mostly

THE SEARCH FOR THE SECRET HEART

characterized by their enormous strength and, in general, by their outstanding stupidity. There are any number of stories where giants are fooled by little men or weak human beings, because too much has gone into their physical growth and not enough into their brains. But in older, pre-Christian Nordic mythology, giants are also very clever, so they have been stupified mainly through the contents which have been repressed since the Christianization of Norway. Giants are mostly responsible for the weather; they create mist and in many countries even now if there are thunderstorms it is said that giants are playing in the heavenly countries and rolling their balls, or bowling. There are thunder giants, lightning giants, and giants responsible for landslides and for boulders or rocks falling from the mountains; when the giantesses have their big washday then the whole country is covered in mist. From these associations we can see that they represent the brute, untamed power of nature, a psychological dynamism mostly of an emotional character which is stronger than man. Therefore we could associate them with overwhelming emotional impulses which overcome the humanity of man as does a giant.

The connection of the giant with emotion and affect is practicably visible in the fact that whenever one gets emotional one begins to exaggerate: we make, as we say, elephants out of lice. A little remark by the other person, or any detail, becomes an enormous tragedy as soon as we are overwhelmed by our emotion. The emotion itself is what is powerful and magnifies everything in our surroundings. In the *Apocrypha of the Old Testament* in the Book of Enoch there are stories that giants desired human women (Genesis VI, 4) and mated with them, producing a generation of destructive half-giants which destroyed the surface of the earth. Dr. Jung interpreted this in one of his comments as a too-quick inrush of unconscious contents into the realm of collective consciousness.

In Germanic mythology giants are the in-between figures between Gods and men. In many creation myths all over the world giants were created before men and were an abortive, not very successful, attempt of the Gods to produce human beings; then came the generation of man who was, at least seemingly, a slightly more successful invention.

In certain versions of Nordic mythology, giants, on the contrary, came even before the Gods. They are the oldest beings in nature. In Nordic mythology there are ice and fire giants. Here again the giant is associated

207

with symbols of emotion, on one side fire, a symbol of emotionality, and on the other ice, the opposite, which is identical with it. Only people who are tremendously over-emotional can be also terribly ice-cold. Ice characterizes the climax of an emotional state where it snaps over into coldness or rigidity. You probably have experienced that one can get into a state of hot anger. If that is intensified one suddenly feels nothing any more, emotion subsides; one becomes absolutely ice-cold from rage, frozen and rigid. In place of the hot emotional reaction one is petrified in rage, or in being shocked, or whatever the original emotion may have been. One literally gets cold hands and becomes shivery, for all the blood vessels contract and one is cold, instead of having a hot red head and feeling a fiery emotion. Ice is a further step, when emotionality falls into its other extreme. So it is fitting that the giants in mythology are the rulers of the domains of ice and fire, since both states are inhuman and completely out of balance.

In Greek mythology the same role would be completed by the Titans, the children of the earth, who have this same in-between position between the Gods and men. In Mediterranean mythology they are responsible for earthquakes. One is bound under Etna; every now and then he rolls over a little and Etna has another eruption in Sicily. There again is the connection with untamed emotional nature, for the outbreak of a volcano is a well-known symbol for a destructive emotional outbreak.

Regarding the position of the giants between Gods and men, you know that we interpret the figures of Gods as symbols or as archetypal images; that is, they are manifestations of the archetypes, which are the basic structures of our unconscious and possibly of the universe. In our psyche there are nuclei of a tremendous charge of dynamism, but as long as they manifest as archetypal images they have a certain order. Every God in mythology, for instance, has a function: he rules over a certain domain of life, he demands from man certain rules of behavior, sacrifices, and so on. So one can say that an archetypal image has a certain order which it conveys, or imposes, on the human being. Gods in a polytheistic religion can fight with each other and then the different orders collide, but at least each archetype has a certain aspect of order.

When an archetypal content approaches human consciousness it can happen that only the emotional charge is experienced and the order aspect is not realized. That would be the giant; one suffers from the influx of an overwhelming emotional affect of the charge of the archetypal content without realizing its ordering and meaningful aspect. That is why the giants between the Gods and man are generally destructive. Their stupidity is easily understandable if we look at them from this angle, because everybody who falls into a state of affect becomes automatically stupefied. You have probably experienced being swept away by an affect and doing the most idiotic things, which, had you been able to reflect in a cool or quiet manner, you would never have done. But giants can be useful too, for being sheer psychic emotionàl libido, if they are still ruled by human intelligence they can perform the greatest deeds. All over Europe there are innumerable medieval legends in which some saint fools a big giant into becoming his slave. Then the giant builds the most wonderful churches and chapels for him — in the service of the saint. So as soon as the giant is subdued by human intelligence or is again integrated into some spiritual order he gives us a tremendous amount of powerful and helpful psychic energy.

This reminds me of what Dr. Jung often told happened to him when he tried to write his book *Psychological Types*. As he says in the Foreward, he corresponded with a friend about his problems and collected all the enormous wealth of historical material which is gathered together in this book and then wanted to begin to write, feeling that now he should go beyond the stage of just collecting material. But he wanted to write in a clear, logically accurate form, having in mind something like *Le Discours de la Méthode* by Descartes, but he couldn't do it because that was too refined a mental instrument to grasp this enormous wealth of material. When he arrived at this difficulty he dreamt that there was an enormous boat out in the harbor laden with marvellous goods for mankind and that it should be pulled into the harbor and the goods distributed to the people. Attached to this enormous boat was a very elegant, white Arab horse, a beautiful and delicate, highstrung animal which was supposed to pull the ship into the harbor. But the horse was absolutely incapable of this. At that moment an enormous red-headed, red-bearded giant came through the mass of people, pushed everybody aside, took an axe, killed the white horse and then took the rope and pulled the whole ship into harbor in one *élan*. So Jung saw that he had to write in the emotional fire he felt about the whole thing and not go on with this elegant white horse. He was then driven by a tremendous working impulse, or emotion, and he wrote the whole book in practically one stretch, getting up every morning at three a.m.

Here you see that when the giant is cooperative, if he is not autonomous, he is like this libido, this amount of energy which can enable a human being to do something supernatural, achieve something which one has not the courage to do in a normal state of mind. One might say that a certain amount of ecstatic emotion and inflation, a kind of heroic enthusiasm, is necessary to achieve something, for that would be the giant when he is cooperative or collaborating with human consciousness. But if he gets out of hand then he does all the mischief described above.

In this story our giant came out of the rocks and without further ado, one has the feeling that it was out of sheer wickedness, petrified the six princes and their brides so that they couldn't go home. Petrification is a step further than the ice stage. If emotion becomes too great, one becomes cold, and if it goes a few degrees further still, one is petrified. This corresponds in psychiatric terms to a catatonic state. One might say that a patient in a catatonic state is petrified by unconscious emotions. On coming out of that, the first stage is coldness, followed by a terrible emotional outbreak. To unwind this tragic event one has to go through all the different stages leading up to the petrification. In Greek mythology it is the Gorgon Medusa whose face and head covered with snakes is so terrible that she can petrify every hero who looks at her. Perseus has to kill her while not looking at her directly, but through a mirror. He has to put the element of objective reflection between himself and the emotional shock which he would get by looking at her directly. This wisdom our princes don't know. They look at the giant directly and get petrified.

Question: I thought it was because they had forgotten to take back a wife for their youngest brother. They haven't a heart themselves!

It may be that this is a punishment because they haven't thought of anything but their own pleasure. On the other hand, if they had, this bride would have been petrified also. Then the youngest wouldn't have had any princess to meet, so it turns out not to be such a bad trick. But certainly they display tremendous naive egoism, as you point out. They just take their brides and forget about everything else, and that coincides with walking into the giant's trap, because of their lack of reflection or thoughtfulness. I think you are quite right, there is a connection between those two facts in the fairy tale.

When the youngest son wants to go look for his brothers there is only one shabby, miserable little horse left, but the prince goes off with it and that has a meaningful connection; one feels less sad when he later lets the wolf eat it, exchanging the horse for the wolf. If we take that psychologically, we see that the king, representing the dominant content of collective consciousness, has not much instinctual energy left. He has lost his wife, probably long ago, his six sons, and his six horses are dead. There is an increasing impoverishment at the king's court, which will naturally charge up the position of the unconscious powers.

The youngest son therefore rides off in a low state of mind, not at all feeling that he is going to accomplish a big deed and swing the business like a great hero. Right from the beginning the disease has been the overemphasis of masculinity, so we see why being a hero would be wrong: it would be again on the line of the old ruling attitude, stressing masculinity against instinct and love and the feminine principle. The youngest has a better chance by having such a shabby horse, which deprives him of the possibility of a masculine heroic attitude. Then he meets a raven which is desperately hungry and he gives him some of the small amount of food he has with him.

The raven in European mythology is generally a messenger between the ruling God and mankind. In Nordic mythology it would be like Wotan's two messengers, Hugin and Munin, who sit on Wotan's right and left shoulder and tell him about everything which goes on in the universe. We could say that they were Wotan's ESP, his extrasensory perception, or his absolute knowledge, his information as to what goes on. Ravens seem to know when there will be corpses for them to feed on. In former times they always accompanied armies, hoping for food. They were Wotan's messengers and the direction of their flight portended victory or defeat. They not only conveyed to the God what was happening on earth; if one could read the signs, the *auguria,* one could read the intention of the God through the behavior of the ravens.

In Christian mythology the raven has an ambiguous role. When Noah was drifting in the ark after the flood he first sent a raven to find whether land had appeared again, but the raven got busy eating all the corpses and forgot to fly back. Then Noah sent a dove, which brought him a twig, so he knew there was land again. From this the Church Fathers in the Middle Ages took the raven to be representative of the devil and of the evil principle, and the dove representative of the Holy Ghost and the good principle in the Godhead. On the other hand, St. John of Patmos was fed by a raven which came from heaven. It brought him supernatural bread and fed him in his hermitage. It was difficult for the Church Fathers to unite these two aspects, but they finally said that the raven represented the deep, dark and invisible, those unofficial thoughts about God which St. John had, or which came to him in his lonely hermitage on the island of Patmos.

Remark: And Elijah too!

Yes, Elijah too was fed by a raven. So in the Middle Ages, as in many other mythological fields, this archetypal symbol of the raven has been cut in two, into a light and dark aspect. It is both a symbol of the devil and of a dark mystical spiritual connectedness with God. In Greek mythology the raven belongs, amazingly enough, to the sun God Apollo and again represents his winter side, his dark Boreal side.

The raven is thus a messenger of the more unknown, the darker, less shining and more invisible side of the great God. Melancholy, deep thoughts, and evil thoughts are very close to each other; the effect of loneliness is both a pre-condition for possession by evil and, for exceptional people who know how to behave in it, a pre-condition for reaching the inner center. The raven might lead either to possession by evil or into essential inner realizations which are always the dark side of the sun God, i.e., thoughts not dominant in collective consciousness at the moment, which the collective would look upon as evil. Whenever someone leaves the collective and goes alone into his own depths, he or she will bring up new contents which will be disturbing to the light, lazy attitude of the ruling conscious attitude. Then the question becomes whether they are really evil or just the dark realization needed for that time. Here the raven represents this helpful side of the human psyche which is now completely starved. In other words, it is the side which has been neglected, but the youngest son feeds it.

Then he meets a salmon which is stranded on dry land and in despair. He pushes it back into the water. In Celtic and Nordic mythology the salmon represents something similar to the raven, namely wisdom and the knowledge of the future. In Celtic mythology there is a salmon of wisdom in a well which the heroes consult and from which they get information about the other world and the Beyond. But the salmon has another quality. Formerly it was a main food in these countries and it therefore represents a nourishing element. It gives vitality and gives not only dark information about unknown facts in the background of the psyche, but an influx of nourishing insight.

Remark: In my country we have a Gaelic toast: May you be as healthy as the salmon which swims up the river in the springtime!

Yes, that would be the nourishing aspect! It is a symbol of healthy vitality. The amazing behavior of the salmon which in springtime go up the river to special mating places, many dying on the way, represents a terrific heroic performance which the salmon carry out every year. It has given root to the idea that the salmon, because it can swim against the current and do something unreasonable from the utilitarian standpoint, is a symbol for such *contra naturam* efforts of man against the flow of nature. It represents the heroic effort against tendencies of laziness and of having it the cheap way, which certainly would convince a salmon never to go up the river. Salmon try to leap the falls of a river ten or twenty times. They become exhausted, swim around and then try again until they make it. It seems natural that they should suggest the idea that man, in order to reach wisdom and a level of higher consciousness, needs to make that same effort.

The salmon has this highly symbolic meaning, representing divine wisdom and leading man in his effort towards a higher level of consciousness, but it also represents an erotic feature. The salmon makes all this effort to get to the mating place. So the salmon in spring represents vitality and the love principle in the same form, the wisdom which includes love.

The salmon needs a push back into the water. That it is stranded is typical of the state of affairs, for before the prince takes a hand, everything in this kingdom has gone wrong. Even the salmon of wisdom has lost its contact with the water.

Compared with the salmon, the next animal is still closer to man. The wolf is warm-blooded and a close brother to us. It is so hungry it can scarcely walk. For two years it has had nothing to eat, and it begs the

213

prince to let it devour the horse. In Nordic mythology the wolf, like the raven, is one of Wotan's animals. It is also a companion of the battlefield, for wherever an army went in those days, the raven followed in the sky while wolves followed behind in the woods. They represented the dark threat of death which accompanied armies in the past. Probably because of his kinship with the dog with its attachment to man, the wolf not only carries the projection of a dark threatening animal, but often of an amazing natural intelligence as well. Again in Greek mythology the wolf belongs to Apollo, the sun God, the principle of consciousness. The Greek word for wolf is *lykos*, which is akin to the Latin word *lux* – light (German: *Licht*), possibly because of its eyes which shine in the dark. In spite of being a nocturnal animal, it is therefore an animal of the light. The real wolf has an amazingly developed intelligence. Probably this, among other things, caused it to carry the projection of the light of nature.

In its negative aspect the wolf is dangerously destructive, representing the principle of evil in its highest form. In old German mythology, the end of the world and of all the Gods in the universe will come when the Fenris wolf gets loose at the end of days. He will devour the sun and the moon and that will be the beginning cataclysm and the end of the universe. So the wolf is the demon of utter destruction. There is a saying that if one speaks of the wolf it appears, just as when you speak of the devil and he comes. In order to avoid mentioning the wolf by name, it was called *Isengrimm* which means iron-grim, grim being the state of rage or fury or anger which has turned into cold determination. To say something with *Ingrimm* means to say it with cold, hard iron determination which stems from a hidden rage or affect. Naturally, if applied in the moment where one needs a merciless determination which comes from a "holy" anger, this can be positive.

The wolf is also one of the devil's animals and an animal of all the war Gods. In Rome, for instance, it belongs to Mars, one of the chief Gods of the Roman Empire, which is why a female wolf mothers Romulus and Remus. The animal has a secret relationship not only to the dark God of war and the dark side of the light God, but to the feminine principle. In "Little Red Riding Hood," for example, the grandmother, the Great Mother, turns into a wolf and threatens to eat little Red Riding Hood in that shape, before the hunter, who is also an aspect of Wotan, comes and kills her. There the wolf becomes an attribute of a dark feminine Goddess and of dark nature. In the dreams of modern women the wolf often represents the animus, or that strange devouring attitude women can have when possessed by the animus. In many mythological connotations the wolf simply represents hunger and greed. In English one speaks of "wolfing" food, eating with a kind of passionate greed.

Remark: In Brehm's Tierleben *there is a wonderful description of the fox and the wolf. It says that the wolf is every bit as intelligent and cunning as the fox, but that it gets hungry and then loses everything; and it is always hungry!*

Yes, exactly. That is why there are many tales and stories in which the fox outwits the wolf by catching him through his greed, for that's the moment where the wolf loses his cunning reflection and gets caught. Greed or hunger brings about his downfall. From our standpoint that's where he gets caught in destructiveness. From our standpoint that is where one can catch him. In *Grimm's Fairy Tales* there is the story of "The Seven Little Goats" where the wolf is greedy and they put stones into his stomach and throw him into the water. There again he is outwitted through his greed.

In man, the wolf represents that strange indiscriminate desire to eat up everybody and everything, to have everything, which is visible in many neuroses where the main problem is that the person remains infantile because of an unhappy childhood. Such persons develop a hungry wolf within themselves. Whatever they see they say – me too! If one is kind to them they demand more and more. Dr. Jung says it is a drivenness which cannot be identified clearly with power, or sex. It is even more primitive; it is the desire to have and get everything. Give such people an hour a week and they will want two, if you give them two they want three. They want to see you in your spare time and if you gave that they would want to marry you, and if you married them they would want to eat you, etc. They are completely driven. It is not really that *they* want it, *it* wants it. Their "it" is never satisfied, so the wolf also creates in such people a constant resentful dissatisfaction. It stands as a symbol of bitter, cold, constant resentment because of what it never had. It wants really to eat the whole world.

215

Remark: St.Columba, the great sixth century saint, was baptized Columba or The Dove, but later acquired a second name, "Crimthann," a Celtic name for wolf, thereby becoming a more useful Christian by combining aggressiveness with gentleness.

So the wolf turned into a luminous thing, into higher consciousness! Yes, that is a relevant and very fitting association.

Question: Doesn't the wolf stand behind the dog with Hecate? There could be a connection there if you connect the wolf with the feminine principle.

Yes, but with Hecate, strangely enough, it is mostly the dog. The wolf comes more in the Nordic fairy tales where it is the companion of witches and of great women Goddesses. In Greece the connection was not so easily possible because the wolf was Apollo's animal, but there *are* late Greek magic papyri where the wolf appears among the dogs with Hecate.

Question: And would you think that this driving greed, when mastered, turns into the positive, luminous aspect?

Yes, naturally, that is why the wolf is called *lykos*, light. The greed when mastered or directed onto its right goal is *the* thing.

In this fairy tale the negative features of the wolf are not displayed, probably because the aspects of greed and lack of self-control are already parked in the giant. The wolf is from the beginning a positive and helpful animal.

Remark: There is another Greek story about the raven which says that at first it was white, but when it told Apollo that Coronis had betrayed him, Apollo, hating it for this, turned it black, and if you really look at the raven in the sunshine there is a lot of white among its feather.

I think mythological symbols always contain their opposite. You are right, but Coronis, the crow, is more the feminine aspect. The crow in mythological terminology is the wife of the raven, his more feminine counterpart, just as the cat is the wife of the dog and the cow the horse's wife. That was the child's idea of coupling animals.

Here the wolf, in contrast to its normal nature, eats only the horse. Then it is capable of stopping its greed and can be saddled and bridled to

216

become the youngest son's horse. Now the carrier is an impetuous desire which does not go beyond its proper boundaries. The shabby horse gave no heroic *élan*, but now the prince is carried by the fiery desire to reach his goal, to find his brothers and their brides. The wolf, who has the secret knowledge of nature, brings him straightaway to the giant's castle and tells him simply to obey the princess. She then really manages the whole problem. The prince has only to hide under the bed.

Mr. Braga has told me something which I think worthwhile, if he will repeat it.

Mr. Braga: Dr. Herzog Dürck of Munich describes in a book several types of neuroses, among them the witch, a person who refused what was called the sadness of being finite and was possessed by this drive to enlarge the dimensions.

Yes, that would be being possessed by the wolf. That reminds me of all the different mythological versions and half-true stories which Kipling made immortal with his *Mowgli* story, of the child who was thrown out and was adopted by the wolves and later returned to human society. If I remember rightly, about five or six years ago such a thing actually happened again in India, or was supposed to have done so; a boy lived for a long time among wolves.

Such actual events are not frequent, but I think this myth, or event, plays such a tremendous role because though only a few real children are adopted by wolves, it happens to millions in a symbolic way. Children are unhappy in their homes and become de-humanized. Or rather, they are not allowed to be human because their parents have an inhuman unconscious. Therefore they fall into the attitude of the lonely wolf. Thousands of children become lonely wolves, suffering from isolation and greed and the inability to make human contact. That is probably why the few stories of where it happens in reality make such an impression everywhere. And all over the world there are stories of were-wolves, people turned into wolves by witchcraft in the night, who perform destructive activities. These amount to the same thing.

If we look at the behavior of our prince, he is in a strange double position. The wolf, which has accepted being saddled and bridled and has not the measureless greedy nature it has in other stories, tells him to be com-

217

pletely passive. And at the end of the story — don't forget that our main
theme is the problem of coping with evil — the decisive step in destroying
the giant is made not by the prince but by the wolf, which says to crush
the egg. So there is a strange doubleness of attitude. The prince is completely passive, hiding under the princess' bed and doing nothing except
listening to what is being said. The wolf carries the whole action through,
so when finally the giant is overcome, it is by the wolf. The prince functions as an instrument, stepping into the story so that the wolf can overcome the giant.

The theme of lying under the princess' bed and listening to a love
conversation will be repeated in another story, so I will only discuss this
briefly now.

The place under the bed generally carries the projection of the personal
unconscious. It people are not very clean, look under their beds, and see
those nice woolly clouds of dust which assemble there together with the
chamber pot, the old shoe and what not. It is the place where one shovels
things away and it makes an ideal hook for what one would call the personal unconscious.

I remember all through my childhood a hunter lived under my bed, and
a yellow dwarf, and Negroes in the space between the bed and the wall.
They put up black paws so that I had to lie stiffly in the middle of the bed
where they couldn't get at me. Other children with whom I shared such
experiences thought that animals and devils and all such thing were under
the bed.

In the Chinese Book of Wisdom, the *I Ching*, Hexagram No. 23, "Putre-
faction and Splitting Apart" — the decay of death out of which comes
resurrection — there is the image of the bed being undermined. Its legs
give way and finally the whole bed collapses. That is described as the
forces of evil which have not the courage to fight openly the forces of
good but which, secretly, slowly undermine them until the bed collapses.
There again "under the bed" is the hidden place where the repressed complexes and problems live, slowly undermining the conscious condition and
finally even one's rest. That's why a bad conscience, worrying thoughts
or repressed things actually disturb sleep and keep people awake. Those
are all evil forces which live under the bed.

Here the prince is the secret dangerous force hidden under the bed, but to undermine the dominating giant he takes on the other role. He goes into hiding and becomes completely passive; by that he slowly learns how he can depotentiate the giant. He can only weaken and overcome him by not fighting him openly, but by getting at the core of his being whence he draws all his secret energy.

It is really the same thing when one is confronted with somebody who is in an overwhelmingly emotional state. It is of no use to openly fight another person's emotion. Trying to talk somebody out of a rage will just send them sky high. But if one can get at the secret core behind it, at the basic motif, which the person generally does not know, then one may get at something to make the whole thing collapse. It is the same thing with oneself. If one becomes exaggeratedly emotional about anything it is usually because one's unconscious vitality and libido are not flowing in the right direction or going where they belong.

People who have a creative side and do not live it out are most disagree-, able clients. They make a mountain out of a molehill, fuss about unnecessary things, are too passionately in love with somebody who is not worth so much attention, and so on. There is a kind of floating charge of energy in them which is not attached to its right object and therefore tends to apply exaggerated dynamism to the wrong situation. One can ask them why they exaggerate, why it is so important, but the over-importance or over-emphasis is not made consciously. The charge goes into their personal foolishnesses because a part of the dynamic center is not parked or not in connection with the right motivation. The moment these people devote themselves to what is really important the whole overcharge flows in the right direction, ceasing to heat up things not worth so much emotional attention. Repressed creativity is one of the most frequent reasons for such an attitude but repression of the religious function in the psyche often results in this tendency to one-sided exaggeration as well.

The religious function is probably the strongest drive in the human psyche. If it is not directed towards its natural goal it loads up the other areas of life and gives them an unmerited emotionality. Laurens van der Post points this out in *Journey into Russia* where he shows that because the religious function of the psyche is mutilated by an atheistic ruling system, this exaggeration is sometimes applied most ridiculously: in certain country regions the peasants have made electricity their God and will call their boy "Voltage" and the girl "Electra." They talk about new dams, or currents, or dynamos which have been built with the same awe with which in former times they would have spoken of religious matters. He also describes a pathetic scene he observed when visiting Lenin's mausoleum. He was quite struck by this rather badly embalmed little bourgeois of the nineteenth century, lying there with his neatly cut beard and having sometimes to be re-embalmed because the worms still ate him. He saw some simple country folk come in, a Russian peasant and his daughter. The man looked in a rather stunned way at this corpse in the glass coffin and took off his cap. Presently he gave a pious look to his daughter, intimating that they should go. After making the sign of the cross, they went quietly out again. If there is no God, we make one out of a dead man!

Whenever a main current in the psychic development of an individual is blocked, you might use a simile and say that the water flows into side tracks, fills up side currents, or if completely blocked, fills the swamp in the human psyche with snakes and mosquitoes, for the flow is not directed towards its real goal. That's why to overcome this destructive emotion the princess has to find out how the giant is connected with his heart. After two wrong attempts she finds out that it is "far away" in water in which is an island, on which is a church, in which is a well, in which is a duck, in which is an egg, and in the egg is his heart.

In certain other parallels of this story, the word heart is replaced by "death." In a Russian parallel a black magician says, "In the island is a church, in the church is a (I don't think it is a duck, but it is some kind of a bird) bird, in the bird is an egg, and in the egg is my death." In a way it is the same thing, because if you have the egg in your hand you have the death possibility of the giant in your hand, and that is probably the connection. The heart here carries the symbol of the feeling function, the vulnerable spot, the Achilles heel, where this invulnerable demonic figure can be hit.

Now we come to this exciting fact, which has puzzled me no end, of the symbolism of water, island, church, well, duck, and heart. Those among you who are acquainted with Jungian psychology know that all these objects are symbols of the Self, one in the other. In mythology, the far away island generally carries the projection of a lost paradise; the garden of the Hesperides is on a far away island, and in Celtic mythology there are all

220

sorts of fairy islands. In the later Middle Ages the Island of Thule was identified with remote Utopic islands as being the place to which the Gods, or the fairies, or the sea Gods, retired. In Greek mythology, Kronos, the old God deposed by Zeus, retired onto an isolated Nordic island and lives there in the Boreal countries. Generally an ideal past state is still subsistent on this island. The golden age, for instance, still continues on the island to which Kronos has retired.

In the late Middle Ages there were innumerable seafarer stories — the journey of St. Brandon and others — in which sailors in a storm drifted out of their course and came to a strange island where amazing magical adventures happened. There the island has simply the symbolism of a far away realm of the unconscious, unconnected with consciousness. The word "isolation" comes from the Latin *insula*, island. In psychological terms an island represents an autonomous complex with a life of its own, which has none, or almost no connection with the rest of the conscious personality. It is literally an insulated area about which the individual sometimes has a certain amount of knowledge but does not connect it, with a kind of compartment psychology, or has no knowledge at all.

I am reminded of the case of a man with a sneaky, slow, chronic schizophrenic situation. He lived imprisoned with his mother, who did not allow him to marry till he was far over forty and incapable of ever making contact with women. He was able to do his office work but had to go home at once after the office. He was incapable of getting out of the tyranny of his old and completely destructive mother. The analyst brought me terrible dreams which showed that this man could commit suicide or have another schizophrenic episode at any moment; scenes where he was sawing himself into bits, and so on, but again and again in those dreams came the motif of an island with luxurious tropical vegetation. Women were there, but from that island always came a poisonous snake which threatened the dreamer in many forms. I guessed right away that he probably masturbated with luscious fantasies and had there a private, secret erotic life of his own, literally quite insulated. In a way, that was positive; at least there was a certain amount of normal life — he didn't have any other sex life till he was forty-five — but on the other hand it was negative, because it eliminated his wish to get away from his mother, which without this would have been stronger. So this masturbation paradise had also its poisonous snake.

221

I told the analyst this was the meaning of the motif but it took a whole year to get it out of the analysand. One day he dreamt that he had again been bitten by a poisonous snake from that island and was seriously ill, and he saw on the floor a bit of the snake's head and a part of the back and he said, "Yes, I must bring that to the doctor so as to get a serum against the poisonous bite." After this dream he finally agreed to talk about the tropical island where he lived at night.

You see how the island is a symbol of a split-off area, an autonomous complex, so to speak. In this case the normal sex had been isolated and split-off by the negative mother complex. The dreamer knew about it but had made up his mind never to mention it to the analyst. He kept it strictly apart from the rest of his life problems. So sometimes the island is known, but there is a great water of unconsciousness between it and the conscious area, and sometimes it is unknown, which means that there is an autonomous complex which is somehow in a fantasy corner, but consciousness does not know enough about it to report on it.

In this split-off, far away, insulated area of the psyche there is a church. Now note: *insula* — feminine, sea — feminine, church — feminine, well — feminine! Here, in a nutshell, are all the feminine and mother principles which were lacking in the kingdom where there was no queen, but they are completely insulated and cut off from the rest of life.

It is interesting that the church should be in this split-off area. Even that aspect of the Christian religious attitude, the church as a feminine containing place where religious worship is held, is split off onto this island, along with the well (in German — *Brunnen*) , which would be a system by which one can connect with the unconscious. The well would stand for the walled-in place from which the water from the depth is brought up. A well in this sense represents a human construction which allows man constantly and without danger to contact the depth of the unconscious. If we put the two together, a church containing a well, it shows that what is repressed in the church aspect would be the living function of the original church.

In the first centuries of the Christianization of Nordic countries the church conveyed the possibility of a mystical religious experience. In later centuries it became more and more a social formality. If I may be so disagreeable, I can say that my impression of the Christian church in Scandinavia is of a completely lifeless affair, a conventional social nonsense which entirely lacks its original function as a mediator between consciousness and the inner depths of the soul.

Question: Is there here some connection with what you said at the beginning about the giant being connected with repressed pagan ideas?

Yes. In the realm of the giant that would mean that when the Nordic people were converted it was for them at the beginning, at least as far as they were not forced by military processes, a genuine religious experience and a progress in consciousness. One sees this by the old chronicles. But then the psychically true aspect of Christianity faded again, leaving only a conventional crust, a social affair with no deep religious meaning. The religious function of the psyche fell back into paganism, but since paganism itself is far away, it is both connected and disconnected with it.

Remark: There are more and more conversions to Catholicism in Scandinavian countries.

Yes. That points in the same direction. They are looking for symbols. Also the Catholic church made a less severe cut between past paganism and its new message than did Protestant denominations. They have still, to my heart's delight, a St. Priapus among their many saints, and isn't that a grand way of rescuing and saving paganism! One should really write to the Pope that St. Priapus should again be put in the front line.

Remark: I think also that they have a more feminine side in the Catholic church.

Yes, because they have a Goddess, or nearly a Goddess, in the Cult of the Virgin Mary. The feminine side is more included and all the pagan past can have an influx into that rich Catholic symbolism, while the Protestant denominations mutilate or warp this side of the psyche. That is why all the symbols are so feminine in this tale.

In the well is a duck and in the duck an egg. Now the duck, strangely enough, especially in fairy tales which are concerned with the problem of evil, comes up as a saving factor; and, at least in our countries, the duck seems to be connected in one way with the principle of evil and in another way with that which rescues one from evil. In Indian mythology it is connected with the sun. When the sun goes down in the evening it swims as a golden duck in the pond in the West and comes back in the East in the morning.

In our countries, ducks and geese have a definite connection with devils and witches, who often have ducks' or geese feet. There are many folk stories where all sorts of beautiful women and beings come along, but if you look at their feet you see that they have ducks' or geese feet and then you know that you have to do with some kind of evil fairy creature.

The duck is a remarkable bird. It can move on land, in the water, and in the air. It moves on land less well than in the water, but better than heavy swans and those completely helpless water birds, so it represents a principle which is at home in all realms of nature and often stands for a symbol of the Self. The duck can overcome what would be a natural obstacle for man. Man cannot fly and needs technical help for swimming, but the duck can do all these things. Therefore it represents what we, in Jungian psychology, would call the transcendent function, that strange capacity of the unconscious psyche to transform and guide the human being, who has been blocked in a situation, into a new one. Whenever human life gets stuck and arrives at a shore from which it cannot proceed, the transcendent function brings healing dreams and fantasies which construct on the symbolic fantasy level a new way of life which then suddenly takes shape and leads into a new situation.

Within the duck is an egg and there, says the giant, is my heart. The egg means a new germ, a new life possibility. That's why at Easter and in all spring festivals eggs symbolize the renewal and the possibility of new life. If you think of the many cosmogonic myths where the egg is the beginning of the world, it acquires the dignity of a cosmic principle. It is the very beginning, something out of which the whole universe can be born; according to many creation myths the world was hatched out of an egg which split apart, as in Indian creation myths, Greek Orphic creations and many others.

In alchemy the egg plays a tremendous role. It is equated with the philosopher's stone because, as the alchemists said, it contains everything in itself and needs no addition, except some slight amount of vital warmth or even temperature. Giving birth out of itself without addition, it symbolizes the innermost nucleus of the individual, the Self, to which we cannot add or take away. If we give it daily attention it is capable of developing by and out of itself.

This amazing series of religious symbols with an essentially feminine connotation, this is the secret heart or depth of the giant.

CHAPTER VI

MAGICAL CONTESTS

The hero finds the duck and the egg in the well in the church on the island. While holding the egg in his hand, he blackmails the giant into turning his brothers and his future sisters-in-law back into life. When the giant has done this there comes the moment of decision: shall it be fair play and let him go, because he has now undone the wrong he committed, or what? And there the wolf steps in and says to squash the egg. The hero squashes it and the giant dies.

I would like to read you a paper Dr. Danelius has written on the problem. He has sub-divided it into two possibilities: first, what it would mean for a woman, if the princess represents the human personality, when the giant would be a stony-hearted, cruel animus figure; she would ferret out in the night the vulnerable spot and hand the information to the prince who would be her positive animus. (I am just giving the essence of the paper.) Sentimental pity with her past master would endanger all she had gained, so her old cruel master has to die to open the way for her real life. From the side of the man, he interprets the egg as the great goal, the justification for his entire life. The egg in the duck would refer to a layer of his unconscious that had never been conscious (meaning the giant), a true goal for inner development. That he has found and bound himself to the finest princess proves that under his stony aspect are greater possibilities, all seen from the giant's standpoint. The princess, as his anima, the mediatrix to the world of the unconscious, leads him towards his goal, his own living heart. Here the finding of the heart means discovery for the giant himself. At this moment his life is fulfilled and it is the right time to die, for as a stone giant with a heart of stone he cannot go on living.

There I am a bit doubtful because it looks at the whole thing from the standpoint of the giant and not of the prince. Seen from the standpoint of the stony giant, it is the end of his life. His fulfillment has come because he is now closer to this church-duck-egg symbol; therefore it is time for him to die. But if we take the giant as this kind of pagan, partial soul, an incomplete thing, then I think things are more complicated. Also, I feel unhappy because I don't quite see how it all can be brought together with the psychology of the prince, or what it means for him, for he would represent the male personality of the fairy tale.

To make things still more complicated before discussing this story in detail, I would like to tell you the opposite story. This is a Lithuanian fairy tale called "How the Woodcutter Outwits the Devil and Gets the Princess."

A woodcutter, when cutting wood in the forest, saw a marten. He at once threw away his axe, but though he ran and ran he only lost his way. When it got dark he had to climb a tree to spend the night. In the morning he heard a violent quarrel. Looking down, he saw a lion, a whippet, a cat, an eagle, an ant, a cock, a sparrow and a fly (eight animals) who were all quarrelling over the dead body of an elk, because each wanted to sing its funeral song. They fought all day long and finally one of them spied the woodcutter and said he should decide. The woodcutter climbed down from the tree and, after thinking a bit, said he would have to sing. Otherwise the elk would never get buried. The others were delighted and said they would reward him for his clever decision by giving him the capacity to turn into any of them, just by thinking of the particular animal.

So the woodcutter sang such a burial song that the whole wood echoed. Then he turned himself into a lion and hurried to another part of the forest. There he met a swineherd who was crying bitterly because the devil was shortly going to eat all of his pigs. The swineherd explained that this was the king's fault for the king had lost his way in the forest a few days ago. A strange man had appeared from God knows where and had promised to show him the way out, on the condition that he gave him a pig every day. When there were no more pigs, the king must give him the princess, his own daughter.

The king now promised his daughter to whomever killed that monster. In that case, said the woodcutter, the pig-eater must be caught and *I* was meant to be the king's son-in-law. So he took charge of the pigs and towards evening the devil came along, seized a pig and disappeared into the wood. The woodcutter quickly took his remaining pigs home, changed into a whippet, and went after the devil. He told him that a little further along, in the eighth wood, a man wanted to hang himself but hadn't the courage to do it; the devil should hurry to get him and leave the silly pig. The devil hurried off, the whippet turned him-

227

self back into a man and brought the pig back unhurt.

The next evening the same thing happened, but this time the woodcutter took the form of an eagle and mocked the devil for eating pig. He said that in the other wood a child had been drowned by its mother and he should rather take that than eat the pig. The devil tried to make sure of his pig before going after the child; he tore an oak apart and left the pig caught in that, but the woodcutter rescued the pig and went home with it.

The next evening the woodcutter got the pigs home and into the pigpen. He thought he would have to sit on a perch like a cock all night and, sure enough, at midnight the devil came, starving with hunger. But the cock began to crow and the devil made off without a sound. He saw that he had been outwitted and got very angry. He went to the king's castle and yanked the princess out of her bed.

The king was in despair, but the woodcutter told him not to worry. He went to the mountain where the devil had taken the girl and there found a tiny hole. He changed himself into an ant and sat on a grain of sand and slid down into the depths. There he came to a great plain where he turned himself into a fly and flew straight to the other end. He saw a crystal palace and the king's daughter sitting at a window crying. He then resumed his original shape and showed himself, but the princess was terrified and asked him how he got there. She said the devil might come any minute and would tear him to pieces.

In a very short time the devil did appear, but the woodcutter turned himself into a lion and attacked him. There was a terrific fight, skin and flesh flew about, but the lion ate the devil up, skin, hair, and all.

The princess was overjoyed. Of course, so was the woodcutter, but now came the question of how to get out of the underworld. They thought of all sorts of things. Finally the princess had an idea for she remembered that in reading the devil's books she had read that in a certain tree was a diamond egg and if one brought that to the upperworld, the crystal palace would come too.

Immediately the woodcutter changed himself into a sparrow, flew into the tree, took the diamond egg out of the nest, and brought it down. That was all right, but how was he to get it to the upperworld?

"Wait," said the princess, "the devil has a doorkeeper who can't bear cats. If he finds one he throws it into the upperworld. Try that.!"

So the woodcutter changed himself into a cat, took the egg
into its mouth and crept purring round the doorkeeper's feet.
No sooner had the doorkeeper seen it than he seized it by the
tail and carried it up a very long staircase. After a long time
they came to an enormous iron door which the doorkeeper unlocked. He gave the cat a kick and threw it out. It landed
exactly where the ant had sneaked in before. But scarcely had
the cat changed back into the woodcutter and laid the egg on
the ground before the crystal castle appeared, together with
the king's daughter. Afterwards they got married and lived
happily in the crystal palace.

I don't want to go into detail over this nice trickster story, but I wanted
to show that it is not always necessary to squash the treasure which the
devil, or the evil power has. Here something happens which would be
more natural, at least to a Jungian; the symbol of the Self is saved, brought
up and integrated into reality. It is brought to the surface, into consciousness, and only the evil power which took possession of it is destroyed.
That coincides with our natural feeling that if the devil has taken possession
of the center, of the greatest treasure of the Self, it is a question of extrica-
ting that from him. This corresponds to the usual pattern of getting the
pearl away from the dragon, or the treasure difficult to obtain out of the
hands of evil powers.

This is an especially close parallel because we have the same motif with
opposite rules of ethical behavior. In the Scandinavian countries Christian
religious life was partially sucked back into the unconscious. In the island-
duck-story the giant represents destructive emotion. Had the giant and
this church-duck with the egg in it lived nearer each other, had they been
closer together, they would have been incompatible. That Christian church
with the symbol of the Self in it is incompatible with the giant and his actions. So the giant is connected with something with which he can only
stay connected by having it far away. The giant resembles people who
draw their real secret of life, their power and their life possibility, from
something with which their actions do not coincide. In everyday life there
are people who may be heads of the church and of societies and who draw
from that their whole position, while in their everyday actions they live a
completely different life. They draw their whole life possibility from

229

something with which their everyday actions are utterly incompatible. In a human being one would call that compartment psychology.

In many mass movements the same thing is evident. People are stirred up by some kind of highly religious ideal, some symbolic ideal of the Self and its great attractiveness, while the actual purpose and actions of those who maneuver them lie in a completely different direction. Recently in Germany many people were lured at the beginning of the Nazi movement by an archetypal dream of bringing Paradise back on earth. The Third Empire was to be a kind of Utopian ideal state in which peace would be established, the right people would govern, all symptoms of decay and de-generation would be overcome, etc. The ideal of Nazism was a naive, child-ish type of Utopia or Paradise which lured people into the movement; what happened was more on the scope of the heartless giant.

If you read van der Post's book on Russia you will see that the same idea of a Utopia or a Heavenly Jerusalem is working there again. This time it is not to come at the end of the days, however, but right now. The promise of established peace and heaven on earth is still one of the great propaganda tricks with which naive people are lured. They give a religious devotion to the Communistic idea because of the attractive archetypal image, while those who maneuver the movement have short-sighted and worldly purposes in mind. In practical life this is one of the most unfor-tunate combinations; criminal action and destructive activity are often secretly combined with an unreal, unrealized religious ideal. What I ex-amplify here in collective movements one sees as well in an outbreak of psychosis. Psychotic people often have somewhere in the innermost re-cesses of their souls a kind of childish Paradise dream which estranges them from life; yet from this they draw all their passionate impulses. It is really the secret behind their completely self-destructive emotional behav-ior. It even enables them to commit terrific crimes with a completely clear conscience.

I always remember a case I once read in the paper of a schizophrenic man who had made such progress in the asylum that he was allowed to be relatively free and was employed as gardener. He made friends with the little girl of the director of the clinic. One day he took the child by the hair and slowly cut off her head. When asked about it in court he said that the Holy Ghost had ordered him to make this human sacrifice.

Afterwards he had not the slightest emotional reaction. He felt convinced he had committed a religious sacrifice, an heroic deed to overcome his own sentimentality about the little girl. There was nothing to be done but to intern him again, for obviously he was raving mad. There again is the same combination of a highly religious ideal, for one could say that a man who thought he was obeying the voice of the Holy Ghost was childishly religious, but he did not see that it was incompatible for the Holy Ghost to order such a thing.

The combination of giant and church typifies such madness; one sees in psychotic dissociations that there is nothing to do but also destroy the childish ideal nucleus which is the secret source of all destructiveness. The prince in our Norwegian story is not asked to make a decision and obviously is not capable of judging what should be done. It is the wolf who takes over at that moment and orders him to crush the egg. We spoke of the wolf representing grim determination, a cold rage, in opposition to the inhuman heartlessness which the giant would represent. The wolf symbolizes dark, dangerous firmness which, used at the right moment, is sometimes absolutely necessary in the process of individuation in order to bring up the right values against evil. If, however, you are confronted with a situation where the opposites are not so far apart and so completely incompatible, then there is the possibility shown in the woodcutter story of destroying the devil and bringing the giant's egg to the surface.

In the Circumpolar Shamanistic rituals some of the tribes say that only a potential murderer can be a good Shaman; sometimes to cope with a turning point in an individual or collective type of illness, that kind of iron firmness is needed; but it is on the razor's edge, for one step further would mean murder or destruction. A Shaman who has not integrated that capacity is not up to the problem of evil.

In analytical work one meets with this in the end phase of the treatment of a severe neurotic dissociation as in our fairy tale; when people have tremendously improved, then, as in a physical illness, the whole problem works up to a climax. The patient suffering from dissociation from the problem of the opposites, cannot at once bring them together, but as he becomes slowly more conscious of the real reasons for the neurotic symptoms, the possibility of further consciousness and of cure slowly becomes constellated.

There are a few people, those of a candid and innocent nature (like the

231

simpleton with the peasant) who at this moment simply shed their neurotic symptoms like an old skin and are cured. There the analysis is very short, for at the moment when the patient realizes what is the matter with him the whole illness falls off. The analyst is happy and would love to publish the case and make a big howl about how wonderful things are. But in actual reality things are rarely so! Only by the grace of God do things go like that. Generally with the increasing improvement there is also an increasing attachment to the neurotic behavior, to the extent that exactly when one believes one may have a psychotic or compulsive neurotic or schizoid person out of trouble and might say that now he or she is *practically* all right — that's the moment to watch out for suicide; for now, with a kind of growing terror, the analysand will realize that in the future a normal life has to be lived. Often that so disgusts him that at the last moment he prefers to fall out of the window or drown in the lake. So this is a moment of climax where things, becoming better, are also more dangerous. Watch the bubbles on your coffee: they attract and dance round each other, get closer and closer, can't quite meet but then, suddenly, they come into one bubble. That is how opposites in the psyche behave. They are attracted to each other, they circle round and approach each other, but the moment when they become one is always a moment of shock, and even great shock, when a neurosis has lasted a long time.

Dr. Jung once said of a patient that at this moment he put up a terrific resistance against the treatment because he could not admit that he had wasted twenty-five years of his life! If you drag along in your life, escaping yourself and everything else for twenty-five years, it is hard to admit that all that has been a neurotic dance. That is why people sometimes can't make the step, but snap back into their former illness at all costs.

At such a time one needs this merciless wolf-determination, the hard cruelty of the surgeon's knife. If twenty-five years of your life are lost, do you want also to waste the next few years you still have because of that? A kind of mercilessness with the disease in a person who has a tendency towards indulging his sickness is absolutely necessary. Sometimes, however, this is not possible and that means a terrible decision as to what is to be done.

In some cases cruel determination is needed when the person has a latent psychosis. If a relatively small area of the person's psyche is psychotic and the conscious personality is ethically strong you can treat it as if it were a neurosis and try to integrate the sick and autonomous part of the psyche. That will lead to great crises but also to complete healing, or becoming total, or integration. But there are other cases where the sick area is big and the conscious personality small and weak; if one were to bring the two together it would be the sick part which would assimilate the remaining sound part, and the latent psychosis would turn into a manifest one.

In such a case, from our standpoint, a treatment of the so-called regressive institution of the persona is indicated; get the person away from the unconscious, away from psychology, help him adapt to collective social standards in a purely outward, persona way. Let sleeping dogs lie. One is usually helped by the fact that such people themselves feel this and will say, "Don't you think that analysis makes one morbid? Don't you think that occupying yourself with your own inner nonsense is not healthy? " In this case one must have the courage to say, "Yes, you are quite right. What we are doing here in psychology is all junk and only for neurotic people. Healthy people like you should return to the world, get a job, or do something else,'" and cheerfully talk them out of an approach to the unconscious.

In a seminar, Dr. Jung gave an account of a case in which he was consulted by a medical doctor who wanted to stop being a general practitioner and become a psychiatrist. He wanted a training in analysis with him, and in one of the crucial dreams which made Dr. Jung come to a decision, the dreamer went into an empty house and walked through one room after another where the was an uncanny dark atmosphere, and neither human being nor animal, pictures nor furniture. He went through a perfect maze of empty spaces until he arrived in a final end chamber; when he opened that door, in the center of the building, there was a tiny child sitting on a chamber pot smearing itself with faeces. Dr. Jung realized that the nucleus of this forty-five-year-old medical doctor had stayed in this infantile state and that the distance between his pseudo grown-up consciousness and this inner-most childish nucleus of his personality was too great. These opposites could not be brought together and, what was worse, in between the child and his consciousness, there was nothing — no figures, no pictures, nothing — just the one pole and the other! Dr. Jung convinced this man that he should return to his profession as a general practitioner and leave the unconscious alone. He obeyed, returned to his profession and thereby evaded a catastrophe.

In such a moment one needs grim determination, the decision of the surgeon who has to cut off a limb to save the rest of the human being. This is what the wolf represents here, the surgical determination to cut something where there is no possibility of evolution. The combination of egg and giant has to be destroyed as a whole and then a new life begins away from this area.

Also this was a squashy egg, while in our opposite Lithuanian story it was a diamond egg. The diamond egg is the indestructible thing, *par excellence;* it is a symbol of the Self in its highest indestructability both in Eastern and Western alchemy and philosophy. Therefore that could not be destroyed but had to be brought up into the upperworld.

If you look more closely at the two fairy stories you will see that they are not contradictory. The common thing is the symbol of the Self, the egg, which is in the hands of a destructive underworld. In one story, because of its mature state as a diamond, the egg has to be brought up; while in the other story it is a slimy, sloppy thing which has to be destroyed. In other ways the Lithuanian story is different. The woodcutter has eight animals with him at the beginning and so has a symbol of totality in an instinctual form; it becomes a question of bringing the other more spiritual part represented by the diamond to the surface of consciousness.

In both stories it is the princess who helps find the solution. In the Norwegian story, in an intimate situation, she finds out where the giant has his heart. In the woodcutter's story she has read the devil's books on magic and so knows where the diamond egg is and how it can be brought to the surface of the earth. It is also the princess who has the idea that the woodcutter should turn into a cat to be brought to the surface of the earth. In both stories the anima, the feminine principle, is the decisive factor in the battle with the principle of evil. Only heroes who have the animals and the anima on their side have a chance to survive; also, the hero in decisive moments does not do much. It is the animals and the anima who take over the action.

These fairy tales all belong to the Christian realm, to European countries. Therefore we have to see this in its relative value. It is a compensation for a too-active extraverted masculine outlook in consciousness. These stories compensate the conscious attitude of Christian European tradition, the heroic chivalrous ideal that man has to fight evil, be involved in fighting it actively — doing something about it! Whatever negative or destructive things we have in our social life, or realm of nature, you will always read in the newspapers: "What does the government intend to *do* about A-B-C-D? Something must be *done* about it!"

That one should watch and study such destructive factors first, getting at the heart or core before doing something, is foreign to us and comes only as a second thought. The first idea is to *do* something about it and that increases the dark power, giving it more and more libido. The art of letting horrible things happen without being seduced into extraverted action is something we have not yet learned. The great problem of the white man, I would say his illness, is his wish to cure evil situations by interfering action. Again it is a paradox, for there are times in inner and outer life where it is right to do nothing but wait and watch, while at other times one has to interfere; but to know when to act and when to let things happen, when to wait till they mature and move towards a possible turning point, is a wisdom about which fairy tales can teach us a lot.

I have been asked to return to the motif of *Frevel*. According to the rules of paradox, *Frevel* must sometimes be right, too. This woodcutter is a marvellous example of being carelessly impertinent, interfering everywhere, stepping boldly and tactlessly into every situation and getting rewarded for it. Here is a wonderful example of how trespassing into the realm of evil, out of no inner necessity but out of sheer bold impertinence, is rewarded.

This leads us to the next step, also implied in the woodcutter story. If the princess had not read the devil's books on magic and the woodcutter had not first acquired the capacity to transform himself into different animals, they would never have overcome the devil. Therefore our next problem is that of magical competition. Should one deal with evil on the level of magic, and if not, then how. This is a favorite theme in many international fairy tales where the question is who wins out in the end. It is not a fight of brute force and affect, as with the woodcutter who in the form of a lion eats the devil. The lion, by the way, is a symbol of the devil. The problem of evil in these next stories is fought on a spiritual level, as a magical contest between the devil, who is a magician, and the hero as a counter-magician. One could think of black and white magic, but that is an arbitrary distribution of colors. I would rather say one magic against another, not naming one black and the other white beforehand.

I will tell you a Russian fairy tale and then an Irish one which we will discuss in detail, taking the Russian only as comparative material so that you have a bit more variation in your minds. The Russian story is "The Black Magician Czar" (Der Schwarzkünstler Czar).

There was a czar who was a black magician and a very powerful ruler and who lived in a country as flat as a tablecloth. He had a wife and children and many servants. One day he gave a dinner party for the whole world, for all the nobility, for the peasants, for all the citizens, for everybody. After an enormous dinner he said, "Whoever can run away and hide himself from me shall have half my kingdom and my daughter as his wife, and after my death he can rule over my whole empire." Everybody who sat there remained silent and turned pale. But a very bold young man got up and said, "Czar, I can hide from you and escape." And the czar answered, "All right, bold young man, hide yourself. Tomorrow I will hunt for you and if you don't succeed in hiding yourself, your head must come off!"

The bold young man left the palace and went out into the city. He decided to hide in the village priest's bathroom.

Early next morning the magician czar got up, made a fire, sat on a chair beside it and began to read his book of magic to find out where the youth had gone. "That bold youth," he found, "has left my white palace and has gone to the city and to the bathroom of the village priest and has decided to hide there." So he sent his servants and told them to fetch the young man from the priest's bathroom. They found the youth lying in the corner and they brought him to the czar. The czar said to the youth, "Since you didn't succeed in hiding yourself from me your head must come off." And he himself, the czar, took a sharp sword and cut off the youth's head. (The important sentence is that the czar found great pleasure in his evil game.)

The next day the czar again gave a big dinner party and invited everybody to it. Again he said the same thing, that whoever could hide from him should have his kingdom and daughter. Again a bold youth dared to say that he could do it and again the czar warned him that if he failed his head must come off.

So the youth left the white-stoned palace and went out through the city and on until he came to a great granary. He thought he would creep into the straw and the chaff, for how could the czar find him there! So he crept in and lay still.

Again the czar went through the same procedure and consulted his magic book. He found the youth and beheaded him.

On the third day there was another dinner party and the czar made the same offer. There was a third bold young man who said he could escape him, but only on the third attempt. He went out of the city and turned himself into a weasel with a black tail. He ran all over the earth, crept under every root and into every stack of wood. He ran further and further and at last came to the palace window where he changed himself into a little drill and danced round the window. Then he changed himself into a falcon and flew in front of the czar's daughter's window. She saw him and opened the window and he flew in. Inside her room he turned himself back into a young man and had a nice private *chambre séparée* dinner with the czar's daughter. Then he turned himself into a ring she put on her finger.

The next morning the czar got up early, washed in spring water, dried himself on his hand towel, lit his fire and consulted his magic book. Then he told his servants either to bring his daughter to him or to bring her ring. The czar's daughter took off the ring and gave it to the servants who brought it to the czar. The czar took it, threw it over his left shoulder and there stood the young man. "So," he said, "now your head must come off your shoulders!" But the youth replied that it had been arranged that he should have three tries, and the czar let him go.

So the bold youth left the palace and went out to the open fields and changed himself into a gray wolf. He ran and ran over the whole earth. Then he changed himself into a bear which ran through the dark woods. Then he changed himself into a weasel with a black tail. He ran and hid under all the roots and in all the piles of wood and finally came back to the czar's palace where he changed himself first into a drill and then into a falcon and flew into the czar's daughter's room. When she saw him she opened the window for

237

him and in her room he turned into his own form. Again they
had a nice feast and spent the night together and tried to plan
a way to escape the czar. In the morning he turned himself
into a falcon and flew far out into the open fields where he
turned himself into a blade of grass among seven hundred and
seventy other blades of grass.

But the czar magician again consulted his book and then
told his servants to bring him armfulls of grass. The servants
went out and brought back the grass and the czar sat on his
stool and hunted for the right blade of grass. He found it
and threw it over his left shoulder and there stood the youth.
The czar said that now he had found him and that his head
must come off his shoulders, but the youth said No, he still
had another chance to hide, the last one, and the czar agreed.

So the youth went out of the palace and out into the
street and on to the open fields and changed himself into a
gray wolf. He ran and ran until he came to the blue sea
where he changed himself into a pike and jumped into the
water. He swam across the water, climbed the bank, changed
himself into a falcon and flew over mountains and cliffs. On
a green oak tree he saw the nest of the Magovei bird (a magic
bird in Russian fairy tales) and he dropped down into her
nest. The bird was not there at the time, but when she came
back and saw the bold youth sitting there, she said, "What
impertinence!" She seized him by the collar and flew with
him out of the nest, across the blue sea and put him on the
magician czar's window. The youth changed himself into a
fly, flew into the palace and changed himself into a piece of
flint, a fire stone, and lay down by the fireplace.

The black magician czar slept through the night, got up
early in the morning and began to read and search. He sent
his servants to the open fields and across the blue water to
hunt for the green oak and to cut it down and find the nest
with the youth in it and bring him to the czar. The servants
went and found the oak and the nest, but there was no youth
in it. They came back to the czar and told him that they had
found the oak tree and the nest but no youth. And the czar
looked in his book and thought that he *must* be there.

(See how interesting this is, for as long as the hero was
active the other could find him, but the return journey this
time was made by the bird Magovei.)

The czar himself joined in the hunt. They hunted and

hunted. They cut up the green oak tree with the nest and burnt every bit of it till not an atom of it was left. The czar thought that even if he had not found the youth he could no longer be alive on the earth.

So they went back to the empire. The second and the third day passed. One morning the maid got up and started to lay the fire. She took the flint stone and rubbed it on some steel; the stone flew out of her hand and over her left shoulder and there stood the youth.

"Good morning, mighty Czar," he said.

"Good morning, bold young man. Now your head must come off your shoulders."

"No, mighty Czar," the youth said, "you have sought me for three days and had given up the search. I have now come voluntarily. Now I should have half the kingdom and your daughter as my wife!"

The czar could do nothing so the two were married and had a wonderful wedding feast. The youth became the czar's son-in-law and got half the empire, but on the death of the czar he was to ascend the throne.

An Irish story of the same type, but a bit more complicated, is called "The Prince and the Bird with the Beautiful Song."

In the old days, before the cursed foreigners came to our country (as the Irish always said and still say), there was a king who, when he was twenty-one, married a very beautiful woman and they had a son called Ceart. But soon after his birth the queen developed a strange illness and died. About a year later the king married another queen who was kind to her stepson until she herself had twin sons. From that day on she hated him for he would naturally inherit the kingdom and take it away from her sons. The twins were very wicked, but for all their mischief, it was always the stepson who was punished. One day they killed a puppy belonging to the king and accused Ceart of having done it, though Ceart said he hadn't.

"Don't tell me lies!" cried the king, "Art and Neart and your stepmother saw you do it."

But Ceart said he had not touched the dog with hand or foot. The king would not believe him and beat him unmercifully.

But an old woman, Nuala, who had promised the first queen to look after her son, went to the king and told him he had been unjust, for Ceart had not killed the dog. She had seen how Art and Neart had killed it and the queen had watched from her window.

The king said he was sorry. On looking at the twins' clothing he saw that they were splashed with the dog's blood. The king apologized to Ceart and gave him money for the old woman.

But things continued in the same way and the prince had to suffer very much.

When the three sons were grown up they once went with the king to hunt in the forest. Before they had gone far they heard the most beautiful music that man had ever heard. They followed the song and came to big tree in the middle of the forest. On the tree they saw a large bird which made the lovely music.

The king was enchanted by the bird. He said that whoever brought it to him should have his kingdom, and that he could not live without it.

The three sons set out on the quest and followed the bird. It flew from tree to tree until it finally disappeared in a hole under a giant oak. This they told the king, but the latter repeated that without the bird he did not want to live and that he would give his kingdom to whomever got the bird for him.

"If I had the right things, I'd go after him," said Art.

"Then get them. I will stay here and guard the hole," said the king.

The three sons went off and soon came back with a big tub and a long rope. The tub they made fast to the rope and Art got in, saying, "If there is any danger I will call out so that you can pull me up."

It wasn't long before they heard him cry out to pull him up. As soon as he could talk he said that there was a great giant who had tried to spear him with a blood-red lance and that he would never go down again even if the whole of Ireland were allotted to him.

Neart then drew his sword and said he would go down, but the same thing happened.

"I will go down myself," said the king, "for without this bird I do not want to live."

"You shall not go down until I have had a try," said Ceart, "and I shall not return without the bird."

With that he drew his sword and said, "If I live, I will be back before nine days are up and then you will hear from me. Keep the things ready to pull me up."

So Ceart was let down in the tub and before he had gone far

240

he saw a little man with a spear. He sprang out of the tub and seized him by the throat.

"Let me go, Prince," said the little man, "I am not an enemy. The two men who came before you had no courage."

So Ceart said that if he was a friend he should tell him where the beautiful bird was which had flown down a little while ago. "My father cannot live without it," he said.

"That bird is now far away," said the little man. "It is the princess of this country and is called the Bird with the Beautiful Song. She and her father have magical powers. Many kings' sons have lost their lives in the hunt for her. But if you follow my advice you can catch her without losing your life."

"I will follow your advice and be grateful," answered Ceart.

"Good," said the little man. "Here is a sword and a cloak for you. Go that way until you come to a large house on the left. Go in and the woman in the house will welcome you and will give you a little white horse which will bring you to the king's castle. Do everything the horse tells you and you will be in no danger. When you have got the princess, the Bird with the Beautiful Song, go back to the woman in the big house."

It happened like that and the little horse was given him by the woman who told him that he should follow exactly what the little white horse said to do. The horse took him very quickly, and with the setting sun they arrived at a big castle.

"Now," said the little horse, "this is the king's castle. He will soon come to talk to you and you must pretend that you know a lot of magic, and don't eat or drink anything in the castle."

Soon the king appeared and Ceart told him who he was and that he had come in search of his daughter, the Bird with the Beautiful Song. The king replied that he thought it would have been wiser if he had stayed at home, but should he deserve her, he would have her.

"Now listen," said the king, "three mornings running I will hide myself and the following three mornings you must hide yourself. If you find me and I do not find you, you shall have my daughter, but if you don't find me and I find you, then you will lose your head."

Ceart agreed to the conditions and the king asked him to come in and eat, but Ceart said that he only ate every nine days. He put the little horse in the stall and gave him oats and hay and water.

241

Then the horse told him to put his hand in its right ear, pull out the tablecloth that was in it and lay it on the ground. Ceart did this and the moment the cloth was on the ground there was food and drink in plenty.

"Now," said the little horse, "put the cloth back in my ear and lie down by my head. I will watch over you till morning." He did this and slept as though on a bed of down without waking until the next morning.

When he was up he gave the horse oats and hay and water. Then he pulled out the cloth and ate and drank until he was satisfied. When he put the cloth back the horse said that the king had hidden but that there was no need to hurry to find him for he knew where he was. Ceart must wait a bit and then go into the garden behind the castle. There he would see a tree with two apples on it. The king was in the middle of the highest apple. He must take it and cut it in two with his knife and the king would come out.

It happened just like that and the king said that the prince had won this time, but that he would not do so the next day. Ceart said that they would see.

Again in the evening he fed the horse and got fed by it and was watched over while he slept. In the morning he got up early, fed the horse again and ate and drank himself.

The little horse said, "The king has hidden, but I know where. Don't worry if he remains hidden until midday. He is in the stomach of a little trout in the lake behind the castle. When you come to the river bank, throw in a hair out of my tail and the trout will swim to the bank. Catch it, take out your knife, cut it open and the king will come out."

About midday Ceart went to the lake, found the trout and took out his knife. He was about to cut when the king sprang out and said, "You have won twice, but you won't get me tomorrow!"

The third time the king hid in his daughter's ring.

Again about midday Ceart went into the castle. The princess asked him in and he began to make love to her and got a bit fresh. He got the ring away from her. She became furious and said that if her father were there he wouldn't dare to do that. Ceart answered, "Well, if you are so angry I'll throw your ring into the fire," and then out sprang the king.

The king then had to admit that Ceart had won again. But, he said, tomorrow and the following days he would find the

242

prince, although he had to admit that the prince was a clever fellow.

At night Ceart once more looked after his little horse, ate and drank and lay down to sleep. In the morning he got up, fed his horse, and had his own food.

"Now," said the little horse, "it's time to hide yourself. Pull a hair out of my tail, step into the hole and pull the hair back after you."

He did so and remained hidden until sunset. Then he came out and presented himself to the king, and said the sun has set and you didn't find me.

"But it won't be like that tomorrow," said the king.

The next morning the little horse told the prince to put his hand in its mouth and pull out its back tooth, then to get into the hole and put the tooth back.

Again he remained hidden until sunset when the horse told him to come out. So the prince went to the king and said that now the second day had passed and the king hadn't found him.

"Wait till tomorrow and I'll find you even if you get into Hell. I know where you want to go," said the king.

The next morning the little horse told him to pull a nail out of his left hind hoof, to get into the hole, and put back the nail. He said that the king would come at once to kill him (the horse) for the blind seer whom he had to advise him would tell him that the prince was hidden within. But it said that it could come back to life again and Ceart should do as it told him: when the sun sank in the evening he was to come out of his hiding place. He was to put his hand into its right ear and take out the little bottle. If he would rub the tongue of the little horse with some of the liquid it would get up as well as ever.

Ceart did what the little horse told him. He was not long in his hiding place before the king and the blind seer appeared. They killed the little horse, cut it open, and hunted through every inch of it but they couldn't find Ceart. The king was very angry and said to the blind seer that for twenty-two years he had paid him and now he couldn't even say where the man was hidden. "On your advice," the king said, "I have killed that man's horse. I thought I could cut off his head and instead he has won my daughter."

(A detail I forgot to mention is that the seer was always supposed to look things up in a book of magic. He now tells the king that the young man is worthy of his daughter, because he

243

has the most magic.)

Ceart then restored the little horse to life as he had been told to do and the horse told him to go to the king and tell him he had won his daughter and that he should give her to him or he would reduce the king's castle to dust.

He reproached the king with having killed his horse which he, the prince, had brought back to life. The king was terribly frightened. He gave the young man his daughter and told him to go. The horse brought the two back to the house where he had first been given to the young man, and the woman in the house sent them to her brother who was at the bottom of the hole. The little man greeted the young man and the Bird with the Beautiful Song.

Ceart called up the hole to where Art and Neart were standing and told them to let down the tub, as he had the bird which was a princess and the most beautiful woman in the world. So the princess was drawn up and when the brothers saw her they both wanted her. Instead of letting down the tub again for Ceart they fought until they killed each other in front of the princess. She, now that she was in Ireland, had no more magic and she called to Ceart and told him what had happened.

The old woman went to the king and told him to go to the forest where he would find his son Ceart. He went and found at the hole his two dead sons and a beautiful woman. He asked her who she was and who had killed his two sons. She told him that she was the Bird with the Beautiful Song, that the two sons had killed each other in fighting for her and that Ceart had won her from her father and now was at the bottom of the hole.

The king let down the tub and drew up Ceart, who told him all that had happened. The king took him and the princess to his castle and sent people to bury his other two sons. The queen, when she heard that they were dead, went mad and drowned herself.

So Ceart married the princess and they had a grand wedding. When the king died Ceart was crowned and he and the Bird with the Beautiful Song lived long and happily together.

This story is more differentiated than the Russian story. It has more nuance. Also both parties hide from each other, the hero from the king and the king from the hero, each three times. The common factor is that there is a kind of incestuous situation between father and daughter in the underworld. The czar does not want to give away his daughter, and this

244

Irish subterranean fairy king does not want to give away his daughter except to a son-in-law who can overcome him by black magic. The czar seems
more evil than the Irish fairy king. The latter does not want to part from
his daughter but wants to keep her in the underworld, while the Black
Magician Czar has pleasure in beheading people.

The daughter's ring is a favorite hiding place. It is interesting that in
the Russian story it is our hero who hides in the ring and in the Irish story
it is her father who hides there. In both stories it is the animal which helps
decide the question; without his little white horse the Irish hero could
never have succeeded, and in the Russian story if the bird Magovei hadn't
interfered, carrying the hero away from where *he* had thought he would
hide and taking him back to another place, he would have been found.
There is a difference in that Magovei is furious and only wants to get this
impertinent intruder out of the nest, while in the Irish story the white
horse is really the cooperative helpful animal as we know it in other stories. In the Russian story the hero turns into different animal shapes but
finally is saved in the form of a flint stone. In the Irish story it is the king
who turns into symbols of the Self, such as the apple, the trout and the
stone in the ring; the hero simply hides in an empty space, and a very small
one, in the body of his horse.

If we compare the two stories, the decisive factor in our Russian story
is the fact that the hero is finally saved in the shape of a flint stone. That
is where the czar cannot find him and from where he comes out voluntarily at the end of the tale.

The flint stone has magical qualities to a primitive mind, for fire can
come out of it. It is a widespread symbol of the Self. The Western alchemist speaks of it as the stone which has a spirit within it. As you know, the
philosopher's stone in alchemy is the stone in which dwells a spiritual
power, and because a flint stone produces something so utterly different
from itself, a spirit of fire, it has always carried the projection of a supreme
union of opposites. The dead matter carries the symbol of the spark of
the Divine fire. In many stories in many North American Indian myths,
for instance, the flint stone is the symbol of different saviour figures and
represents the Divinity appearing on earth.

In some Iroquois myths when divine powers appear on earth they take
the shape of a saviour figure whose name is Flintstone. If you dwell in

your imagination on the tremendous importance of a flintstone to a lonely hunter in the woods and to people having no electricity, the flintstone is a life provider. It easily carries the projection of the divine helper of man. Thus we can say that whoever can dwell within the Self, whoever can lose his ego personality and retire into the innermost nucleus of his personality can, so to speak, retire into the invisible castle of the Self within him and be inaccessible to the attacks of evil. The Self, with the possibility of retiring into it, is the only hiding place when evil tries to involve one in its powers. The stories look like a magical competition in which the important fact is who can become invisible to the other person. This story is extremely compensatory in civilizations and countries where the ruling dominant and collective ideal is one of heroic action.

This is strongly reminiscent of Eastern Buddhistic ideas. Buddha, too, did not fight evil. He retired from it and made himself invulnerable by invisibility. There is a famous Indian legend in which Mara, the ruler of the demons, finally had enough of Buddha and his teaching, which was weakening his powers over man. He planned a general attack of all evil powers and mobilized all the million devils he had in the underworld. All armed and in a well-organized manner, they went to destroy Buddha. But Buddha did not let himself be crucified like Christ, nor did he fight like a sun hero. He simply was not there! In temples you can see the famous sculptures with the empty lotus throne of Buddha and all the twenty-thousand demons brandishing their weapons, looking most disappointed because Buddha was not at home and they couldn't find him! This introverted way of not fighting evil or getting involved in its emotional or other effects, but of simply stepping back into the inner emptiness of the Self has become in the East a conscious collective teaching. In Western stories we find it mainly in the realm of fairy tales as a kind of compensatory trend against more active hero ideals.

The Irish story is to my mind more interesting than the more primitive Russian story because both the king and the hero hide and it is interesting to compare the differences. The fairy underworld king gets his knowledge by technical means. The Black Magician Czar has a book. The Irish king, like the czar in the Russian story, has a blind seer, a druid we would say, a priest personality. Such seers, poets and mediums were often blind — think of Homer. A blind seer with mediumistic insight and the help of a magical book advises him. The hero in the Russian story has his own magical capacities which do not help him very far, but he has no other advice. He can turn himself into all those different shapes, while in the Irish story, the whole counter-magic is carried out by the little white horse which Ceart receives in the underworld from a feminine figure. He has the support of a feminine principle against the masculine one, and of the animal against magical knowledge. Here the fairy tale puts instinctual spontaneity, the knowledge of the animal or the horse, on a higher level than the mediumistic magical book knowledge of the fairy king.

Book knowledge means some kind of tradition, a knowledge of psychic laws and events which have already been codified to a certain extent and handed down through the generations. Long before the introduction of writing, the different civilizations in our countries had a body of traditional knowledge, and we must assume that the blind seer had his druidic Celtic and medicine-man teaching of the past. For although we are in the Irish underworld, in a completely pre-Christian layer of the collective unconscious, there is already cultural knowledge. Even in the most primitive tribes, in Polynesia or among the Bushmen in Africa, there is an oral tradition of stories and known facts, knowledge which is handed down through the generations.

This wisdom strikes us as being of the highest value, the highest wisdom, being close to the essence of all psychological functioning. The more primitive such knowledge is the more revealing and worth-while it is for us to study, because it is so close to the functioning of the unconscious psyche in modern man. But still, it is already formulated and handed down within a certain tradition. Therefore it is already partly adapted to the conscious life of such nations. In comparison, the horse and its magical knowledge is more immediate and personal. It is a spontaneous reaction which springs from the deepest instinctual layer of the individual personality. It is each time unique, because it is always improvised and springs in new form from the spontaneous living basic nature of the psyche. That is why the horse's advice proves to be superior to the great wisdom handed down by the blind seer and his books and traditions. It is superior because it cannot be figured out by anybody else. As soon as you have traditional codified knowledge of some kind, it can be misused. Evil forces can take possession of it and use it for their own purposes. But creative, instinctual spontaneity can never be foreseen and the other can never tell what's going to happen. It is completely creative and essentially unforeseeable, and thus superior to other knowledge.

As long as Dr. Jung lived, we, the people around him, said among ourselves that he was someone whose reactions you could never figure out. You always knew that whenever he came into a situation or intended to say something about, or even interfere in, a situation, you never could know what he would say or do. It was always an utter surprise — sometimes, as he said with a grin, even to him! Because he did not know what he was going to say or do, he rarely planned his actions in a conscious way; he answered to the situation and questions on the spur of the moment. He let the "horse" give of its wisdom and therefore nobody could think out ahead what could or should be said. I often tried to think of what he would probably say in such and such a situation but I always fell out of the clouds when confronted with reality. It was always different from what people, even those who had known him for a long time, could have figured out.

This creative spontaneity which springs from the essential depths or center of the personality and which has to be represented by a horse, because it is a kind of semi-unconscious reaction, is the one thing which can overcome the attack of evil when that has taken form, when it has combined itself with a certain intelligence and with the tradition of the past. We are now, to my mind, in such a situation. Mankind is not threatened by brutal murderous impulses, though they break out here and there as probably always will occur where the mob gets wild and animal forces get loose. The real danger for us is when these forces combine with high scientific intelligence. In atomic physics they combine with the highest achievements of scientific knowledge. This combination cannot be compared practically, but our story says there is, in spite of everything, one thing superior to it: a return to the innermost genuineness of the depths of our own psyche with its invincible clairvoyance and natural knowledge. With that we can possibly overcome even these diabolical forces.

CHAPTER VII

THE NUCLEUS OF THE PSYCHE

The stories in the last chapter illustrated the problem of magic competition, or magical contest, as one form in which the principle of evil is fought. One was a Russian story in which the Black Magician Czar promised his daughter to whoever could hide from him. Three young men took up the challenge, two of whom were beheaded, while the third succeeded thanks to his greater magical power; but even he would not have escaped if the bird Magovei had not carried him back to the czar's court where he assumed the shape of a flintstone. In the Irish fairy tale, "The Bird With the Beautiful Song," the Irish hero has to go into the underworld and find this bird for his father. Here there is a double competition. The underworld king, the father of the bird which is really a beautiful woman, hides three times: in an apple, in a trout, and in his daughter's ring. Then the hero hides three times in the white horse which he had previously obtained from a benevolent underworld woman. The king has a blind seer as his advisor and the hero has the white horse as his.

The archetype of the magical competition is to be found in almost all societies and on all levels of civilization. In primitive civilizations it is in the form of different medicine men, smaller and greater, who compete with each other, each one establishing a realm of power and influence over a certain group in the tribe or over a neighboring tribe, while trying to eliminate their rivals. The same thing exists in the rivalry of shamans in the Circumpolar tribes; smaller and bigger shamans challenge each other as to who is more accomplished in magic and try to block each other out in this way.

There are traces of this even in Christian legends. The Gnostic Simon Magus claimed to represent the Godhead on earth. He was not only a rival of Christ but of St. Peter, as well; the two met in Rome to have it out with each other. Simon Magus tried to demonstrate that he could fly and St. Peter used magic against him so that when he went over a cliff with his wings spread he fell down and was killed.

There are later stories of saints who fight with wizards or witches in a similar way. So one finds it practically everywhere. One could say that it is the archetype of trying to fight evil by one's wits and intelligence and through knowledge, instead of by brute force. Knowledge, if linked with a state of higher consciousness, is perhaps the greatest means of fighting evil; dissociated from consciousness, it is just one magical trick against another.

The rival whose knowledge means wider or deeper consciousness will probably win against the rival who simply uses traditional knowledge without knowing its real meaning, not being essentially connected with it. Anything in this sense can be used as black *or* white magic. That is why I avoid speaking of black and white magic, for each rival will contend that he is the white and the other the black magician.

This reminds me of a childhood dream of an analysand who had been the victim of a destructive mother. The mother was a nurse and, like many nurses, had a definite suicidal complex. She was a bitter, pious, power-driven woman with hidden suicidal tendencies. She had married just to marry, without the slightest love, and she told her children from morning till night that it would have been better for her not to have married and that they never ought to have existed. You can imagine the constructive atmosphere in which those children grew up! The childhood dream of one of the girls was the following: When about four years old she dreamt that she got out of bed with the feeling that her mother was doing something very mysterious in the neighboring room. It was half dark and she looked into the room where her mother sat with the Bible. In came a huge black man, and the mother took up the Bible, which had a cross in gold on the cover, and held it up against the black man, who fled. The girl woke up with a cry of horror, not because of the black man, but because she had seen or caught her mother using the Bible as a magic means.

Now that was pure black magic. The mother repressed the problem of evil, which in her case had taken the form of a completely destructive power animus. She split herself off from her destructive animus by using the Bible as a trick, not as something to read or meditate upon or to incorporate in any way, but as a kind of outer magical, technical trick to keep herself from a confrontation. Thus the whole problem of evil and of having it out with her animus was put onto her children.

That is why I do not use the words black or white magic, because even the Bible can be used for black magic against dark powers. Whether magic is white or black depends on how and with what attitude you use your weapons.

I have often been struck by the fact that even in Zen Buddhism, in conversations between enlightened masters or those in which the masters test other unknown monks to see if they have acquired Zen, there is sometimes a disagreeable tone of power or magical competition. I mentioned this to Dr. Jung. He said, with a grin, that a lot of the old shaman's power competition had sneaked into some of the Zen competitions. Naturally this is not a general statement; it refers to certain forms and doesn't cover everything, but it is a danger which lurks in the background. And, last but not least, in psychology one meets the same thing in the disagreeable way in which most analysts relate to their colleagues and, on the subjective level, in the relationship between the ego and the unconscious.

Often people approach the unconscious with an inner utilitarian or power standpoint; they want to exploit the unconscious in order to become more powerful themselves, to be healthier, to dominate their surroundings, or to learn how to get things in their own way. Or they approach it with a secret ambition to acquire a mana personality. This is especially a pupil disease; if somebody in lonely work upon himself has acquired a certain superiority, the pupil wants to acquire it in the same way. If he is intelligent he thinks, "Oh well, I'll follow exactly the same method and do exactly the same as the Master and I'll get the same results." Such a person does not notice that he is deceiving himself. His approach to the unconscious is not genuine but contaminated with a trick, or with an exploiting attitude. The unconscious is something like a beautiful forest whose animals he wants to catch, or a field he wants to take possession of.

When consciousness assumes such an attitude the unconscious becomes trickster-like too. The dreams become contradictory, they say Yes and then No, left and then right, and one feels that the archetype of the trickster God Mercurius is dominating the phenomenon of the unconscious, leading the ego in a thousand ways up the garden path. Such people, sometimes after years of fighting with their own unconscious most honestly and desperately, finally give up and say, "Well, the unconscious is a hopeless abyss and misleading, something one can never get to the end of, for the dreams say both this and that."

251

Such people do not realize that they constellate this trickster quality in their own unconscious by the trickster attitude of their ego, that is, by their own attitude towards it. They want to cheat and exploit the unconscious, they want to get it into their own pockets with a slight, subtle power attitude and the unconscious answers with a mirror reaction. There are even people who, after reading Jung, try to force individuation in this way. They think, "If I do as Dr. Jung did, write down every dream, do active imagination, etc., then I'll get IT," so to speak. They put a forcing, pressing ego attitude into the enterprise which tricks it from the start and gets them into endless trouble. This is a modern variation of the age-old archetypal motif of the magical competition or contest.

Both in the Russian and in the Irish story, the one who wins is the hero who can make contact with the black magician's daughter. It is the feminine element which decides the problem or which steps in and decides in favor of one or the other party. In the Russian story the hero succeeds in flying as a falcon to the window of the Black Magician Czar's daughter and having an affair with her, and in the Irish story the hero wins the help of an underworld mother figure and her horse, and with that feminine part wins out against the underworld king. This has to be understood as a compensatory factor, because whenever consciousness gets itself lost in a magical competition it means that it has been caught from behind by a power attitude; the princess represents the counter-principle of power, love or Eros, against the drive of domination. Therefore the one who has Eros instead of a power attitude wins against the other party.

In the Russian story this is very clear. The Black Magician Czar when sitting at the table promises his kingdom. One sees how completely he is caught in a power attitude. Those first two boys who get up and say, "I am going to do it," walk into the power attitude trap, taking it on themselves; in a way, it serves them right that they are beheaded. They should have shrugged their shoulders and watched the Black Magician Czar shooting off nonsense.

The third hero, on the contrary, knows a way to approach the feminine principle which is a captive of the Black Magician Czar. He wins through his contact with her and the bird Magovei, which must be a female bird because it is sitting on eggs. Three times he is helped by the feminine: by the czar's daughter, by the bird Magovei, and by the maid who takes the flintstone from the fireplace and throws it over her shoulder by mistake, allowing him to turn back into human form. Three times touched with the feminine principle, he escapes, so it is really the same as in the Irish story where, through contact with the feminine principle, the hero also gets out of trouble. Somehow the Black Magician Czar cannot follow the ways of the hidden feminine mentality. If somebody has a power attitude he cannot understand the attitude of love, of Eros. He will always misinterpret it, looking for some hidden trick, and will get onto the wrong track.

In the Irish story it is even more interesting. There the enemy has hidden, black magic knowledge, the old magical traditions which have been handed down through mankind from the stone ages. Magic is probably one of the oldest of man's spiritual activities. Whenever a new conscious attitude arises, the old knowledge, the previous attitude, sinks onto the level of magic. Magic is therefore the older form of spiritual and religious knowledge and activity which has been superseded by a new spiritual religious attitude and therefore has sunk back into a more unconscious condition.

In the Irish story the magic of the horse wins against that of the blind seer. This is a Celtic story and the underworld country is obviously the famous Celtic Beyond where the fairies and elves live, where the dead go, where the beautiful damsels on the lake, and others, come from, and where the knights of the Middle Ages got lost. There Merlin, the great magician himself, got bewitched. The land of the Beyond in Celtic mythology has a romantic character which is what has been lost in the upperworld.

The king had first a positive wife, the mother of our hero. But then she dies and he marries a second time and up comes the stepmother with her two sons who try to supplant the hero. The stepmother has a poisonous power attitude; she wants to eliminate the first son and get her sons on the throne of Ireland. So the whole world of feeling, of love, and with it art, song, and beauty, disappears into the unconscious. The hero is the one who can bring this up again. While in the upperworld a destructive stepmother rules, when he goes to the underworld the hero finds a positive mother figure who gives him the white horse which helps him along. The counter-balance is thus found in the unconscious, the world of Eros; the hero who is not afraid to go down can get support from there.

The rest of the fight happens within the unconscious itself, for it is actually a fight between the white horse and the underworld magician king. The hero has only to do what the white horse tells him.

I tried to interpret the horse in commenting on the problem of spontaneity, for the horse represents the completely unconscious spontaneous life force, the genuine instinctual reaction on which the hero can rely. We can elaborate further, for the hero hides in the hole made by a pulled-out hair, in the hole made by a pulled-out tooth, and finally in a hole made by a nail pulled out from the hoof. He has to put the hair, the tooth, and the nail back and hide in that practically non-existent little space. Psychologically this shows that the ego and its own conscious planning and activity must be practically annihilated; the whole mental activity of the ego has to vanish. By an entire renunciation of self-will the horse and its divine spontaneity can come forth.

The horse is white, which shows that it is an instinctual impulse which has its natural direction towards consciousness. The sun God's chariot in Greece and in Rome was pulled by white horses, while the chariots of the night or the moon were pulled by dark horses. White animals were sacrificed to the Olympian Gods and dark animals to the subterranean Gods. In the Irish story it is constellated that certain instinctual, positive impulses are naturally pulling towards consciousness; therefore the ego can trust it to the extent of doing nothing, just letting itself be carried along. With another constellation, with black horses, the problem would be quite different.

In mythology black and white are not an ethical designation. They have become so only in late Christian allegory as a secondary, artificial interpretation. In comparative mythology black generally stands for the nocturnal, the unworldly, the earthly, belonging to what cannot be consciously known, fertility, and so on. White, on the other hand, stands for daylight, clarity and order, but either can be negative or positive, depending on the situation. The white horse here would mean there is a natural carrying force which tends to bring things up into consciousness, probably the Bird with the Beautiful Song. In this case consciousness has nothing to do except not be in the way; it must not block the positive processes in the unconscious by making plans of its own.

The last time the hero hides under the horse's hoof, under the horseshoe which, along with the hair and the tooth, is an old means of defending oneself against the devil. In the *Handwörterbuch des Deutschen Aberglaubens*, the horseshoe is described as a relatively recent luck-bringing symbol, inherited from the older symbol of iron nails. Iron in general has the magical capacity for chasing away devils and witches and has healing magical power in all the agricultural countries of Europe. The Irish hero goes into the nail hole in the horseshoe and has the horseshoe as a protection over him. The magician of the underworld cannot catch him because the horseshoe is nearly a circle consisting of iron. The iron has an apotropaic character and is also a shoe, which in certain magical practices also has an apotropaic character. So the horseshoe is three times a symbol of luck and a symbol of apotropaic power of the devil. It is especially amusing if one recollects that the devil often has a horse's foot himself. There again is the strange fact of *similia similibus curantur.*

What disappoints me is that the white horse at the end of the story stays in the underworld. When Ceart comes up from the well the white horse disappears; it returns to the mother figure from which it came and stays below. Only the Bird with the Beautiful Song is brought into the upperworld. This means that the healing process has taken place without the conscious realm having completely realized what has happened. One can compare this to somebody who by a short analysis has been cured of certain symptoms and then walks away without reflecting on what happened, being simply glad of the healing process. This occurs often and quite legitimately among young people who come for some minor symptom and who get out of the trouble relatively easily. They thank you nicely, walk off and only years later come back and say, "I would like to understand better what happened there." At the time the natural tasks of life, getting married, having to build up a profession, etc., take them away into the outer world. They haven't time to realize the processes which have occurred.

Once Miss Barbara Hannah got such a young person out and into a happy marriage, said Goodbye, sent flowers to the wedding, and wrote a nice letter of congratulations. The young woman wrote back, thanking her, but saying that she hoped this was only the first chapter and that one day she would come back again. For the moment she had to return into life (she was still very much in the first half), into her marriage and having children, but she knew that a lot had happened which had touched her somewhere.

255

At the moment she felt she could not go into that, but would save it up for the second half of life.

Healing processes can take place more or less consciously, but here something has remained unrecognized in the depths. In this case it is our white horse. There is a Persian story which tells a bit more about the horse. The story is entitled "The Magic Horse" (*Das Zauberross*) and is to be found in *Märchen aus Turkestan*.

> There was once a king who had a beautiful daughter. When she was old enough to get married he invented a very clever riddle. He fed a flea so long that it became fat as a camel. Then he killed it, took the skin and showed it everywhere, and said that whoever recognized what animal it came from should have his daughter. (Here again is a possessive father, like the Black Magician Czar and the father in the Irish story.) Naturally, nobody guessed that it was the skin of a flea. But one day an ugly beggar came and said he wanted to solve the riddle. They wouldn't let him into the palace but he insisted that he had the right to guess. As soon as the king showed him the skin of the flea the beggar said, "but naturally, that's the skin of a flea!" The king was furious but had to give his daughter to this horrible man.
>
> The beggar turned out to be a div, a destructive demon who eats people, an ogre. He took the girl and the princess was in great despair. She went down into the stable and cried on the neck of her favorite little horse. The horse said it would help; she must take it with her, as well as a mirror, a comb, some salt, and a carnation. When they came to the div's cave it was full of human bones because he had already eaten a lot of people. The horse said they had to flee. The div came out of the cave and followed them in a snowstorm he had caused. The princess, instructed by the horse, threw behind her first the carnation, then the salt, then the comb, and last the mirror. Always they turned into some obstacle — a thorny jungle, and so on — which delayed the div, but in the end he always caught up with them again. The mirror turned into a river (that was the last thing she threw away); the div came to the river and called to the princess asking her how she crossed it. The princess said that she bound a big stone round her neck and jumped into the water. The div quickly did the same, but even that didn't help. Finally the horse said that there was nothing else to do but go and fight the div itself. So it jumped into the water. The princess stood on the bank

and saw how the water foamed and turned red and she thought that her beloved helper, the horse, had been killed. But after some time it came to the surface and said that now she was safe; it had killed the div, but now she had to kill it, the horse. She had to throw its head to one side, its four legs in the four directions of the horizon, its intestines on the other side and then she had to sit with her children under its ribs.

The princess said, "How can I kill you, when you have saved me!" But the horse insisted. And when she did, out of the legs came golden poplars with emerald leaves, and out of the intestines came villages with fields and meadows and under the ribs came a golden castle. From the head came a beautiful little silvery river and the whole neighborhood turned into a kind of paradise. There the princess also found her husband.

I have skipped the part about her marriage and her children because it is a very long oriental story and I am only concentrating on the transformation of the horse. Here again the horse wins the fight with the black magician who this time is a div who can perform all kinds of magic. At first the horse also uses magic, saying that the princess should throw the carnation, the salt, the comb, and the mirror behind her, but the magic alone does not help. Then it comes to a real battle. So here we have the combination of both behaviors — the magical contest and the *corps à corps* fight.

Sometimes we have had magical contests and sometimes a fight, as in the story of the Lithuanian woodcutter who turned into a lion and devoured the devil. Here we have both motifs in the same story, first a magical contest and afterwards a physical heroic fight to overcome evil. This is satisfactory because, as you know, there must always be a paradox and always both things. First you should not fight, then you should fight; you should use your wits, you shouldn't; you should use strength, no, you shouldn't. That all belongs to what I told you in the beginning; every rule of behavior which you can deduce from the unconscious is usually a paradox.

But what leads us further here is the recognition of what the horse really is. It turns, in Jungian terms, into a mandala after it has been killed. As this is a Persian story we have to reckon with Indian influence. The skinning of the horse reminds one of the old Hindu horse sacrifice which was the central ritual at the creation of the universe. You might therefore say that this princess repeats the old Hindu horse sacrifice and a new world is again created. But what does that mean in psychological language?

The horse is one of the purest symbolic forms of the carrying instinctual nature, that energy by which the conscious ego is supported without noticing it. It is what makes the flow of life, directs our attention onto things and influences our actions through unconscious motivation. It is the whole feeling of being alive, the flow of life which we do not make but upon which we ride along, so to speak, into and through life. Most people accept this carrying force without question. They let themselves be carried through life by their impulses, desires, and motivations and only try not to be thrown off conscious plans. But the force constitutes a kind of unconscious health of following unconsciously one's own animal pattern without questioning it in any way. The horse sacrifice therefore means a complete renunciation of all the libidinal flow which attaches one to any life impulse; in other words, an artificial, complete state of introversion. There is much more about the symbolism of the horse sacrifice in Jung's *Symbols of Transformation*. What I now sum up so briefly is described there *in extenso*, especially in connection with the Indian horse sacrifice.

The princess reacts to the horse's request with great sadness and says, "How can I do that to you who have saved me? " This shows how difficult such a sacrifice is, for it means cutting off everything which is most natural. The spontaneous, innocent life impulse is destroyed at its very base. But through this comes forth the Self which was lying hidden behind it. To give you a modern analogy I can tell you the dream of an analysand.

The dreamer was a man who drank heavily, which is unusual for people of his type; he had the kind of simple genuineness which I mentioned formerly. But he got sick of drinking, and was told by one of his friends to go into analysis. He turned up, quite lively, and said that he was sick of drinking and now wanted to be cured.

You know how honest that usually is! There is a proverb which says, "Wash my fur, but don't make me wet!" That's what people generally mean when they say such things. But this man really wanted his fur washed and didn't mind getting wet. His dreams showed very clearly what the trouble was. He was living with an old witch who ruined his pleasure in life. Drinking was partly a surrogate for the life from which she kept him. When a dream showed that this was so — I hadn't even to say anything to him — he went back, gave up his room, had a terrific fight with the witch and took a room somewhere else. In this way, naively and genuinely and without argument, he did everything his dreams indicated and therefore experienced what one might call a miraculous cure. For several months he didn't touch alcohol and felt much better. He also got engaged. His life was going all right in every way and there seemed nothing more needed. I thought he would leave analysis, because, practically speaking, there was no need for it any more. He was a gay, good-natured extravert, and I imagined how he would go off into life and never give a second thought to what had happened to him. But at this moment came the following dream:

He was in a boat on a river. It was Sunday and there was music on the boat, just as we have here. There was a good atmosphere, the sun was shining and he went along with the people, looking at the river and enjoying himself. From time to time the boat stopped at a station and then went on again. Though he wanted to go further in the boat, at one of the stations he thought he might get out and look at the boat from the outside to see what its driving force was. So when it next stopped he got out and stood on the shore and looked back. To his absolute amazement he saw that the boat was carried by an enormous dragon in the water underneath. That was the driving force. The dragon was a very benevolent creature with a tiny little head and as he stood on the shore it came and tweaked his sleeve saying, "Hi, you!" It was quite friendly and he woke up amazed.

Because of that dream he decided to stay in analysis and find out what was below his miraculous cure, what the secret of life could really be. Then, to my surprise, he went into great depths and far into the process of individuation. Through that he became a quite remarkable personality.

There one could see the turning point. The question came: "Shall I sail along again, carried by the unconscious life force or shall I ask some deeper question? " And then the dragon tweaked his sleeve and said, "Won't you see who I am? Won't you take up the deeper contact? " which, in this case the man did.

Then it turns out that the deepest nucleus of the psyche, the Self, is behind this life force of the horse; it is the Self travestied, or covered up, or only appearing as an unconscious urge. The urge towards individuation is in our view a true instinct, probably the strongest instinct of all. Therefore it first appears as an animal, because it is a spontaneous instinctual force in the unconscious. But it needs the sacrifice, or the having it out with this force, to find out the deeper forms and go beyond experiencing it as a kind of divine carrying impulse.

A German fairy tale in the volume *Deutsche Märchen seit Grimm*, Vol. I, entitled "The King's Son and the Devil's Daughter," illustrates this problem still more deeply.

> There was once a king who in a great war lost all his battles, one after the other. All his armies were destroyed and he was in great despair and ready to commit suicide. At this moment a man turned up and said, "I know what's the matter with you! Have courage and I will help you if you will only give me *en noa Sil* out of your house. In three times seven years I will come and fetch it." (The king understood this as a request for a new cord, or rope, though in high German it could also mean a new soul.) The king thought that was a cheap price and gave his promise without hesitation. Then the man cracked a whip with four tails and magical armies appeared. With the help of these the king won all the battles so that the enemy had to beg for peace.
>
> When he got home his joy over his victories became still greater when he heard that a son had been born to him. After three times seven years this son was twenty-one, strong and beautiful. But the king had completely forgotten his promise. Then the strange man turned up again. He turned out to be the devil who demanded the *noa Sil*. The king went to his store chamber and brought him a new rope but the devil laughed at him and said he wanted *eine neue Seele* — a new soul — that was what he had meant. The king tore his hair and his clothes and nearly died of misery, but that didn't help. The boy in his innocence tried to comfort his father, saying that this devilish prince couldn't do him any harm. But the devil was furious and said he would pay for that. He seized him and bore him through the air and into Hell.
>
> In Hell the devil showed the prince a hellish fire and said that's where he would be roasted tomorrow; but in the meantime he would give him a chance. He showed the boy an enormous pond and said that if he could dry that up in the night, turn it into a meadow, mow the grass, make the hay and stack it up so that it could be brought in in the morning, then he could be freed. Then he shut the prince up. The prince was

very sad and ready to say goodbye to life, but the door opened
and in came the devil's daughter, bringing him food. When she
saw this handsome prince, his eyes red with crying, she said,
"Eat and drink and don't be discouraged. I will see to everything for you."

In the night when everybody was asleep the devil's daughter
got up quietly and went to her father's bed. She stopped up
his ears, took his magic whip and went out and cracked it in
all directions. All the devils in Hell appeared and did the work.
In the morning when the prince looked out of the window he
saw to his joy and astonishment a lot of ricks in place of the
lake. The devil's daughter, as soon as the work was finished,
had taken the wool out of her father's ears and put back the
whip. When he woke up, full of anticipation of his wickedness
and the thought of seeing the prince in the fire, he was amazed
to see that everything had been done. Thereupon he became
even more furious and he went to the prince and gave him a
further task. He should now cut down a big wood and make
it into piles so that it could be carried away early in the morning. Then the wood should be replaced by a vineyard in which
the grapes were ripe and ready for the vintage. Again the devil's
daughter got the work done for the prince by stealing her father's magic whip.

The third time the devil smelled a rat and got suspicious.
But he said he would let the prince go if the next night he
could build an entire church out of sand, complete with dome
and cross. The devil's daughter tried the same trick but this
time the devil's servants could not do it, for they couldn't
build a church even with stone or iron, let alone sand. All the
same she made them try; sometimes they got as far as half a
church, but then it collapsed. Once they finished it, but when
they put the cross on the dome the whole thing collapsed again,
so in the morning the work wasn't done. Then the devil's daughter quickly turned herself into a white horse (the white horse
again). She said to the prince that there was nothing else to do
but run away and that she would take him home, and off they
galloped.

When the devil woke up everything seemed very quiet. He
looked round for his whip, but it wasn't there. Then he yelled
at the top of his voice till the whole of Hell trembled; at that
the cotton wool fell out of his ears and he could hear that outside everybody was at work. Then he thought of the prince and

went to his room, but found the door open and the prince gone. He found his whip in the corner and cracked it so that all the devils in his kingdom came running, asking what he wanted done now. They said that they had been hard at it all night and were tired. He asked who had given them the order and they told him it was his daughter. The devil cried, "Ah, now I know! This is all my daughter's work" (*die Menschengefühlige*), for she had sympathy with human beings! (That is the important sentence.) Then the devil turned himself into a black cloud, determined to bring the two back. He soon caught sight of the white horse and its rider and he yelled to his devils to catch it and bring its rider to him, dead or alive. The Heavens became black with the crowd of flying devils and the horse called out to its rider that the black cloud following them was her father's army. She changed herself into a church and the prince into a parson, and she told him to stand at the altar and sing the Mass and not to give any answers. The army drew near and was astonished to find the church, the doors of which were open, but nobody could cross the threshold. The prince stood at the altar singing, "God be with us, God protect us" and didn't hear the devils' questions as to whether he had seen the flying couple. Finally they went to the end of Hell and back and told the devil they couldn't find the horse.

The devil was furious. The next morning he got up and again went up in the sky. He saw the church and heard the singing and he said, "There they are, now I'll get them, they won't get away this time." He collected an even bigger army and told it to destroy the church and bring him back one stone and the priest, dead or alive. But this time the devil's daughter turned herself into an alder tree and the prince into a golden bird which had to sing all the time and not be afraid of anything. So when the devil's army got there, there was no church, only an alder tree with a golden bird on it which sang continually and was not afraid. Again the devils did not catch him, but returned.

Again the devil raged. He flew up in the air and saw the alder tree, seven hundred miles away. He collected a still bigger army and gave it instructions to cut down the tree and bring him the bird, alive or dead. But the tree and bird had become a horse and its rider and were a further seven hundred miles away. When the prince looked back and saw the army the devil's daughter turned herself into a rice field and him into a quail which had to keep running continually over the field, singing "God with us, God with us" and not listening to any questions.

The next morning the devil in his rage flew over the rice field and heard dimly the cry of the quail. He thought that now he had them. He told his servants to mow down the field; but then he thought that this time he should go after them himself, for if they could get further away than four times seven hundrèd miles his power over them would be gone. So he flew once more up into the air, but the horse and rider had gone on. They had only seven miles to go to reach the earth when they heard behind them a terrific storm. The prince said that behind them he could see a black spot in the Heavens and in it fiery lightning. The girl said that was her father and if the prince now didn't follow her instructions exactly they would be lost. She said she would turn herself into a big pond of milk. He must be a duck and always swim right in the middle and keep his head under the milk and never look out; if he looked out for one second he would be lost, and he must never swim towards the shore. Soon the old devil was standing on the shore but he couldn't do anything until he got the duck into his power and it was swimming in the middle of the pond too far away for him to reach. He didn't dare swim for he could be drowned in the milk. He tried to lure the little duck and said, "Dear little duck, why do you always stay in the middle of the pond? Look around, and see how beautiful it is where I am."

For a long time the prince resisted, but finally his curiousity became too great. He peeped out once, and in that second he became stone blind and the milk became a little cloudy. A voice out of the milk called out, "Alas, alas, what have you done!" But the devil danced with wicked joy on the bank and said, "Ah, now I'll soon have you!" And he tried to swim in the cloudy milk but just sank, so for a long time he kept trying to entice the duck out, but it wouldn't come. Then the devil became furious and lost patience. He changed himself into an enormous goose, swallowed the whole pond with the duck and waddled home.

"Now everything is all right," said a voice out of the milk to the duck. The milk began to ferment and the devil began to be more and more uneasy and frightened. He could only move with difficulty and longed to be home. He took a few more steps. Suddenly there was a loud crack and he burst open. There stood the king's son and the devil's daughter in their youthful beauty.

Then the two went home. It was the seventh day since the devil had abducted the prince when they got back home. There was great rejoicing in the whole land and a wonderful wedding. The old king handed over the kingdom to his son who became as wise and just as his father and is still reigning, if he has not died in the meantime.

The beginning of this story is a common one. A king who is in difficulties, knowingly or without knowing what he is doing, promises the devil the child born in his absence. Then it is the child's task — the girl's or the boy's — to free itself from the grip of evil. The king, or in other stories the merchant who has lost everything, is in some kind of trouble when he does this.

If we compare this with personal psychology and do not for the moment take it on an archetypal level as we should do, it can be easily illustrated — by the way parents sell their children to their own unsolved problems. We saw this in the case I mentioned before where the mother, instead of having it out with her own destructive animus, kept the animus at bay with a Bible; therefore her daughter had to cope with the problem of the dark man. This daughter ran completely wild. She had several illegitimate children, she had abortions and other unpleasant experiences of evil and she landed in analysis a complete physical and psychological wreck. That was what the black man did to this mother who sold her daughter to him, so to speak, for she, by trickery, got rid of him through the Bible.

On a more general collective level the king represents the ruling conscious attitude and the underlying ruling collective conscious idea, which also means the dominant image of God in the collective set-up at a certain time. Again, as practically every myth begins, this king has become deficient and is no longer capable of keeping the destructive and deceiving powers at bay; the ruling religious and sociological order, its ideals and images, are no longer psychologically powerful enough to present an attractive goal for human behavior. Therefore part of the psychic energy flows into all sorts of dissolving channels. The process of dissociation has already gone quite far because, as we see later, the devil possesses the symbol of the Self, the whip with the four lashes which, when he cracks it, produces any kind of effect he likes.

This whip with the four lashes is a primitive royal sceptre. One finds it in the hands of the underworld kings in Egyptian sepulchral images. Osiris has such a whip. The sceptre was originally the cattle herder's staff. The whip is a similar symbol and represents royal power and the king's ability to rule. The four lashes refer here to the totality. As this power has fallen into the hands of the underworld ruler, the upper king is lost and has no chance. The only thing he can do is to abdicate in favor of his son or let himself be killed. This belongs to the archetypal figure of the king who has to be ritually killed and revived after a certain time, a reference to the inevitable aging of all conscious principles which must be destroyed and renewed so that they do not stop psychic evolution and life.

The king in the story does the same thing parents often do to their children personally; he unconsciously sells his son to the devil, in this case by misinterpreting the devil's request. But unconsciousness is no excuse in the cruel world of psychological facts. Therefore the devil comes back and asks for the son, now twenty-one years old and an innocent simpleton, completely incapable of coping with the problem. The redemption action therefore rests with the devil's daughter, of whom we hear that she has feeling for human beings. She has human sympathy (*sie ist menschengefühlig*).

The devil's daughter is a parallel to other feminine figures who sometimes live with the devil. He does not live in a celibate state, except in the dogmatic view. In folklore he always has a female with him, generally his own grandmother. The word grandmother does not imply kinship, however, but means that he lives with the Great Mother. In the fairy tale world he actually lives in marital relationship with her, as you can learn from the fairy tale "The Three Golden Hairs of the Devil" where he goes to bed with the grandmother and in the night she pulls out three golden hairs from the devil's head to give to the hero hidden under her skirt.

The mother or daughter figure who in folklore is associated with the devil is generally more friendly towards the human race than the devil himself. She usually plays an intermediary role. In this case the devil's daughter leaves her father and comes to live in the upperworld and becomes the queen of the next generation. This is a typical story compensatory to the too-patriarchal order of the Christian religion ruling in the upperworld. A part of the feminine principle is repressed, together with the devil, into the underworld. It only waits for an opportunity to come up again and take its ruling place on the surface. In the Sumerian Babylonian Gilgamesh Epic, the hero is not supported mainly by feminine figures but by the sun God Shamash and, in the Beyond, by the ancient flood-hero Utnapischtim. The feminine Goddess Ishtar is his great enemy. So you see these constellations change with the cultural frame in which they belong. In Sumerian Babylon there was a civilization where the reinforcement of masculinity and of the masculine principle was intended by the unconscious. If in our story the hero is mostly supported by a chthonic feminine principle, this has to be understood as a specific late European problem where the masculine form of life has been exaggerated and constellated a destructive masculine counter-position. This locking of the light and dark masculine powers, as exists in Christianity, can only be undone by the unexpected mediation of the feminine principle which comes up in these stories.

The devil's daughter has not only feeling for mankind, she represents the feminine principle *par excellence*, Eros. The love principle undoes the stiffening position of the masculine world, and she solves all the tasks for the king's son. It is interesting to look at what the devil's daughter actually does. First the devil sets the king's son enormous Herculean labors, which only a very powerful and strong man could manage, or somebody with tremendous magical power. He challenges the power of the king's son and we can thank God that he cannot meet the challenge, because that would probably not work. The devil's daughter does not use her own power, she uses her father's magical whip. She does all the tasks with her father's own power. By feeling, she turns his power, the magical whip with the four lashes, against himself and succeeds three times. But she cannot build a church.

The first and second tasks are what one could call the civilization of nature, turning a lake into a meadow and cutting the hay, then turning a wood into a vineyard and gathering the grapes for the wine. This is a deep and amazing picture, for in more primitive societies it is the hero who performs such civilizing tasks. Here, however, this activity has become evil, for the devil suggests it and wants it done.

In light of this story, one cannot help questioning our technological exploitation of nature and reflecting on who is inspiring this kind of activity. It was once a civilizing task, but now, overdone, it has fallen into the autonomous hands of a devilish destructive unconscious activity, an extraverted restlessness which goes on and on beyond natural measure. In this story it goes so far that the devil wants a counter-church built. God and the Trinity have churches on the surface of the earth, so the devil must have a church in Hell, a proper church with a cross. But that doesn't succeed, even with his fourfold whip. Here again, in an uncanny way, one is reminded of certain totalitarian movements which have robbed the church of its idealism and of various forms of activity and organization and have tried to use them in a counter-manner.

Hitler actually studied the procedures of the Jesuit Order to build up his set of activities and proceedings. The Communistic State is practically a youthful replica of the Catholic Chruch. So this has come true; the devil is trying to build a Christian church in Hell as a counter-principle. But, and that is why I love this story, it is not built on solid ground. It will crumble, for it is built of sand, sand representing a mass of tiny particles. One cannot build anything from human beings whom one has reduced to mass particles. If you grind the human individual into a grain of sand and want to build something which holds, the prospect is not promising. That is a most satisfactory insight to be obtained from this story.

The two have to run away from the attack of the devils; again there is the motif of transformation-flight with a kind of magical contest in which the couple transforms three times in a mandala of a specific form. The first mandala is closest to collective consciousness, for it is a church with a parson in it reading the Mass. This represents the more traditional way by which the devil has been kept at bay in our civilization. It works as far as it goes, but it does not go very far. The next picture goes deeper into nature and there is no longer a civilizing symbolism; it is an alder tree with a golden bird on it.

The alder tree is a famous old magical tree apotropaic against witchcraft and the devil. Its twigs are put into the fields and stables by the peasants as protection against the devil; the tree itself is devilish. So it is like the wolf against the giant; a devilish tree against the devil. It is devilish because it generally grows in dark places in the woods or in marshlands. As its wood is useless for mankind, it is assumed to belong to witches and demons. Alder wood quickly turns red and this, it is said, is because the devil uses it to beat up his grandmother, i. e., his wife. So in folklore it is sometimes red. On the other hand, as always with this strange double aspect of apotropaic symbols, with alder twigs one can oneself beat up the devil. He beats his wife with it, so you can use it to beat him. The wood is useless and is akin to what is dark and useless in nature; because of that, because of its closeness to the devilish principle itself, it can save the hero, who, as a golden bird in it, sings "I am not afraid."

But even so the two don't escape. The third symbol is the rice field with a quail in it which walks up and down calling, "God with us." The rice field is again a nature symbol but this time principally a symbol of fertility. Rice in many countries is one of the most fertile products of the earth and is a basic food. Even nowadays rice is thrown at couples at a country wedding. It is an old folklore custom to guarantee fertility for the couple, who in return throw sugar candies for the children.

So here the fertility of mother earth, something which belongs neither to the devil nor to the Christian God but is a feminine divine realm in its own right, is the saving factor. In it the prince, who is always the one in danger, walks up and down like a quail calling "God with us." The German word *Wachtel* in popular etymology is connected with the word *wachen*, to stay awake, to be on watch. There is a widespread old Indo-Germanic superstition that the quail stays awake continually, declaring its presence by its restlessness and crying in the night, especially on nights of the new moon. If the quails call often, the crops will be good and vice versa. Here this ability to be inwardly alert and awake is the decisive factor. It needs constant, concentrated inner alertness to escape attacks of evil. Even if one watches one's shadow or one's animus, if one is not constantly on the alert these figures get one in a moment of fatigue or in an *abaissement du niveau mental*. That, as in this dangerous situation, is naturally a crucial point.

If one has an outer fight with evil, often one sees how if one gets emotional and thereby slightly unconscious, one loses one's own arguments. I remember myself once going to a session where I wanted to get the best of some enemies and had all my documents to prove my points in a paper right beside me. At the last minute when I left the flat I left them home and had to talk without the written proof. That's typical of what happens when one is involved with some problem of projected evil. Where one projects one easily becomes emotional; already one has an *abaissement* and because of that, without wanting to, one defeats one's own objectives. That is usually how one loses the battle in such cases. Generally not being alert plays a certain role. At the decisive moment one becomes stupefied and forgets either one's best arguments or leaves the documents at home. This is always a sign that some of one's own evil has been projected into the situation; not that the whole evil is one's own — there is objective outside evil — but one has become involved through projection of one's own evil. This entails a loss of soul. In such instances, because a part of oneself is involved with the enemy through projection, one is no longer on the alert, but half asleep, and so one plays against oneself.

So this alertness of the quail is important. But even that does not help in this case. Therefore there is a fourth task; the devil's daughter turns herself into a pond of milk and the prince into a duck. Then comes the decisive necessity that he swim in the middle and keep his head under the milk.

Milk, because of its innocent white quality, has always been one of the most widespread apotropaic means against evil. On the other hand it is very easily attacked by witches and devils. If somebody wants to practice witchcraft on a peasant, almost anyone can, with the evil eye or *malapion*, bewitch a peasant's cow so that it will produce bluish or watery milk; or the cream, when churned, will not turn into butter. Milk is a sober drink in contrast to wine. In old Greece and Rome it was frequently used in sacrifices to the Gods of the underworld, who should not be aroused but appeased. If you gave them wine they became more active and enterprising, while if you gave them milk they became soft and mild. Therefore the divinities of the dead and of the underworld must have milk, while wine could be given to the upper Gods. That is why milk sacrifices were called *nephalia*, sober sacrifices to the Gods of the underworld and to the dead.

The prince had not only to swim in the middle of this milk pond but had to hide his head and not look at the devil, whatever the latter might say to him. This is a wonderful illustration of what, to my idea, is the only possible attitude if one is confronted with evil coming from the outside. If one looks at it there is already projection. The word projection comes from *projicere*: something is thrown unconsciously out of oneself into the

269

other object. If one looks at something evil, Plato once said, something evil falls into one's own soul. One cannot look at evil without something in oneself being aroused in response to it, because evil is an archetype and every archetype has an infectious impact upon people. To look at it means to become infected by it. That is why this prince had to keep his head dipped down into the milk right in the middle of the pond. He had always to swim close to the innermost center which is beyond the problem of good and evil, beyond the split and therefore beyond the opposites. Without one second of aberration he had to keep close to that inner center and avoid getting involved.

That in itself would be an eastern solution. It was practiced long ago in Buddhism and many other eastern philosophies. It means stepping out of a problem of evil by getting beyond the problem of the opposites, getting close to an inner center beyond the duality of good and evil and its fight. But here a battle is fought all the same, not by the conscious attitude, not by the prince, but by the devil's daughter who destroys her own father when he swallows her.

There is a famous alchemical saying which was a favorite quotation of Dr. Jung: "All haste is of the devil." The wonderful thing about that is that the devil himself easily gets into a hasty attitude. He is hasty by nature and that's why all haste is of the devil. If we get hasty we are in the devil; if we are in a hurry-up mood we say "things must be decided today," "this evening I have to post the letter," "I must come out in a taxi so that you can sign it, because tomorrow morning will be too late," etc. If you get a phone call like that you know who is behind it. Dr. Jung had a wonderful way of losing such a document on his writing desk, not even consciously putting the thing off, but just losing it on his desk. The devil *is* personified haste. Here he gets hasty and can't wait any longer; he becomes a goose, which, among other things, is stupid, and which in Greek antiquity represented a special aspect of Mother Nature or the nature Goddess, Nemesis.

Nemesis comes from the word *nemo*, which means to distribute, to attribute to each one his right lot. Nemesis is a principle of natural justice by which everyone gets what they deserve. We cannot avoid seeing that there is such a principle in the unconscious which has a curious way of giving to people exactly what one feels is somehow deserved. It is not justice in the human sense of the word, but there is an uncanny regulating force in nature which acts like justice and strikes one as being meaningful. So one could say that the devil executes himself; he becomes a goose, he personifies that justice which people get. He drinks the milk and it begins to boil in his insides. You know that milk has this nasty quality of boiling over, even if you watch it — worse if you watch it — and that's why the boiling over of the milk is a general and famous expression for getting into an uncontrolled rage. In France they say, "*il monte comme une soupe au lait*," he boils over like a milk soup. People who are inclined to get into sudden fits of anger are called a milk soup because they boil over so quickly.

The devil's daughter is now his own anima, the emotionality and feeling from which he has split off. Here we link back to the heart of the giant. The devil's daughter is his heart. She has a heart and feeling, she is his feeling side. Now in hasty forgetfulness he incorporates his feeling side, the emotionality he had coldly split off, and he gets nicely what we would call anima possessed. He becomes moody and explodes; with that he is weak and overcome. He is as finished as a man is when he gives in to his anima' moods. He is undone in his innermost nature, dissociated. So the couple steps out unharmed, the reborn new principle of consciousness which now begins to rule on the surface of the earth.

The destructive emotionality which is so easily connected with evil in a masculine type of civilization causes the feminine principle to be destructive. It functions as an unconscious blind emotionality in men which constellates at the wrong moment. If that principle — the anima or feminine principle — is brought up from Hell into consciousness, it overcomes the specific form of evil represented here as the devil. The new principle of consciousness then dwells, so to speak, in a center of totality beyond the split between good and evil. In that sense one could say that according to this fairy tale the innermost center, the divine nucleus of the human psyche, is the one thing beyond the problem of good and evil and is an absolute factor which can lead us out of the situation with which that problem confronts us.

It is a very profound, mystical solution offered by this fairy tale; but fairy tales only seem to be innocent stories. They are so profound that one cannot explain them superficially; they require that one dive into deep waters.

INDEX

Abraham/Isaac, 91.

active imagination: 55, 58, 74ff; as witchcraft, 76f; in meeting devils, 152; in overcoming affect, 183.

Adam, 109.

Adonis, 13.

affect, as giant, 207.

African tales, 170.

aggression, 88, 122.

Aigremont, symbolism of shoe, 22.

Aion, C. G. Jung, 174. (CW 9 Part II)

Alchemical Studies, C. G. Jung, 38, 47. (CW 13)

alchemy, 45.

alder, apotropaic, 267f, 262.

Armor and Psyche, 31.

amplification, 28,34.

analysand: sick of drinking, 258f; sudden death of, 132; intellectual, 145f; compulsive, 165; with negative animus, 172.

analysis: of charwoman or half-wit, 28f; resistance to, 42; danger, 61; analysand's development, 82; by brutal intervention, 87; of anima, 87; of elderly people, 107; swindle, 165f; decisive factor, 186, 231ff; against all rules of, 188; and wolf-determination, 232ff; dream leading to individuation, 258f.

analyst(s): feeding demon, 172; outgrown by patient, 177, 221; woman as, 198f; eaten by analysand's shadow, 163; and black magic, 251.

Anderson, Hans Christian, his neurosis, 83.

angel, guardian of children, 194f.

anger, 179ff, 214.

anima: 48; Goddess, 55; creative, 56; secret traditions of, 57ff; and active imagination, 58; possession, 60; poisonous, 68ff; and religion, 69; seed ideas, 70; repressed, 71; as hysterical liar, 71; and Protestantism, 71, 79ff; as dream, 81f, 83; as living reality, 84; poles, 85ff; and sexuality, 87; as religious attitude, 93; as great entangler, 107; ending destructiveness of, 107ff; and repressed sex, 116; as feminine principle, 234; moods, 271.

animal behavior, 13, 121f.

animal(s): helpful, 119f; ghost, 131f; hunted, 157; coupled, 216.

anima/animus, 5.

animus: 7; arguments, 42; working against life, 173; possession, 195f, 199ff; as wolf, 215; positive, 226, 264.

Answer to Job, C. G. Jung, 175f. (CW 11)

anthropos, as tree, 39.

272

Christian: shadow, 7f; era(s), 41, 89; civilization, 89; civilization extraverted, 107; legend (and magical competition), 249; symbolism, 82; *Weltanschauung*, 22; infantilism, 192f.

Christ: King of Kings, 25, 36, 40; and Wotan, 41, 53; married (to) the church, 108.

Christianity: amongst slaves, 30; king as symbol of, 31f; and repressed female principle, 72; re: evil, 174; Norway, 206f, 222; and masculine powers, 266.

chthonic, male, 13.

church, Catholic, 26f, 222f; in Hell, 261, 267.

clothes, and persona, 21.

cock, 137.

colt, 16.

compensation, in fairy tales, 120ff.

competition, ego vs. unconscious, 251f.

complex(es): mother, 19; polarization, 31f; as forbidden chamber, 71; Oedipus or Electra, 91; repressed, 218; as island, 221f; autonomous, 222.

conscience: as experience of voice of God, 115; eye as, 169; bad, 156, 165.

"Conscience, The", C. G. Jung, 113, 169.

consciousness: as seen from the unconscious, 81f; collective, 81, 207; on earth, 87; in fairy tales, 81; petrifying effect of, 89; unrealized, 177, 223; reborn, 271.

contamination, 78.

corn, 159, 162.

creation myths, 207, 224.

creative, solution of shadow problem, 60f; creative power, unused, 177.

creativity, repressed, 219.

cross/gallows/tree, 36.

crow(s), 16, 19, 43f.

crown, 17, 46.

curse, 89.

daimon, 113.

daughter(s): 18, 138, 158ff, 264; incestuous situation, 244f.

death: hostility after, 131ff; sudden, 132; as enemy of, 170f; death wish, 171f.

death pull, 132.

deer, 127.

Demeter, death and resurrection, 162, 165.

demons: and anima, 68; nature, 134; "IT", 144f, 153; therianthropic, 146; fed by analyst, 172.

devil: 9, 80; grandmother of, 105; shadow of, 116; and introversion, 151f, 182; as lion, 235; as grip of evil, 260, 264; and Great Mother, 265.

Jung, Dr., M.-L. von Franz' personal references to: 12, 87, 105, 114, 165, 177, 192-7, 201, 215, 270; on Zen competitions, 251; as control analyst, 172; the memoirs, 187; and forcing individuation, 232, 252.

Kali, 105.

keys, Janus and Peter, 53f.

Khidr, 72f, 79.

kindness, to the dwarf, 193.

king: 17ff, 20ff, 202ff, 244; in decline, 30; in *Mysterium Coniunctionis*, 24; new/young, 24, 62; sons of 202ff; old, 51, 62, 81, 83; as instinctual energy, 211; in difficulties, 260, 264; as dominant image of God, 264; ritually killed, 265.

King Arthur, 197.

King/Queen, 89; in alchemy, 108.

Koran, 72.

Kronos, 221.

lamb, 108, 191f.

Lenin's Mausoleum, 220.

libido, 45, 210.

light, 171; devilish, 178.

lion, 235.

Logos, 206.

loneliness, 142, 150ff.

Lorenz, Konrad, 121f.

love. 211, 253.

Madonna, Black in Einsiedeln, 105.

magic: 58; in competition, 234f; black, 73, 75ff, 131, 184, 250ff.

magical powers, as protection, 162.

magician, black, 249.

man, primitive, 121.

mandala, 153, 257, 267.

Mars, 214.

masculine/feminine, interaction, 266.

masturbation, 221.

Maya, 107.

medicine man, 26, 131, 249.

Mercurius, 20f, 73, 79. 91, 251.

Merlin, 253.

milk, 263, 269f.